Seamless

Seamless

Successful B2B Marketing, Selling, and Account Management

Peter D. Bayley
With
Kimball Bailey, Tom Cairns, and Michael S. K. Grant

BUSINESS EXPERT PRESS
Leader in applied, concise business books

Seamless: Successful B2B Marketing, Selling, and Account Management

Cover design by Charlene Kronstedt

Interior design by Exeter Premedia Services Private Ltd., Chennai, India

First published in 2023 by
Business Expert Press, LLC
222 East 46th Street, New York, NY 10017
www.businessexpertpress.com

ISBN-13: 978-1-63742-477-3 (paperback)
ISBN-13: 978-1-63742-478-0 (e-book)

Business Expert Press Selling and Sales Force Management Collection

First edition: 2023

10 9 8 7 6 5 4 3 2 1

Description

A unique guidebook to B2B marketing and sales for practicing and aspiring managers.

In *Seamless: Successful B2B Marketing, Selling, and Account Management*, the authors and 20 successful businesspeople share their practical experience and the valuable lessons they learned at the sharp end of branding, selling, and marketing.

Expert opinion, academic theory, research, and practical advice are summarized with explanatory graphics and "Dos and Don'ts" lists for each topic.

Essential for students of business and managers of any size or type of firm, *Seamless* will educate and guide you through the marketing, sales, and account management process to business success.

Keywords

best; guide; successful; seamless; marketing; advice; branding; selling; B2B; sales process

Contents

Foreword

Sales and marketing are two professional disciplines which rank alongside engineering, law, and accountancy as vital components of any business. Unfortunately, unlike engineering, law, and accountancy, too few people—and even fewer businesses—appreciate this.

This has always been a mystery to me.

Intelligent business leaders have no problem appreciating that engineers make sure their products are safe, lawyers make sure that the company's activities are legal, and accountants make sure that the numbers add up. And yet, all too often, those same leaders see salespeople as a necessary evil and marketing as a luxury.

I will never forget the country manager in the company where I once worked who, in a fit of irritation when asked why his marketing spend was so low, said:

"I'll spend money on marketing once sales pick up."

Symptoms of companies that don't get it are:

- No one has "sales" in their job title.
- Marketing budgets are consistently raided, as underbudget revenues call for urgent expense reductions.
- Salespeople are selected on the basis of little more than a sunny disposition and an ability to read a brochure.
- The marketing department's two principal responsibilities are the website and the staff Christmas party.

When I began my career in sales and marketing at IBM, we spent years training in the classroom and on the job, learning about our markets, our prospective customers, and our products before we were allowed out to play our part in bringing in the revenues on which the company depended.

The mantra which was drummed into us then was "Need, Feature, Benefit."

- Need: What is the problem that you are trying to solve for the potential customer?
- Feature: How will our product satisfy those needs?
- Benefit: Why is our solution the best one available for the customer?

Three simple words which belie the complexity, creativity, and effectiveness of a well-run sales and marketing machine.

This book debunks the myths that sales is a necessary evil and that marketing is a luxury by unpacking and explaining the three principal disciplines of an efficient sales and marketing machine.

Sir Kenneth Olisa, OBE, Chairman, Restoration Partners

Sir Kenneth Olisa, OBE, CStJ, FRSA, FBCS, FIoD, Chairman, Restoration Partners. A Nottingham native, Ken is an IT businessman and philanthropist with a 40-year international career at IBM, Wang, and Interregnum (which he founded and floated in 2000). Ken has advised or invested in some of the United Kingdom's more interesting computer technology entrepreneurs. A diversity pioneer and enthusiastic mentor, his principal cause is social inclusion and, in that capacity, he chairs the Powerlist Aleto Foundation, whose mission is "sharing success with tomorrow's leaders."

Acknowledgments

The authors thank their interviewees for relating their considerable experience and allowing the use of their interviews:

Mike Ames, sales and marketing consultant; *Joy Armstrong*, Executive Account Director/PPD/Thermo Fisher Scientific; *Carlo Tortora Brayda di Belvedere*, CEO/Gorilla; *Judi Edwards*, consultant; *Andy Heyes*, MD/ Harvey Nash; *Mark Robinson*, entrepreneur; *Professor Andrew Sturdy*, Research Director/The School of Management at the University of Bristol; *Greg Adams*, consulting group partner; *Kenton Turner*, Chief Technical Officer/BPD Global Group; *Steve Lockwood*, VP/VENA Solutions; and *Iebe Ypma*, Director/Alastor Consulting.

Peter Bayley thanks the following individuals for their insights and expert comments, quoted in this book: *William Agush*, Founder and CEO/Adsonica; *Chuck Besondy*, President and Author/Besondy Publishing LLC, Founder/Besondy Consulting & Interim Management Inc.; *Jane Frost*, CBE, CEO/the Market Research Society; *Steve Lavelle*, Managing Partner/NGS Global; *Juan Pablo Pazos*, President and CEO/XmarteK; *Chris Raman*, serial venturepreneur, Founder/Ventures4growth; *Jacqui Rand*, Founder and Director/The Channel Consultants Ltd; *Nick Ray*, CEO, Director, Founder/NXD of Software and Technology Firms; *Nichola Thurston-Smith*, sales leader in large corporates such as Microsoft and Vodafone, and *Sir Kenneth Olisa*, OBE, for his foreword.

Introduction

In this book, you will find valuable experience, clearly expressed expert opinion, references to the best academic theory, published advice and research, and the wise words of top professional men and women, about techniques used and lessons learned at the sharp end of B2B marketing and sales.

The role of head of marketing or sales has changed. As well as its traditional functions, marketing is now seen as the core entity managing the customer experience. Sales is the center of customer relationship management. The conventions of work have also changed, with less traditional office-based time and completely flexible working hours. Marketing and sales have had to adapt quickly to virtual selling, digital and automated marketing, the dominance of social media for communication, and dramatically different phases of decline, growth, and development in different industry segments. In small companies, one individual may be in charge of these functions and will need multiple skills.

But some things remain constant: the need for strong, consistent branding and strategic thinking; the focus on and business insight into the needs of the customer and their buying process; and the essential collaboration between these two vital business functions in particular: marketing and sales. *Seamless* looks in depth at these issues (Figure I.1).

"This is the best product out there and can easily be sold to anyone, anywhere!" If only that were always true. (There's nothing like an enthusiastic product manager.) Business history is full of examples of the failure of the best product, technology, or service to win the day. When the company that wins the deal or secures the account is not offering the "best" solution, why did it win?

The answer is usually that the winning product was supported by the best, most consistent, and most integrated sales and marketing process. It was the most thoroughly researched; the most sharply targeted; and the most relevant or personalized for the buyer. It was the easiest and most comfortable one for them to engage with: the least threatening or risky purchase and the one most easily justified as a good business decision by the buyer, to the users of the solution. It's the quality and comprehensiveness of the process that can give you the competitive edge. In the 21st century, that process is no longer linear: it's a complex, iterative one for buyer and seller and is the core subject of this book.

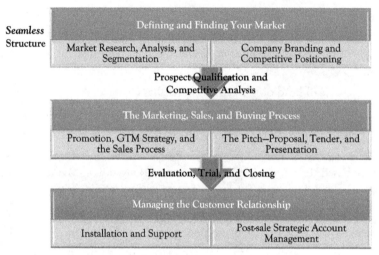

Figure I.1 The three key areas and eight chapters

There are multiple disciplines involved, most often viewed as being part of either sales or marketing. Often, marketing and sales are viewed inside larger firms as two "sides" and there is conflict. Isn't that odd, when their essential objectives are the same? There is no room for that conflict in today's B2B world. These two essential but disparate business functions must be mutually supportive. Effective execution comes from a jointly well-understood effort to find the right market and buyer, position your product and company competitively, communicate that to the customer well, sell them the right solution, and develop a long-term, profitable customer relationship. Then everyone wins!

Seamless presents the marketing and sales professional or the student of these business disciplines with a concise and exhilarating combination of expert opinion, proven methodology supported by fully referenced academic theory, real-world experience, and up-to-the-minute, practical guidance. With memorable quotes from highly successful business people, a succinct summary on the content of each chapter, and a concise

"Dos and Don'ts" table for every topic, it will be an inspirational, useful guide and reference for those concerned with driving businesses—large or small—forward.

I have managed the sales and marketing function—sometimes with a team, sometimes alone—in many types and sizes of business. This highly accessible book would have been very useful to me at any stage of my career, as it uniquely takes the reader on the journey from market selection to long-term profitable customer relationships, using candid and revealing interviews with leading practitioners in each element of the art and science of modern marketing, selling, and account management.

I hope you enjoy it and use it to bring success to you and your business.

Peter D. Bayley

CHAPTER 1

Market Research, Analysis, and Segmentation

Overview

In this chapter, we're going to define your target market, its nature, and its business potential. As stated in the Introduction, it's thorough research and sharp targeting that makes for a successful product or service offering, one that is relevant or personalized for the market and the buyer. We'll consider the role of traditional primary market research, as well as the world of information available online, in providing the vital data that can become actionable market intelligence. We will then discuss using that intelligence to select your target market, by analyzing and understanding the needs of specific market segments and their strategic fit with your business plans. This applies whether your firm and ambitions are small, medium, or large. Then come the formulation of products and precise marketing and sales messages. We'll also touch on the salesman's curse: the need for precision prospecting to find the prospective customers worth spending your time on. Senior practitioners will discuss their relevant lessons learned in the field and we will draw some conclusions on how you can make use of segmentation to capture your market and to focus your marketing and sales process effectively.

Why is this important? This early stage in the marketing and sales process is the one that will define your business for a considerable time. Think of it as the map for your journey. Even the smallest company can demonstrate that time spent in high-quality reconnaissance is never wasted. Get it right and from the start, you will be a focused and efficient business with increasing market share and expanding expertise in your chosen field of operation.

Market Research and Analysis—Defining and Finding Your Market

The ease with which the Internet allows anyone to access data from around the world might seem to make formal and sometimes costly primary market research redundant; it does not. The B2B market demands that you gain and utilize considerable depth of knowledge about your chosen prospects. The process of examining markets in detail, then deciding how to approach them before making major commitments, is fundamental good business practice, whether you are a start-up using only free online sources or an established company with a sizeable research budget. 100 percent market knowledge does not exist, but diligent research will provide considerable and essential market understanding. Are you an innovator in product, price, positioning, or your route to market? Are you out to capture a new market or to provide something new to an established one? Either way, going head-to-head in competition with established players will be something you need to be prepared to do. Michael Porter's work on competitive strategy and his much-practiced "Five Forces" and "Generic Strategies" frameworks have guided many companies in their approach to gaining market share from market leaders. These frameworks remain worthy of study as you develop your strategy. More recently, "Blue Ocean Strategy," a theory developed by Kim and Mauborgne, has been very popular in guiding the thinking on a different approach to market selection and entry. Although its basic premise is not original, it expands in a very accessible way on the premise of "first mover advantage" the advantage conferred on the first company to move into a particular market.

Two years before "Blue Ocean Strategy" Adrian Slywotzky and his coauthors in *How to Grow When Markets Don't* argued that "demand innovation," or the creation of new growth by expanding the market's boundaries, is key to expanding a business or finding a place to thrive when markets lose their fizz. His demand innovation theory is very similar to Kim and Mauborgne's Blue Ocean model. Being a market pioneer is a risky business, however, and this aspect of what Blue Ocean strategy entails is now much criticized as being underemphasized in their work. Side-stepping the competition in "red-ocean" market conditions—where competition is rife, fierce, and too much of it can lead to oversupply and weakened demand—is a nice theoretical idea, but there are many instances of companies failing by making that move. It's high cost and high risk, no matter how good your research. It's instructive that it seems to be mostly deep-pocketed, large corporations that have attempted to follow this path, rather than smaller ones.

At the core of a Blue Ocean strategy is "value innovation," meaning the attempt to identify and build aspects of a business that make it competitive and able to outreach marketplace competition. That value could be in the shape of the product offering, the way it is packaged, the way it is sold or delivered to the buyer, its pricing, or a combination of all or some of these attributes. Your research will help you in deciding about shaping product and company positioning to be attractive in that specific target market (more on that topic in the next chapter). But "making competition irrelevant" (as Kim and Mauborgne put it) is no easy task. It's also worth remembering that many of today's current market leaders were by no means first to their markets—early, maybe, but not first. Google—today's leading Internet search engine, of course—was in fact a late entrant to the market. Alta Vista and Yahoo! were there before them. The AMP MP3 Playback Engine got to market four years before the Apple iPod, which then quickly took pole position. Getting there first does not guarantee market dominance. Blue oceans do not stay blue indefinitely; if you're not there first, following a market leader (who has spent the time and resources to create a market), while learning from their mistakes and examining their weaknesses, can also be very effective.

Market research in the 21st century is not, as is sometimes now implied, a matter of DIY "Big Data" collection alone. Although there are a wealth of sources and tools for in-house marketers, it is "smart data" that companies need. The analysis of that smart data, together with the strategic insights and actionable tactics to utilise it, is what the best market research professionals can provide.

Jane Frost, CBE, CEO, The Market Research Society

Making an assessment of what does not exist is hard. That's where primary market research can the solution; no one is talking on social media or blogging about the market that's not there, yet! You can brief an expert market research agency to investigate what you see as a potentially lucrative market space. You will want to establish the value and longevity of the market you can see emerging, what it replaces or complements, the needs and current behaviors of the potential buyers, who they are, and the infrastructure of the business world in which they operate. You may offer a new technology, product, or service that may initiate a new type of usage or consumption, but not create a new market per se. Take the example of JustPark, which sells car parking space. Prebooked parking is not a new market, but using neighborhood driveways as well as multistory car parks adds enormous scope. The innovation is that the whole process is online, through a smartphone app, a platform only possible because of the Android operating system, which relies on fast cellular networks combined with the microprocessor technology that powers the smartphone. The same applies to Uber—the taxi service—and to Othership, the meeting space and virtual office rental company: new ways of buying an established product or service, not new markets. These companies have established a market lead by getting their timing right, but have also committed only to established technologies, have built barriers to competition by quickly signing up providers of the service, and have not had to make disproportionate investments up front. They have been strategic opportunists. Uber has been the one that has transferred its benefits across countries, now operating on a vast geographical scale. We will discuss new and emerging markets strategy later in this chapter. Capturing entirely new markets is potentially highly profitable, but is hard and risky. For existing markets, in B2B in particular, there is an established methodology for market selection based on firmographics: market segmentation. It was Wendell Smith, as far back as 1956, who proposed that market segmentation, rather than product differentiation, should be at the heart of strategic decision making.

Segmentation—Precision Targeting

Market segmentation provides a method of focusing and aligning the entire organization around common targets and objectives. Again, the message is about resource-efficient precision: about *focus*. The very point of adopting a segmentation strategy is to get that focus. No business or product offering will appeal equally to every potential customer in your more broadly identified target market. Customers are increasingly demanding solutions tailored to their most pressing issues and those issues change over time, so your research and market feedback loop has to be a continual one. This approach allows your organization to develop a deeper understanding of those key customer issues and how you can solve them, both now and in the future. From that flows the ability for your firm to prioritize marketing, sales (whether direct or channel oriented), and further product development activities. Really, this is about good marketing practice: making a profit by meeting the needs of your customers with the optimum allocation of resources.

The basis of segmentation is dividing a market into distinct groups of buyers, each of which has differing needs, characteristics, or behavior and which demands disparate marketing mixes to be informed about different products. These groups might be "vertical" or "horizontal." Horizontal segmentation means selling a product to a wide spectrum of a specific type of consumer, across many industries and markets, while vertical segmentation narrows your selling focus to target a usually smaller number of consumers in a smaller demographic. Though it might seem counterintuitive to look at a smaller total number of prospects when you are looking for the highest potential sales for your product or service, focusing on vertical markets—particularly by industry classifications such as health care, retail, education, and finance—is a core part of successful B2B segmentation. B2B markets differ considerably from B2C in that, although personal relationships matter, B2B sales are more complex, usually involving a group of people in a buying team rather than an individual, so that rationality and longer-term justifiability dominate the buying decision, rather than personal choice or short-term thinking. They are thinking about business benefits, not personal ones.

You may immediately think of the term "demographics" in the B2C context; this is segmentation by factors such as age, education, income, gender, and occupation. In B2B, we are talking about firmographic segmentation, which looks at organizations rather than individuals, and considers factors like industry specialization, company size, and number of employees. This *multiattribute segmentation* allows even greater prospecting and targeting precision for your sales and marketing efforts. Part of the function of segmentation is to enable you to provide the material to support buyers in making a rational and justifiable purchase decision. More on this in Chapter 4, when we talk about *core content*. A major advantage from a sales point of view is that each of these segments will be united by a common set of needs. The individuals involved often consult among themselves, outside their own companies, over their procurement of any products or services. Targeting them involves evaluating each market segment's attractiveness and selecting one or more of them to focus on. In the extreme, there might even be an instance of a "single-prospect segment"! We'll deal with what's meant by market "attractiveness" later.

Positioning, which we look at in detail in the next chapter, is about doing all that we can to ensure our offering occupies a clear, distinctive, and desirable place relative to segment-specific competing products in the minds of those target customers. Doing this effectively means considering how it fits into your overall business strategy or perhaps even shapes it completely. The objective is to focus your business model and resources—all of your resources—on a "value-creating" approach to the market, as opposed to a "horizontal solutions" approach, where the market may be larger, but the costs and effort involved in addressing it are much greater. And then there's the increased competition. We have a far better chance of making every sales, marketing, and support dollar, pound, or euro an effective one if we refine our offering to target the specific needs of a particular market segment, in defined geographies, with R&D-tailored products, made available through specific channels. If you feel that you really do have an offering that can *create* a market for you, then the Blue Ocean strategic moves will be appropriate.

Choosing That Target

How do you select which segments to go after? Figure 1.1 shows the issues involved. Statistical analysis techniques geared to helping make these decisions and the people who know how to use them are widely available. Multivariate analysis (put simply, looking at multiple criteria and cross-comparing them to discover clearer trends) can discover the needs of a particular set

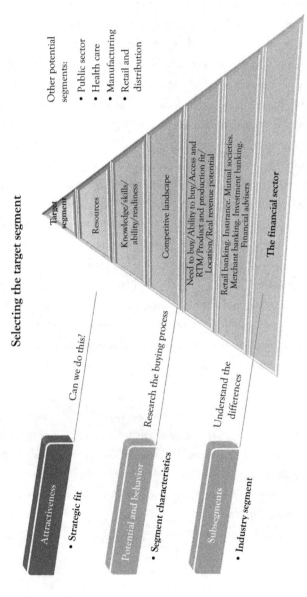

Figure 1.1 Using the financial sector as an example, there are many factors to consider in selecting each target segment

of prospects, with factor analysis and then further cluster analysis enabling more precise understanding of how to group together the common needs of customers within those groupings. What makes a specific segment "attractive"? It might be the case that your sales force will tell you that they have already had some success in a segment and that they feel there could be more business there, if the approach was better supported by the marketing effort, by increased industry expertise, or with adapted products. It might be obvious that your business does well with, say, financial institutions or health care providers. Do you know what those current customers think of your solutions? Are they happy with them and buying more? Do they perceive your company as one that understands the particular challenges of their line of business and how to help them meet those challenges? Integrating and targeting your marketing and sales improves customer perception in those cases; most buyers like the idea that you sell to other "people like me," as they see it. When managers from the same industry are talking positively about you, there's very effective reinforcement of your company brand and positioning going on. Conversely, not having got your brand image across correctly to them (see Chapter 2) will potentially undermine the positive benefits of those meetings. Negative messages, unfortunately, tend to stick in the mind as much as, if not more than, the positive ones. Consistent measurement of your brand awareness is essential when carrying out your selection, just as in any marketing operation, right from the beginning.

> *I've always enjoyed seeing companies that are capable of thinking differently; of defining their market and ideal customer profile as one that only they and their solution can satisfy. By defining their own "sandbox", they can set the rules of engagement precisely to match that ideal customer's needs and do it as if they existed in a "metaverse", setting them completely apart from their competition.*
>
> Juan Pablo Pazos, President and CEO, XmarteK, Miami

How big is our target segment? How big is the current and potential spend in any specific subsegment that we want to target? Is it growing, static, or declining? Who are our competitors and what share of that market do they currently hold? The segment has to be *measurable and substantial.* Understanding the competitive landscape in a potential segment is vital. Focusing on gaining enumerated share in your chosen target segments supports your planned growth ambitions. It helps you to set realistic targets better and to allocate appropriate resources. Sometimes, the juiciest-looking business segment in terms of overall size might not be the wisest choice for you. If your strongest competitors have large and growing market shares there, your cost of entry will be high. You will have to commit more marketing dollars to raise awareness, more sales resources to get through the door, and potentially more of your R&D budget to adapt your product or solution. You will have to offer an advantage, or at least to be on a par with the incumbent supplier, to have a chance of making the customer switch. The segment has to be *accessible and actionable.* On the other hand, if current vendors are not meeting the customers' needs and there is dissatisfaction, there might be an opening for you. The risk is lower than trying to create a market, because you do at least know that it exists and have a feel for its dynamics.

Let's imagine that you find an ideal target segment and look at each of these elements. Your research has shown you that it has a significant spend on your class of product, and that spend is increasing at a rate that is attractive for your business model. You have discovered that there is an appetite for innovation amongst the buyers and that the gap between new technology introductions and the time taken for broad adoption in that industry is short. In *Crossing the Chasm*, Geoffrey Moore established the concept of the gap between early adopters and mainstream users of new technology and discusses how vendors can leap that "chasm". The process of introducing a new technology to an industry—making a few sales that come with intensive and expensive marketing and sales effort—can be slow and resource-hungry for you. You may be able to achieve premium pricing at a low volume, but it's worth it only if you can achieve major follow-on sales into the mainstream on a timescale that fits the demands of your own business model. Examine that market potential and its prospective timing carefully.

Who is already in the game as the incumbent supplier in that segment? If there is a broad list of equally competitive suppliers, well-defined channels from which those businesses buy, and a need for what you sell, what would you need to do to compete effectively? Perhaps your research and previous experience in the segment (no matter how small) convinced you that you have the right product or solution to be competitive. Can you adapt or create unique products for these targets without excessive expense? You will need to ensure that you have an efficient feedback loop from your frontline people, back to your R&D function, so that you can prioritize your development schedule based on the needs of the segment or segments that you have chosen. Reasonableness must prevail, of course. If what you have is just too far from being what they need, you may not be able to justify your investment to adapt it. Sales and support will be up close and personal with the users and managers of your solution and will be the first to hear the good and the bad responses, or simply the suggestions for how it could be made better for them. Being responsive to those requests is what will secure that customer for you in the long term—every internal supporter is a plus! More on this in Chapter 5.

What are the other barriers to entry? It might be the necessity for buyers to do things *around* your own product that is a key to the purchase decision. If you are selling a core product, around which others have to work to be effective, can you identify and strike up partnerships with other companies with the right expertise who would, together with you, provide a compelling total solution? That might help you jointly to develop specific product features for your segments, more quickly. The concept of strategic alliances is one that has gained greater credence over the last few years, for good reason. The interview with Carlo Tortora Brayda di Belvedere in Chapter 4 emphasizes this point.

Part of your earlier research will have told you how these companies buy. Identify the segment-specific channels (more on this in Chapter 4) that supply and have the trust of the buyers that you are after. Striking the right kind of relationship with them—financial and operational—will be one of the keys to your success. What will be their incentive to recommend or promote your products ahead of those of your competitors? Obviously, making money will be uppermost in their minds, but having satisfied customers is a key goal for them, as it is for you. It could be that their product or service is highly dependent on the successful implementation of your own. It's much better for you both if you ensure compatibility and user satisfaction by working together at the earliest stage, rather than having to discover some glitches in front of the user, later on. Then, if that collaboration is particularly positive for you both, you each have a partner to go hunting for the next successful deal. Mutual benefit! If these are channels from which you have discovered those prospects are happy to buy, be prepared to share a slice of your profits with them to gain and secure new accounts. Your payback will be speedier market entry, and you will gain valuable further education in the customers' needs and reasons to buy in that segment. We cover go-to-market strategy—choosing channels—in more depth in Chapter 4.

Why Do They Buy?

Why do these companies spend on your particular class of product? Your segmentation work will have helped to group those whose needs are similar, if not identical, because of the industry in which they operate. But developing a *prospect profile* might not be as obvious as you think. "Value-added" selling does not mean simply add-ons to your product. The best value you can offer will be your understanding of their needs and why it's you that can meet them. Take the example of the health care sector. Its diversity makes it a complex one to sell into. More so in the public sector than private but, in both, health care resources are always strained. Making the very best use of those scarce resources is a constant challenge for clinicians and their staff. It seems obvious that positioning your business as one that understands this and can help them with that problem is the way to go. We cover company and product positioning in Chapter 2. But there may be a higher level of need—and therefore reason to buy—that you should strive to discover. Chapter 3 looks further into this.

Mike Ames in Conversation With Kimball Bailey

Mike Ames grew a fledgling IT recruitment business into a £40M IT services and recruitment group which was sold to a NYSE-listed company in 1998. He then set up another recruitment business, which was sold (as another multimillion-pound enterprise) to one of the United Kingdom's biggest recruiters in 2017. To do it once is impressive; only a handful have done it twice and so share Mike's depth of knowledge and experience in sales and marketing. He now advises and coaches recruitment companies and other professional firms on growing their businesses, and writes and blogs on the subject.

So, what's the secret?

The challenge for any salesperson, says Mike, *is to personalize the sales process and to build a lasting relationship with the client. A relationship-driven sales cycle is very different from a purchasing-driven sales cycle.*

What does he mean by that?

Very simply, if everything else is equal, or even if it isn't, clients are more likely to buy from someone with whom they have a relationship than from someone they don't. It's not about being "in your face" all the time, nor having to be all "hail fellow well met," nor having a substantial golf budget. It's about identifying individuals who are decision-makers, finding out about them—in business terms—and talking to them.

The information you can acquire can include business issues, priorities and even procurement timings—and it is so much easier to do so now than it used to be.

Easy? Really?

Absolutely. There is so much information available these days. Market research will help you to identify a "class," if you like, of potential clients that you can target. From this you can set up an ideal client profile—sector, size, how they buy—but this won't necessarily tell you anything about the individual decision-maker. There has been an explosion of information over the last decade, and we can all use social media—LinkedIn, Twitter, even Facebook. Look at their profiles and posts to pinpoint a client decision-maker or influencer accurately, on an individual basis, to build a "persona" for that individual, and hence to find ways of building a relationship. Social media is now critical to identify targets, to find out information about them and to build credibility and promote one's own services.

It's all about timing. It doesn't matter whether you're trying to sell recruitment services, or the services of a real estate agent, or a new computer system, or a new car. There is a very limited period in the overall client lifecycle when the client will have any interest in buying.

So how do you break into the lifecycle?

Let's say that you are the salesperson looking to sell me a new car. I am currently in the "not interested" zone: I have a car, it works, I don't need a new one, thank you very much. If the seller calls, it's a waste of time—the buyer is unlikely to engage. But there will come a time when my car has a catastrophic engine failure on the M42, which puts me straight into the "buying zone," or when I realize that the cost of servicing is greater than the cost of a replacement vehicle, or I know the car won't pass its next MOT, when I am in the "pre-buying" zone. A random call is most likely to be at the wrong time, when the buyer is in the "not interested" zone; it's the luck of the draw. And worse than that, it may well just irritate. Timing is everything.

So how does the seller make sure that he or she is around in the "buying zone" or shortly before, especially when there is a long purchase cycle?

That is where building a relationship comes in, alongside sensible investigation of an individual on social media. People disclose a lot of valuable information about their business on social media, let alone about themselves personally, and certainly enough to be able to initiate a conversation. To pursue the car analogy, I might spot that the individual is posting a question about the range of an electric hybrid vehicle. And I capture this within the target persona.

So, I am looking to establish how best to build a dialogue with the individual based on their interest, because I want to connect with them—and I can think long-term because most purchase cycles are reasonably long. One approach which has worked for me is based on social media. I want to link my content and service to their potential need, so I send them something, a small piece of research perhaps, and I run a series of expert Zoom workshops based on the content that I believe my clients will be interested in, at any time of the lifecycle. All pretty low-key—perhaps low-threat or low-commitment is better. I invite them along, as my guests and for free, obviously, and can check who has registered and attended. If they don't come, I can invite them to something else because we are already talking. And when I call to ask for feedback afterwards, and most will take a call at that point. And it is human nature to start to talk, so I am cultivating the initial lead. We are more engaged; we are in a dialogue.

I back that up with a series of online videos which are on my website, plus customized LinkedIn and Twitter. They are not expensive—and again I can check clicks and responses.

This is how modern marketing works.

All part of turning a contact into a relationship, changing the narrative without necessarily any overt selling. So, when we are into the "pre-buying" zone, there is a far greater chance that they will talk to me. And on that basis, I can massively increase the chance of converting a burgeoning relationship into a sale.

So, I have got the client's attention and interest, I've begun a dialogue, I've cultivated a relationship whereby the client has started to associate a credible solution with that relationship. This is of course all pre-pitch: the pitch itself is a different beast, but how much more likely it is to be successful with the relationship in place.

We talk about a "relationship bridge." Every time we have a little more dialogue with the prospective client, every time we interact, we put another layer on the bridge, and the more layers you have, the stronger the bridge becomes. And when it is eventually strong enough, you can walk over it—or if you're lucky the client will walk over it to find you.

So the Five Cs still work for me:

- *Capture*
- *Connect*
- *Cultivate*
- *Convert*
- *Care*

Client care is absolutely critical for any sort of repeat sale, of course, so once I have developed the relationship, I take real care to make sure that I don't fritter it away. I'm not going to go too deeply into a gardening metaphor, but a relationship has to be tended carefully—with just the right amount of fertilizer.

The traditional transactional sales cycle—where sellers are focused on end of month or end of quarter targets—leads to bad behavior when it comes to a client relationship. Ignoring or neglecting clients who are not buying now may be understandable in that context—but if you do that, you won't be remembered when those clients are buying. You must care for clients even when they are in the "not interested" zone when they are not actually buying. It may seem quite counter-intuitive, but it really isn't if we are focusing on building a positive relationship.

Everyone, no matter how cosmopolitan or multilingual, prefers to speak in their own language. Subtleties, nuances, and deeper meanings are more easily communicated. We relax, listen more, and understand better when everyone is using the same words and terminology. So it goes in the best segment marketing and sales encounters. Every industry has its own "language" of words, phrases, and the dreaded forest of acronyms that they operate with, daily, in the workplace. Across national boundaries, shared industry terms and common expressions become the *lingua franca* of business, remaining consistent even in different languages. Learn the language of your prospects: it will substantially enhance your credibility and make your sales and market message to any industry segment more attractive and a more effective sales tool. Hire and work with industry experts to expand this form of segment knowledge, and for credibility. Use these experts as advisers, consultants, and spokespeople in your PR efforts. Target key influencers for the segment—sell your solution and segment credibility to them, learn from them, and convince them to retell your story throughout the industry. And pundits: love them or hate them, oft-quoted experts, and industry spokespeople *do* influence your marketplace. As well as ensuring that you develop a positive relationship with those people—they may be journalists, academics, leading proponents of the discipline concerned, or consultants—why not join them? Industry-specific publications of all kinds are always looking for good-quality material; help provide it for them. Train your best technicians or most knowledgeable sales, marketing, or support people on how to speak to the media in the vernacular of the targets. And it's not just about sales and marketing people. Your pre- and post-sales technical teams can often be extremely effective in this regard. More about this in Chapter 4.

Overseas and Emerging Markets

Geography also plays a part in your market segmentation strategy. The Internet has made it possible for every business to instantly become a worldwide one, certainly in terms of visibility, but also—if Internet selling is one of your routes to market—in sales. But not every company can sell to and support its B2B customers remotely—at least not properly. Sometimes, it will be the case that your business model requires boots on the ground—a physical presence wherever your solution is sold. This can be a challenge. Be honest about your own strengths as a business. If you have a major presence in the United States, Canada, and the United Kingdom, but nowhere else, for example, then focus your market entry efforts on those countries. Do you have the people with the skills to do the international sales job? If not, do you have the budget to recruit and pay for them? Can you offer them an attractive career path?

> *The CEO/VP EMEA for a specific vertical niche with a specialised solution offering can be a devilishly difficult role to fill, depending on the target market. Candidates are typically looking for a compelling proposition, including a great role with a sector leading vendor, career progression and a compensation package that combines market rate cash compensation and benefits with a motivational equity element.*
>
> Steve Lavelle, Managing Partner, NGS Global, United Kingdom

As you gain experience, expertise and reputation in your chosen industry segment, you will become equipped to enter new geographies—segmentation expertise makes that easier because it will be largely applicable wherever the industry is located—but focus on gaining a foothold in your established geographies first.

In *Capturing New Markets*, Stephen Wunker considers that "Developing countries contain some of the most enticing new markets." The IMF categorizes these 20 countries as emerging markets:

> *Selling new products into new markets is hard, lengthy and expensive. As the Ansoff Matrix[1] illustrates, although that can be a way to grow the company, servicing existing clients with your existing products is where your high-volume business is going to come from.*
>
> Juan Pablo Pazos, President and CEO, XmarteK, Miami

---

[1] The Ansoff Matrix (referred to by J.P. Pazos) was developed by H. Igor Ansoff and first published in the *Harvard Business Review* in 1957, in an article titled "Strategies for Diversification." It has given generations of marketers and business leaders a quick and simple way to think about the risks of growth.

Argentina, Brazil, Chile, China, Colombia, Egypt, Hungary, India, Indonesia, Iran, Malaysia, Mexico, the Philippines, Poland, Russia, Saudi Arabia, South Africa, Thailand, Turkey, and the United Arab Emirates.

These 20 emerging market countries account for 34 percent of the world's nominal GDP in U.S. dollars and 46 percent in purchasing power parity terms. These countries are also featured in commonly used indices for emerging markets, such as those of J.P. Morgan, Morgan Stanley Capital International, and Bloomberg—enticing, maybe, but still largely a side issue for most businesses. Entering those markets carries higher risk, higher cost of entry, and a level of volatility on too many fronts to be a priority for most firms. That said, there are success stories; it might just be that your chosen segments have a level of globalized uniformity that encourages you to examine their potential. To quote Stephen Wunker (*ibid*):

> *Many people would think first of the $4.4 trillion expansion of China's gross domestic product over the past 30 years—a sum that constitutes more than seven percent of today's global economy. The nation's tremendous growth has led it to become the world's largest consumer of construction equipment, automobiles and more. As impressive as China's growth has been, it presents just one facet of the story. Look at sub-Saharan Africa. More often associated with development aid than high-growth industry, the region nevertheless has seen an explosion in the field of cellular technology.*

He was writing this in 2011; since then China's share of global GDP has risen to an astonishing 18.79 percent, on its way to an estimated 20.31 percent by 2027 (*IMF World Economic Outlook Database April 2022*. Published by C. Textor). I'll leave the topic here, remembering the old adage "In China, everything is possible, but nothing is easy," with a cautionary note from Mark Hedley from B2B International in "China Market Entry Strategy: A Guide to Entering Chinese Business-to-Business Markets":

> *While it is true that China represents a huge potential market for foreign manufactured goods and services, it is also the case that*

understanding where these opportunities lie and how to access them can be extremely challenging. Whether it be the large western multinationals with an established China presence or the first-time market entrant with no previous China experience, foreign companies of all shapes and sizes often find their China success stymied through insufficient lack of local understanding.

The report discusses the many considerations, highlighting the importance of IP protection, trademarking, and due diligence on partners, customers, and employees. China is a classic example of a market that looks—on the surface—like an opportunity not to be missed, but can be a stretch too far for you if you are not properly prepared to enter it. There is no one perfect way to enter a new market, but good research is essential, whatever your tactics. In their *Harvard Business Review* article, "The Core Competence of the Corporation," Prahalad and Hamel suggest an "expeditionary" approach—taking small stabs at optional markets and seeing what works, harvesting and learning from the experience. This, they advise, is better for most ambitious businesses than looking for the "home run," first-time, big success, fueled by a large bet of time and resources. Your core strategy will help you to decide which is best for you.

Industry leaders are usually big companies. Many companies underestimate their abilities as a small concern to supply a large one effectively. If you get your targeting right, then your expertise in your product or service offering can be just as compelling to a very large business as to a small one, regardless of whether you are an SME. In *Bag the Elephant*, Steve Kaplan agrees with, but emphasizes, the hard work involved, stressing that you will have to judge if the extent of that work justifies the end goal. We will talk more about investigating what would qualify as specific large targets for your size of business and how to sell to them successfully in Chapter 3. If your strategy discussions have concluded that you will focus on large accounts in a specific market segment or industry, then you can be confident that your segment expertise will make opening the door to what looks like a forbiddingly large prospect that much easier. Your size becomes irrelevant; your expertise becomes the winning card to play in your sales and marketing. Many businesses focus almost obsessively on gaining an industry "elephant" as an early customer to establish their credentials in an industry. Yes, that's a good idea, but make sure you are ready to do that before you walk through those big, impressive doors. If they are the biggest, they will almost certainly also be one of the most demanding and will test your knowledge, expertise, sales process, and salespeople to the limit. They will likely be at the top of their game, so you must be, too. They will expect the highest level of proof that you really can provide what you say that you can. The real prize in securing such an account—say, the most prestigious investment bank—is as much the kudos that you gain as the revenue. This becomes a valuable reusable tool for your sales process, for other institutions of the same kind.

We will look at the way to make such a relationship a mutually beneficial one in Chapter 8. Managed proactively and properly, that customer's prestige rubs off on your firm, too. If they are a thought leader in that industry, then their competitors will take notice when they see that they have chosen your firm as a supplier. You will be seen as a supplier worthy of their consideration, too. But don't overlook the need for real ROI: no prestigious brand name customer is worth gouging your pricing for or becoming a disproportionate drain on your resources and profitability.

Your tactics for the implementation of a segmented marketing and sales strategy have to be worked out in detail before you begin. Let's use the financial services sector as our example. Having decided that this is our target, the subsegments that we have identified have to be analyzed in order for us to understand what it will take to gain and service them. As shown in Figure 1.1, the overall label of financial services covers a multitude of business types. Marketing and selling to the insurance sector is going to need a different approach to the retail banking one. They are different types of firm, each with distinctive needs and objectives that you must be aware of. We need to prepare—through training and selection—our best sales resources. If—as is likely in this segment—we are intending to use expert partners for our go-to-market (GTM) strategy, they need to be recruited if we do not already have them. Then they have to be extensively briefed on our plans and how they can benefit from them. Have a clear direct-only, channel-only, or mixed GTM strategy from the beginning and stick to it. Chapter 4 explores dealing with third-party channels in more detail. Our field marketing team, those with experience and training in the sector, need to be ready to engage with prospects on behalf of partners. Our sales and marketing teams will be working in lockstep at this point, with marketing responsible for creating compelling core content designed specifically for this purpose: for your partners to use. Sales tools for the channel and internal salespeople should be produced, such as briefing handbooks, online training modules for self-learning on industry "hot topics," and the critical requirements relative to the products and solutions that they will be selling. A measure of success is to get to the stage that your partner salespeople feel as much a part of your company as do your own staff.

Start early with the engagement of the commentators and industry influencers we mentioned earlier, to use their supportive comments as marketing content. Stay highly informed about the hot topics in that industry, so that you know what is on their minds. Get your senior people onto public-speaking platforms in relevant industry conferences and gatherings of those that we are targeting, obviously making sure that they are sufficiently well briefed to answer challenging questions from an expert audience. Your PR machinery should now be grinding into action, as well, using that core content to gain a presence in, for example, financial trade publications, and be preparing easy-to-implement campaigns to broadcast your account gains and successes, when they happen. All the while, be focused on what you have learned about the needs and buying behaviors of the target segment: don't expect to get away with the same generic message to retail banking as to merchant banking. Show deep understanding of their particular world and its current business issues or you will immediately damage your credibility.

Now that we are highly targeted, we can identify precisely who are the "marquee accounts" who not only spend considerable amounts of money on our kind of solutions, but are the thought leaders to whom all others in the sector look for guidance. Let's identify and go after the 20 percent of businesses in our chosen segment who spend 80 percent of the total available market (TAM) dollars. Create a SWAT team that has executive sponsorship and involvement from your most senior people, involving the value-added retailers (VARS), consultants, and system integrator (SIs) that you've selected to partner with you. These channels may have been selling lesser or competitive solutions into the segment already, so be prepared to offer substantial competitive advantage to gain their attention—and more money. Where your partners have been selling at a lower level than you are now targeting—either in the business-critical level of the solutions or the size of company—be prepared to train them to raise the expectations of what they can achieve for themselves with your newly focused help.

Strategic Fit

Your carefully honed strategy, based on your core values as a business (see Chapter 2), has informed your upstream marketing work and sales plan and focused you on the market that will deliver your targeted revenues and give you long-term competitive advantage. Hopefully, your early experiences will be positive ones. But it all has to feel right for your company and continue to motivate you.

Strategic fit is usually defined as when the resources of an organization—human, financial, material, technology, and knowledge—are aligned with its strategic goals and development objectives. Despite my focus on research, data, and judicious, objective customer selection, you and your fellow company leaders will need to feel that the segment you are targeting has a *strategic fit* with your own firm. This is usually viewed as three subsections: financial fit, market fit, and technology fit. Ask yourself some questions:

- Do you have sufficient initial resources and the ongoing financial plan that supports this market entry? Can you afford the right people, infrastructure, and technology that are required?
- Does the market fit with your plan and capabilities? Can you handle either high volumes or very long sales cycles, as this segment demands? Do you already have or can you readily acquire the requisite industry knowledge? Is the geographical reach that will be needed to be a leader in this segment an overstretch for you?
- Are you ready with products or technology that will put you in a leadership position in this industry? If not, will you need to build it, buy it, or partner with someone who has it?

Segmentation is not in itself a guarantee of success. If each of your chosen segments is truly different in a meaningful way, if it is big enough to satisfy your resource/return plan, and you feel that the needs-based analysis you have carried out shows that you can be both competitive and successful in those segments, then you can go prospecting!

Prospecting—Filling the Sales Funnel

In Chapter 4, we examine the sales process: getting from first contact to closing the deal and acquiring a new customer. But at this early stage, let's look briefly at the job that salespeople traditionally dislike: prospecting, making that first contact in the market. Prospecting from "cold" is demanding and can be soul-sapping. The watchword, however, is quality, not quantity. Your objective is to spend the most time with the best qualified prospects. Your earlier work on research and segmentation will have narrowed down your potential targets to those that are likely to be the best prospects for you. Your marketing function will have put your best core content (see Chapter 2) in the places where your target market can see it, in all its forms. This will have changed your prospecting from cold to warm, at least. Some of those you want to contact will have become the subjects of "permission marketing"—a description coined by marketing writer Seth Godin. This is the route to quality lead generation. They will have requested a contact from you via your website, in response to a direct e-mail campaign, through social media, or in some other way. Those are very warm prospects and you can go directly into your proven sales process with them.

It's the prospects you know are there but with whom you have had no contact—the truly cold—that you have to work on. You have a CRM database or system that has the basic contact details of, for example, the universities and colleges that you know could benefit from your part-time online and blended education programs for their students around the world. You know that you use cutting-edge technology, sector-leading teaching methodology, and first-class student support to provide an outstanding educational experience. The prospects you are going to contact—to interrupt at their workplace—don't know that. You know from your research that they are very likely to consider buying your services if you can make them aware of you, get them informed, and then get them to consider your solution as one that meets their needs (see Figure 4.1 in Chapter 4). If your marketing has been as effective as you think, then you may find some level of awareness, but at this point, you have to assume there is little or none, particularly if you are completely new to that market segment and are a low-profile SME. You have to make the contact to find out. However you are going for it, have a clear objective for that contact. Do you want a meeting (face to face or video), an e-mail address with permission to send info via attachments, or links, to offer a presentation or demonstration or get attendance on a webinar? Be specific, but flexible: offer options. Just be sure that you have a clear idea of what constitutes success for that contact.

Let's take four methods of contact as examples:

- Telephone:
  The telephone call as a sales approach is not dead! The proliferation of websites, online chat, automated e-mail systems, social media, and so on does not negate the incisive use of the telephone as a prospecting tool. Don't underestimate two essential elements: that you are interrupting someone's working time, if this is not prearranged; and that you will leave an abiding impression by your tone of voice, message, and how you handle the call. Expect rejection, but press for contact details and permission to get back in touch. Always leave the call on a positive note.
- E-mail:
  Postal mail marketing is almost dead. It still happens, but in B2B, its effectiveness is minimal or negative. It is—and looks—20th century. E-mail marketing is the replacement for it. This has evolved into a marketing science all of its own, with expert practitioners offering complete end-to-end campaign services. Just be sure that it is your own, carefully handcrafted strategy that is driving and guiding the implementation and the measurement of ROI, in terms of the number of well-qualified prospects that you get into your sales pipeline. Have a clear strategy, plan, and set of measurable objectives for your campaign. Get expert help in crafting the form and content of the communication, from the headline,

to the call to action, to the sign-off. Unless your e-mail is opened and responded to, it has failed. Like we described above, you're looking for it to generate a sales conversation, an appointment; an introduction to an influencer or decision maker, or registration for a download of documents, a video, or a webinar.

- LinkedIn messaging:
Prospecting through LinkedIn is increasingly popular. LinkedIn itself provides a set of marketing and promotional tools and services to make the most of your online connections. You need to do this judiciously so as not to be blocked by those who don't know you, but whom you wish to contact. LinkedIn's Sales Navigator and Campaign Manager tools can help you to turn your contacts into prospects in your sales funnel.

  Other forms of social selling media abound, of course, but monitoring Twitter, Meta, Instagram, YouTube, and others is more about information gathering than about selling. Limit your time with them!

- Events:
Trade shows, conferences, webinars, and online live training sessions still have a part to play in your prospecting toolset, so long as you apply the same rigorous tests of focus, applicability, and target ROI to them that you do to the rest of your activities. It's easy to be seduced by the glamour of running or participating in a major event. Objective assessment of cost versus potential is what you need to begin with. We talk more about online events in Chapter 4, but suffice to say here that face to face events are still an effective prospecting tool if you micromanage your time and investment in them. If your segmentation analysis has led you to choose financial services, for example, as your target market, build into your prospecting plan the time and investment to get in front of the specific people that you need to meet with at the specific events that they attend or that you can arrange to draw them to you.

In each of these cases, close collaboration between marketing and sales will prove highly productive. The more that marketing has managed to parade your compelling brand credentials in front of the target market, the more likely that your salesperson's approach will be welcomed by the prospect. Your hunter-gatherers should bring in a continuous flow of prospects into the sales funnel. Ensure that your sales managers have a balanced team of these, closers, and account managers. You're looking for business from qualified prospects for today, tomorrow, and the future. In Chapter 3, we look in more depth at the qualification of those prospects and at understanding who they are, what they want, and why they buy. As a closing point on prospecting, I like Mike Weinberg's comment in his book, *New Sales. Simplified*: "The first rule of holes is when you are in one, stop digging, and the first rule of sales slumps is when you are in one, start prospecting." That instruction is going to be at its most effective when it is your top chosen segment that you are prospecting in, from a base of clear knowledge of their industry and business needs.

Summary

Why is this such an important first step in your marketing and sales process? This is not the glamorous end of marketing or sales, but time taken to select your most lucrative and available target market is time well spent. Get the selection right, based not on emotion but on hard facts and considered analysis, and you will have higher marketing ROI and a more productive and satisfied sales team.

The more tailored to your own objectives your research, the more you will add to your own knowledge and expertise, and that of your teams. If you feel that you can genuinely address multiple segments, that's great, but take it step by step, learning as you go. Have the objective of becoming truly expert in your chosen segment; that's a competitive advantage that you can bank, grow, and draw upon over the longer term. You cannot do this as a semipro. Without developing or recruiting people with the right skills, you risk damaging your credibility and your brand when you approach specialist, expert prospects. As our contributors from recruitment (Andy Heyes, interviewed in Chapter 3, and Steve Lavelle, quoted in Chapter 1) will attest, it is easier to mold an industry expert into a salesperson than to turn a generalist salesperson into an industry expert with real depth.

Encourage your marketing and sales teams to be perfectionists in their prospecting: use any or all of the available tools that we have discussed above, but select and eliminate ruthlessly to get the best ROI for your marketing and sales budgets.

If you avoid or underestimate this early sales and marketing process work, it is inevitable that, later, you will find yourself racking up many hours of wasted effort in chasing or losing deals, correcting your targeting, revising your sales and marketing strategy, and even reconsidering your overall business mission. Get it right the first time.

The Takeaways and Lessons Learned From Chapter 1	Do	Don't
Market research	Use reputable secondary research from the leading companies and if you can afford it, conduct primary research of your own The plethora of online information available is outstanding, but use highly qualified sources and cross-check them	Don't take the DIY approach through the Internet and social media alone Don't assume that research results from studies by vendors—of anything—are unbiased. Many are tremendously useful, but skewed to support their own objectives
Analysis	Apply as much expertise as you can gather in objectively analyzing the data	Don't forget to apply the expertise and opinions of your whole team. The commitment must be company wide
Segmentation	Select your target segments (max of five) by their business potential *for you*, after compiling a realistic strategy that you can execute to meet your business goals Getting your segmentation strategy right will focus your business on achievable goals that support your business plan	Don't be blinded by the big numbers. Your business potential is not the same as the total segment market size Don't underestimate the need for in-depth industry or segment expertise. Recruit it or train it Don't underestimate the commitment to continual monitoring and feedback to marketing, sales, and R&D needed for successful execution

The Takeaways and Lessons Learned From Chapter 1	Do	Don't
	Understand from the outset that this requires a high level of commitment, thoroughness, and persistence, but the big payback is the more effective use of every dollar of resource and the evolution of your company into an industry specialist, with competitive advantage	Relentless measurement and corporate learning are essential
Prospecting	Be diligent and realize that marketing and sales have a continuous shared objective to feed the funnel Use multiple methods, rigorously testing the results of each one Check back with your segmentation objectives that you have a pipeline of prospects that have the potential to meet your sales targets	Don't be tempted to fill your CRM system with unqualified targets just to make the number look good Don't negate future contact in the face of rejection: leave every contact with the potential for a later conversation

CHAPTER 2

Company Branding and Competitive Positioning

Overview

This chapter is a discussion on the importance of establishing your brand and a compelling competitive position before attacking the target businesses in the lucrative market segment that we identified and researched in Chapter 1. Fixing your brand image in your prospect's mind is an essential precursor to your marketing and selling efforts. Consider it a rung on your ladder to success that must not be missing. Establishing your brand and positioning in that market is the next step in developing your marketing and sales process. Then you can begin a highly focused and effective marketing and sales approach. Senior professionals will comment on lessons learned in the field and we will draw some conclusions about the most important actions you can take.

Branding—Making a Name for Yourself

In challenging times for business, when revenue is your top priority, branding is sometimes considered a soft, ineffectual marketing concept. In fact, if you get your company branding right and use it well, you will generate a focus on the strengths of your business, gain more customers, and add long-term value to your company. Rather than the purely conceptual, we are talking here about using branding as a powerful business tool in our sales process toolbox, whether the company behind that brand is huge or tiny. Products come and go but a strong brand goes on forever. It has been said that buildings age and become dilapidated; machines wear out; people die. But what live on are the brands. It's about longevity.

Strong brands are remarkably hardy. The recent trend for the rediscovery and reuse of "retro brands" supports this contention. Kodak, Atari, Harley Davidson, and Rediffusion are examples of long-established brands that have survived and been revived after the companies that they were associated with were absorbed by others, ceased to trade, or simply disappeared. Some, like Kodak, have even gone back to the company's original logo-style to emphasize their strong foundation and valuable legacy. It's not so much about nostalgia; it's a return to a company's roots, showing a commitment to its original mission and the retention in the buyer's mind of the desirable attributes of that brand, which transcend the passage of time. They got it right from the beginning! Investing in a branding campaign that specifically includes long-term strategic asset building as a goal connects with customers, improves brand health, and ultimately drives long-term growth, no matter the size of your business at this stage.

As well as what you are, you have to be prepared to say what you are not: if you stand for something, you will always find some people for you and some against you. If you stand for nothing in particular, you will find nobody against you but nobody for you—in which case you may as well pack up and go home, because you will be anonymous. Your brand states what you stand for.

It used to be the case that the term "branding" would immediately make people think of corporate identity—the "look"—the use of consistent graphics, colours, logos, and so on. Not the case, now. I would estimate that 80% of my real branding work has been concerned with positioning. With diligent work, you can soon establish a position for your business, but really, it's an exercise for the long term. Positioning is the product of ruthless exclusion and is a core element of branding. I agree with Al Ries, who said that "You can't brand what you can't position."

William Agush, CEO, Adsonica Inc., Wellesley, Mass

So, what is a "brand," anyway? This is a big topic! In addressing it, let's try to be comprehensive without being overelaborate. Your brand embodies what your business represents to your prospective market (Figure 2.1).

The elements of branding

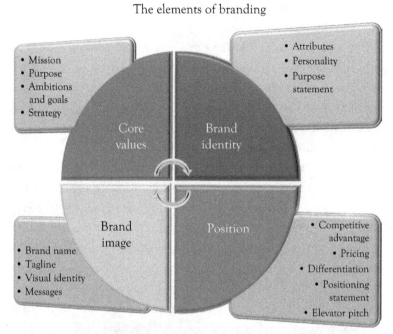

Figure 2.1 Beginning with your core values, to brand and position the business to arrive at a compelling brand image

A strong brand is a badge of reassurance and a guarantee of performance, having both distinctiveness and longevity. It adds value, helps gain and maintain customers, and makes them comfortable in paying what might be a premium price for your product or services. It stirs emotions and prompts them to spread to others the positive experience they have by being associated with it. All of these benefits pay back many times over, the effort of working to get it right. If your salesperson is forced to begin the sales conversation with a new prospect by having to establish the company's credentials because of its weak branding, that's a small mountain to climb right at the start of the selling process. Consider the difference between these two sales meeting scenarios:

"So, I know that you are the company that provides specialist, high-speed global printing solutions for large companies in our line of business. Do tell me more," and

"So, who are you and what do you do?"

Help your sales force with that first call by forming and promoting a strong and clear brand identity.

This is important for growing businesses as well as established ones. The world's top five most valuable brands are technology companies: Apple, Amazon, Google, Microsoft, and Walmart. They had a combined value of $1264.95Bn in 2022 (Statista). Their names and logos are virtually tattooed on your brain. You know what their brands represent, what they each do, and what their products are.

Brand value is not to be confused with brand equity. This latter term refers to the value a company gains from its name recognition when compared to a generic equivalent. Brand equity comprises the following elements: awareness, brand associations, perceived quality, brand loyalty, and other proprietary brand assets. Brand equity has a direct impact on sales volume and a company's profitability because consumers gravitate toward products and services with great reputations. Often, companies in the same industry or sector compete on brand equity. You will be doing this, so be prepared for it by working on that branding.

Brand valuation, on the other hand, is the estimation of a brand's total value. This is achieved by following the International Organization for Standardization's ISO 10668 standard, which maps out the appropriate process of valuing brands by adhering to six key requirements: transparency, validity, reliability, sufficiency, objectivity, and financial, behavioral, and legal parameters.

A brand is defined as an intangible asset (name, term, design, symbol, or any other feature) identifying one seller's product from another. It is often a corporation's most valued asset. Strong brands enhance business performance primarily through their influence on three key stakeholder groups: customers both current and prospective, employees, and investors. They influence customer choice and create loyalty; attract, retain, and motivate talent; and lower the cost of financing. Ultimately, strong brands help shape perceptions and influence purchasing behavior, making products and service less substitutable. Brands, therefore, create economic value by generating higher returns and growth and by mitigating buyer risk.

Let's use the high-tech sector as an example. The market for hardware, software solutions, and services has been much affected by recent economic, geopolitical, and global health uncertainties. Sometimes, this has been hugely positive, Zoom being a prime example of an opportunistic—some would say, serendipitous—success. Zoom's brand value increased by 24 percent (Statista), ranking it in the top 10 for growth in 2021. Its market valuation had reached an astonishing $5,636,865,833, following three years of over 300 percent year-on-year revenue growth. (It has since declined to $23.79Bn by October 2022, showing reactions to worldwide stock market volatility.) It has also entered everyday parlance as a verb—to "Zoom," meaning to video chat or videoconference—a sign of outstanding achievement in brand identity, to match "Google," "Xerox," and "Hoover."

In other cases, some markets for the sellers of hi-tech have virtually disappeared overnight (travel companies, hospitality businesses, the arts, and others). There have been mergers and rapid changes in all categories of high-tech business—consultancies, SaaS companies, cloud solutions vendors, app developers, and PC vendors. This has turned a marketplace that was already poorly understood by its consumers (both B2B and B2C) into one that is confusing and often mistrusted.

High-tech buyers are therefore looking for a brand that offers them certainty, security, and support. Can you convince them—or their equivalent in your own market segment—that you can be that provider?

Core Values Drive Brand Development

If your only branding objective is to establish and use your brand to proclaim your intentions, and to differentiate your firm from the morass of aggressive competition by establishing a sustainable competitive advantage, then that alone is worthwhile. You can achieve success and sustain it over the long term by harnessing the determination and passion that drove you to start your business to develop a deeply coherent and visibly strong brand. Your marketing and sales efforts should be underpinned by your *core values*. Investing in your brand is critical if you want your business to be unique and sustainable in a crowded market place, but authenticity is essential. You will almost certainly know the core values that the founders of your business began with, whether that was you or not. Those values are what drives them and the members of your company team to maintain a clear sense of purpose about where that company is going and how it treats its customers, partners, and employees. Though well known and understood at the top (and often within the business, too), these core values frequently do not get communicated and used as the very bedrock of the company brand. They should be. If they excite and motivate some or all of the people in the company, then why not use them to raise the same emotions in your prospective customers? Use those core values to fashion your own brand values. Your marketing goals, promotional messages, and sales efforts will be all the more cohesive, consistent, and solid if they are informed by brand values of which you are proud. Think of the big brands that you know: could you articulate their brand values?

A good example of getting this right is American Express, representing a company with inspiring core values. This is how they express themselves:

- Customer commitment: We develop relationships that make a positive difference in our customers' lives.
- Quality: We provide outstanding products and unsurpassed service that, together, deliver premium value to our customers.
- Integrity: We uphold the highest standards of integrity in all of our actions.
- Teamwork: We work together, across boundaries, to meet the needs of our customers and to help our company win.
- Respect for people: We value our people, encourage their development, and reward their performance.
- Good citizenship: We are good citizens in the communities in which we live and work.
- A will to win: We exhibit a strong will to win in the marketplace and in every aspect of our business.
- Personal accountability: We are personally accountable for delivering on our commitments.

These statements—admittedly, they can look a bit patronizingly obvious—define a company that is prepared to go above and beyond the normal boundaries of corporate culture and customer support. Do they always succeed? Probably not, but the important thing is whether they are committed to strive to do so. In "18 Core Company Values That Will Shape Your Culture & Inspire Your Employees," Caroline Forsey lists the top six of these as:

1. Integrity
2. Boldness
3. Honesty
4. Trust
5. Accountability
6. Commitment to customers

This is an area where—rather than being unable to match the larger-scale efforts of bigger companies—the small firm can really forge an advantage. How much easier is it for the prospective customer to believe in the integrity of the potential supplier when the owner is in front of him? The SME has the ability truly to personalize its brand. If I personally promise you that I will make this solution work for you and that my business depends on that, you will believe me! A good (B2C) example is Bickerstaffe Bows—who make customized English longbows for archers—a tiny company, yet one which has an enormous presence and total brand recognition amongst its target market for its dedicated expertise and the quality of its products.

The Mission Statement

Imagine beginning that important first sales call with those business values and credentials already established in the mind of your prospective buyer. Powerful. And a great example of how your firm's marketing and sales activities can be mutually supportive and devastatingly effective when properly coordinated, as we discuss in Chapter 4. It's interesting, isn't it, that the six points earlier could be the personal values that make up the personality of an individual, as opposed to a firm. We'll talk about *brand personality* later in this chapter.

It is expected that any corporation will have a clear *mission statement*, and the majority of major corporations do (424 out of the Fortune 500 in

2022). The tone and core message that this gives out will help shape your brand positioning statement and brand identity, which we discuss below. A mission statement is useful to explain, in simple and concise terms, a company's purpose(s) for being. In *Start With Why*, Simon Sinek wrote about finding your "Why?"—establishing the reasons that the business exists. He considers that when you see the value in what you're doing or offering, it becomes easier to leverage inspiration in your and your colleagues' everyday work and to find fulfilment in doing it. Then it is easier for your customers to buy into that mission. The statement is generally short, either a single sentence or a short paragraph, aimed at motivating employees and reassuring investors of the company's future, explaining a company's culture, values, and ethics. Some examples:

Twitter: "To give everyone the power to create and share ideas and information instantly, without barriers."

Harvard: "To educate future leaders is woven throughout the Harvard College experience, inspiring every member of our community to strive toward a more just, fair, and promising world."

PayPal: "To build the web's most convenient, secure, cost-effective payment solution."

Spotify: "Our mission is to unlock the potential of human creativity—by giving a million creative artists the opportunity to live off their art and billions of fans the opportunity to enjoy and be inspired by it."

Tesla: "To accelerate the world's transition to sustainable energy."

This last one is a good example of stating a company's highest global ambitions, going ambitiously far beyond the supply of its products and services. It promotes strong brand recall by evoking the specific emotions you want to generate among your customers and employees. Also, when business growth expands your reach to new divisions and locations, it becomes a reference point around which your senior managers can motivate and inspire their employees. There are many examples of brands who have attempted a brand-extension exercise, lost sight of that reference point, left their brand values behind, and lost their customers.

But branding techniques and imperatives evolve with time and the zeitgeist. The Tesla example is an example of what is now most often called a *purpose statement*. This form of words moves upwards and out-wards from the mission statement, being more about what companies and organizations do best to advance or improve peoples' lives. They tend to be driven by the newly evolving need for an explicit environmental, sustainability, and governance (ESG) strategy. We'll look at this in more detail below. Surveys are beginning to show that customers believe a brand or company should have a purpose beyond making money and warm toward businesses that express their wider purpose.

As ever, these statements can vary in their true reflection of that business. Your purpose statement must be genuine and supportable, a heartfelt and shared mantra about your brand's place in the business and wider world. As mentioned earlier, brand personality is an important element of your brand; your purpose statement—done right—will enhance that. Here are some examples:

BorgWarner: BorgWarner chooses to be a leader—in serving our customers, advancing our technologies and rewarding all who invest in us.

S&P Global: We accelerate progress in the world by providing intelligence that is essential for companies, governments and individuals to make decisions with conviction.

Cognizant Technology Solutions: We innovate to find a better way—for the clients who depend on us, the customers who rely on them and the communities who count on us all.

General Electric: We rise to the challenge of building a world that works.

Verizon Communications: Verizon's core purpose is to give people the ability to do more.

ESG marketing is the activity of promoting the *environmental, social, and governance* attributes of a company's brand strategy to its investors, buyers, and other stakeholders in alignment with those core values that we discussed, with its corporate mission and purpose. This new corporate credentializing has become important to the B2B as well as to the B2C marketplace, particularly as generations Y and Z move further into positions of management and influence in the corporate world. An ESG marketing message builds a firm's brand equity, financial worth, and potential for true social impact. A strong and authentic corporate ESG content strategy puts brands at a competitive advantage, as long as the values expressed are genuinely held ones and those values are well communicated. In a study carried out by the International Business School of The Hague, in the Netherlands, it was discovered that eight of the world's leading brands had largely not succeeded in communicating their corporate social responsibility (CSR) and ESG credentials to their customers, despite the expenditure of much effort and dollars. Though not lacking in sincerity and authenticity, and not being subject to claims of "greenwashing" (hiding poor environmental practices behind a smokescreen of marketing platitudes), they simply had not got the relevant messages across as they intended. The fact that this is the result for companies that are usually held up as a benchmark for branding excellence illustrates the difficulty of getting this right for any firm.

Your marketing team has to be very much in tune with what is required to establish and communicate your ESG credentials. ESG reporting, or sustainability reporting as it is sometimes called, has grown steadily in popularity over the past two decades. And the workforce to which you are communicating is changing. Many millennials (Gen Y) and Gen Zs make decisions about their careers and about where they shop based on their values. A total of 44 percent of millennials and 49 percent of Gen Zs surveyed said that, over the past two years, they have made choices about the types of work they would do, the organizations they'd be willing to work for (they like to say "work with"), and those from whom they would buy, based on their personal values. And as consumers, they often stop or initiate relationships based on how companies treat the environment, protect personal data, and position themselves on social and political issues. As referred to elsewhere, approximately 30 percent of the workforce is now made up of these two generations, and a large proportion of those are owners or managers of the kind of fast-growing businesses to whom you will want to sell. Therefore, some alignment with millennial and Gen Z values is essential for firms who would otherwise risk losing favor with this large and increasingly influential group. Those values encompass concern for change, over issues like racial justice, inequality, and climate change.

Your customers, investors, and employees want to know what your brand is doing to help make the world a better place. It's estimated that around 90 percent of S&P 500 companies now publish ESG reports, with half of them having sourced data enabling sustainability value creation to be tracked, managed, and reported as KPIs. In ESG reporting, based on what is known as ESG discovery (internal evaluation), big questions are asked about the company as a whole: about whether the mission, vision, and values are aligned with business goals. The results then become a vital part of a modern business content strategy—more on this in Chapter 4. Vendors must beware, however, of exposing themselves to the charge of "greenwashing," meaning spouting all the right ESG messages, while continuing to indulge in practices (like running a fleet of executive jets) that contradict their avowed good intentions. Cynicism on the topic has even gone so far as it being labeled as a giant societal placebo by some. You may never have thought that driving societal change was something your business might do, but it's now being seen as good for business as it is for the world.

Brand Identity

Brand identity is the total business idea that the brand owner is trying to communicate. It is not transitory or superficial, but rather is strategic, constituting the brand offer, involving depth, consistency, appropriateness, character, and performance. The reason for having an identity is to secure a desired place in people's minds (a "position"). In other words, to generate an *image* that is brought to mind by any part of your communication. It is vital to establish this solid brand identity and then to work hard to make sure that the image of your firm formed in the minds of your target prospects is the one you intended it to be. A strong brand image will establish, define and sustain the strong, highly focused company that you want to be! Remember that you don't get to choose: neglect the proactive establishment of your brand identity and the market will ascribe one to you. It may not be the one you want! We'll look later, in Chapter 4, at how you reverse unfavorable perceptions when we talk about PR.

What is the *personality* of your company that you want others to recognize? "Personality"? Of a business? Yes; never forget that your entire sales and marketing effort is a series of communications with individuals, not faceless companies. Their emotions, personal prejudices, and preconceptions ultimately guide the decisions about buying what you are selling. Maya Angelou said: "I've learned that people will forget what you said, people will forget what you did, but people will never forget how you made them feel." We look further into why people buy in Chapter 3.

Your corporate (brand) personality can make a big difference in how your company, your people, and your products are perceived. Why think about a brand personality at all? Because it is the unique central part of the brand identity of the business, just like it is for you personally. Everything else can be copied, acquired, or home grown. Personality is different—it reflects a humanized version of what your customers want to deal with and will draw them to you if you get it right. *Dr. Paul Temporal, of Said Business School,* is quoted as saying "Personality accounts for the difference between world-class companies and products on the one hand and also-rans and failures on the other."

A brand is a very emotional thing. The personality of the brand appeals to the emotions, even in B2B. I like to involve everyone inside the company to provide their reference points about who they work for. It also provides the buyer with a personal connection and the confidence that they are making the right decision to be one of that brand's users. I often use the Aaker brand personality model with my clients, listening carefully to their reactions to the different dimensions, to get a good fit for their firm.

William Agush, Founder/CEO, Adsonica Inc., Wellesley, Mass

The leading B2C firms are very good at this and we B2B businesses can learn from them. You know the personality of Virgin, IBM, and Macdonald's because they have each established one (respectively, straight-talking and fun; totally professional and solid as a rock; family oriented and value conscious) and kept to it in everything they do. You can see that personality is a source both of *differentiation* and of *sustainable competitive advantage*. It is also not negotiable, in the sense that you will be *perceived* to have a corporate personality anyway—better to establish it actively and strategically to help take control of the marketing process, as described earlier.

We might consider that certain brands are "sophisticated," "rugged," "exciting," "basic," or "conservative." This set of human characteristics associated with brands is what Jennifer Aaker in 1997 defined as her definition of brand personality. William Agush refers to it in his comment, earlier. More relevant to B2C's individualistic, emotional consumer-buying stimulus than the rational, group-oriented B2B process, this is still a perspective that is worth looking at by all marketers, who understand that decisions are made by individuals with emotions, in groups or otherwise.

In developing your brand identity, it is important to establish your *brand attributes*—those essential characteristics of the brand that make up the impression that you want to create. They must be real and be ones that are not already loudly claimed by your competitors. These attributes might be unrelenting attention to detail, and consistent high quality and ESG commitment, for example. ESG, as mentioned earlier, is environmental, social, and governance—the framework for assessing the impact of the sustainability and ethical practices of a company. Spend quality time on defining those brand attributes: they must be genuine and communicable. Consider all of the words or phrases that communicate your strengths and then select the top five or six; for example, expert; proven to be trusted and reliable; having global vision with local sensitivities; leading-edge technologists; delivering the best complete solution of its kind; and a committed and supportive business partner. Check them against those of your main competitors. You cannot "own" an attribute that is already in the grip of your major rival. Once decided upon, make these your corporate glossary and spread them widely around your company, so that every team member can use them to build whatever form of communication they are delivering.

Then think about *differentiation*—how you will stand apart from and above a crowded and noisy marketplace. No matter how much you have focused down on your target segment (see Chapter 1), you will still need to stand out from your competitors. Think how you can use four simple but powerful marketing words to differentiate your business:

- "First"
- "Best"

- "New"
- "Only"

These are great differentiators to own, for any size of business, but only if they can be supported. They answer the question "So why are you different from all the others …?" Imagine how powerful it is to be able to respond: "Well, we are the *first* company to provide this *new* solution, which is being rated as the *best* one in this field and the *only* one that can fully meet the demanding requirements of your kind of work." This should also be precisely reflected in what your prospect can read in all of your marketing communications. In this context, consistency and repetition are your friends.

In *Differentiate or Die*, Jack Trout reinforces our focus in this book on research and strategic planning, when he says "Differentiating your business does not mean being cute or 'creative' or imaginative. It has everything to do with logic—the science that deals with the rules and tests of sound thinking." His recommended four-step process for successfully differentiating yourself from competitors emphasizes the following:

1. Context: essentially, timing—in relation to market and competitive conditions.
2. Finding the differentiating idea: that is not necessarily product related, but is couched in terms of being a customer benefit or meeting a customer need.
3. Having credentials: to support your differentiating idea, to make it real and believable. Answer the challenge of "Prove it!" We examine the closely related *evaluation* part of the selling process in Chapter 6.
4. Communicate it: the best product on its own doesn't necessarily win; you must build the perception of a strong brand in the marketplace to succeed.

You will want that perception to be one of a business that has a clear understanding of its own position in the market. In a competitive situation, no matter at what point in the sales process, none of your salespeople should be phased by the question, "So, what's different about you, then?"

Positioning—Here's Why We're Different

Positioning is best defined as the creation of the ideal perception of your company and its products in the mind of the target customer, relative to the competition. Sounds simple, doesn't it? Yet this requires time, skill, and attention, not least because you do not have control of your prospect's mind! Before you begin, find out what is the current feeling about your company and product in the target market. You may already have some of this feedback from your earlier research (see Chapter 1), but it is important to establish your positioning starting point. Perhaps you have already made sales into companies in that industry segment. Charge your salespeople with the task of giving you very clear feedback on the level of customer satisfaction that you have there. It may be less than you think, or even be negative. If this is the case, you really need to know about it. Managers of companies in the same industry tend to gather together throughout their working lives, to exchange ideas, best practice, and technical innovations, and to socialize. The number of industry-specific business events is testament to this. You may be better known than you think, so ensure that you are aware of what is being said about you; don't assume that you know. As an "insider," a customer survey has the potential to give you candid and valuable insight into your customers' opinions and future plans. Carefully constructed, a customer survey can also tell you a lot about your competitors. Very valuable!

Don't underestimate the expertise required to get this intricate exercise right, however. As Sascha Eder, CEO at market research firm NewtonX, New York, points out in a recent article on voice of the customer research, you have to be careful about multiple forms of bias. Extreme views, both positive and negative, tend to predominate; your salespeople will be unlikely to give any feedback that looks bad for them personally; former customers can provide insight as valuable as existing ones. Even if you carry out the study with your own resources, it is wise to use a research professional to design it for you and to help to interpret the results.

> *In my experience, start-up companies in any industry come with a clear focus on their products or solutions, but far less on their primary target market. "Entrepreneurship" is a term that everyone thinks they understand, but I have found that the very best and most successful entrepreneurs have skills in understanding what drives their customers, both "physically and psychologically," to purchase from them over another.*
>
> Chris Raman, serial venturepreneur, Founder,
> Ventures4growth, Belgium

Imagine, for example, you discover that your largest customer in health care, though satisfied with the solution that you have provided, is concerned that one of your competitors—who is constantly approaching them for business—claims to be further ahead of the desirable future technology curve than you are. Whether this is the case or not, it is a clear signal that you have identified a competitive challenge or weakness that needs to be addressed: your solution is not considered future-proof and you did not understand the psychology of a customer who rates this highly in a supplier. You will have discovered that technological advantage and future-proofing are important to that type of customer and that you will need to position your own business as being progressive and in touch with the latest R&D advancements. If you don't address it, it could be that your own customer, as an influential member of the health care community, is positioning your company for you—as a technology laggard. If this is the case, then you will need to look closely at your own R&D efforts, address the situation, and then ramp up positive communication around that issue.

Alternatively, it may be that you discover that the number one factor driving supplier choice in that industry is cost, to the near-exclusion of all else. You got the deal because you were the cheapest, which is a competitive advantage easily outmaneuvered by a rival with deeper pockets or a lower cost base. This would drive you instead to emphasize the value for money and wider business benefits offered by your solution, increasing your differentiation away from pure net cost. Put these two findings together and you have begun to build a workable positioning as a "leading-edge provider of value for money solutions, tailored to the needs of (that industry)." Again, this is an example of your marketing and sales efforts combining in the sales cycle to turn theory into profitable practice. The messages you then build into your sales and marketing work—the words and phrases that contain the key benefits and positioning statements for the brand and communicate its key attributes—then also have a basis for consistency.

Interview With Steven Lockwood by Tom Cairns

Steve is currently Vice President of Vena Solutions, responsible for the UKI region and parts of Europe. Vena Solutions is a global leader in cloud financial planning and analysis software.

Steve has been consistently successful over 23 years with blue chip global IT leaders as a sales professional, sales leader, and senior business executive. His consistent achievement is the result, he says, of "continuous learning and a laser focus with his teams on the process of effectively applying solutions to help his customers achieve their desired business outcomes, personal goals and company business objectives."

TC: What made you into a successful professional salesperson and sales leader?

SL: *I look back at my career as having two phases. The first phase of success was based more on my ability to build rapport with my customers than on executing the sales process. The turning point for the second phase was being mentored by a leading professional sales coach. I was taught three enduring principles of selling.*

I ensure continued success by applying these three principles:

1. *Identify the client's true business pain caused by his business problem to help uncover and address the financial impact in the client's business terms.*
2. *Understand that not all projects are good projects, and that "qualification" is key to finding those deals you can win versus those you cannot.*
3. *Trust a good sales methodology, but you must also develop the ability to successfully execute this process by engaging and building rapport with customers.*

TC: Can you describe in general terms, as a senior business practitioner in selling, what you have learned over the last 23 years? What worked and what did not?

SL: *People only buy to make a difference to them, and what you sell must help them achieve their personal and business objectives. Move away from believing that people will buy from you because you're liked. Take off the happy ears. Don't view everything as a glass half full. It's not always good to be unrealistically positive.*

Focus on the needs of the customer and business value in the customers own terms, not what you think they need. You lose sales when you are not able to influence the customer and achieve their desired business outcomes. You must understand that there is a sales execution process to follow and that you will rarely win by taking shortcuts.

Finally, marketing and branding brings people to the window, but in B2B the seller drives the successful transaction. It is therefore critical that sales and marketing work together as a team.

TC: How was success achieved? How was success missed?

SL: *True sales professionals become business orientated sellers and business advisers, to succeed and focus on a deal that is mutually beneficial to both businesses. Don't be afraid to say no to the prospective customers. Work out what is not right for them or for your business and walk away. Your customer will thank you. It can save hours of time for both businesses.*

In other words, if you know that you cannot deliver the best service, then qualifying out is best early on when you discover there is no good fit between the businesses and you.

TC: Can you now specifically relate those observations above to successful business examples, challenges involved, and lessons learned?

SL: *Yes, I would like to use four examples to illustrate those observations on the practical application of my professional discipline.*

The first is a leading world-renowned retailer with an established major competitor as the incumbent. Regular prospecting and marketing to this company always resulted in being told all their needs are being met and no help was required.

TC: What were the key actions in this sale?

SL: *The breakthrough action was when we comprehensively researched this prospective customer's financial divisions which revealed* *they had significant business needs. We created and applied a strategic plan. These key actions helped negotiate and win a strategically import-ant $350k software and services contract which removed the incumbent competitor.*

Key actions and steps were as follows:

- *We discovered an online podcast by their CFO which contradicted the message of "no need" being shared by the business users. We now had unmet need we could focus on.*
- *As leader, I contacted the CFO by liaising directly with his PA, onward sharing this story of misalignment. This resulted in initial meetings with the CFO where he specified his unmet business needs, requirements and outcomes. We had now qualified the probability of a sale.*
- *Multiple product demonstrations were completed, a working party set up, but key influencers and decision makers preferred their existing strategic vendor.*
- *The next key action was to spend multiple days on site documenting the implementation process and risk/reward areas to create a "Business Process Value" document with our unique solution.*
- *This BPV document, supported by the CFO, was shared throughout the company's key stakeholders and executives.*
- *Push back continued from IT and procurement functions, but referral back to the agreed Business Process Value document overcame these objections.*

TC: What were the pivotal moments, the lessons learned?

SL: *The biggest lesson we learned was how to sell against the status quo. There were three pivotal moments. By researching the CFO and his business and needs and using that to obtain a foot in the door, we built trust and showed genuine interest in their business. This earned us the right to challenge their status quo.*

The second critical moment was being able to prove and agree business value with the CFO and then being able to refer to this CFO agreement throughout the cycle, which unblocked issues as they arose.

Finally, having the Business Process Value document agreed and shared with all the stakeholders highlighted what, why and how we would add business value over and above their existing vendor.

The second example is of a large domestic and industrial water utility. As with many water and utility companies, there were significant government and regulatory issues and constrictions. We were tripped up by some of these and our initial approach was rejected.

TC: What were the key actions in this sale?

SL: *The breakthrough action was identifying a user case from a similar regulated industry where our technology added significant business value. We then created and implemented a team action plan based on this user case and ultimately signed a strategic contract worth £100k.*

TC: What were the pivotal moments, the lessons learned?

SL: *We learned how to become a valuable partner and team up with the client. The pivotal moments started with identifying an untapped area for value creation that was equally beneficial for both parties. We linked and created an accurate business value reference document that made the project results tangible and relatable to stakeholders' goals and strategic direction. Critical to the successful negotiation, we used this agreed document to obtain buy in and support from our own company executives and our pricing committee.*

Then there was a large contract up for renewal at a major country household insurer. We needed new content to allow the renegotiation to succeed. Within the client's estate was a small legacy technology that was utilized but undervalued. We also identified a requirement around UK GDPR regulations. Ultimately the contract was signed over a three-year period and a value of $4.5m.

TC: What were the key actions in this sale?

SL: *The breakthrough action was meeting with all three key stakeholders and agreeing:*

- *Financial—do the maths work, and is the deal financially successful to both parties?*
- *Technical—can the tech integrate and co-exist in the architectural landscape?*

- *Operational—will the users benefit from the technology? Are they bought in to the change and supportive of our proposals?*

TC: What were the pivotal moments, the lessons learned?

SL: *We learned how to re-energize a relationship to win a larger renewal deal. This was achieved by obtaining all three key board level stakeholder agreement. Without that agreement, our proposal would not have succeeded. We now had the business and technology teams supporting our negotiations. This was critical to get the deal agreed.*

The pivotal moments were linking strategic goals to an area of current external pain with a tangible business outcome from a technology project. Obtaining the support of the users and the IT and business teams. Obtaining the support of the CIO in speaking on our behalf. This confirmed the business value and that we were delivering a mutually beneficial project.

My last example is of a leading European retailer and wholesaler of pharmaceutical products. The client had an existing footprint of our technology, but the need for additional tech was not required due to the existing technology covering all the bases. There were no easy points of entry, therefore it was important to uncover all areas of value to achieve a sale. We had a good reputation with the client, but it was imperative that we engage in the wider business of the customer.

TC: What were the key actions in this sale?

SL: *The breakthrough actions were:*

- *Researching from annual reports, financial accounts, and their strategy globally, locally, and then by department.*
- *Discovering three key areas where we could help and linking these back to their core strategic business goals.*
- *Creating a plan with best practice templates combined with a competition and industry challenges summary, and sharing this with eight main board members.*

TC: What were the pivotal moments, the lessons learned?

SL: *We learned how to provide business value to the C-Suite executives and how to defend against the competition. The first pivotal moment was being able to build a value-based vision to take to the operational board members. Second, articulating business insights and a co-ordinated vision across the organization demonstrated the power of scale critical to the success of the project was achievable. Finally, the success of the Proof of Concept resulted in a valuable investment of our time with the client that created trust and proved we had the ability to deliver against strategic business objectives.*

TC: Have you any final thoughts and observations on what works and what does not?

SL: *High performing sellers understand how the business they are selling to must map onto their products and solutions. In addition, unless you have sponsorship and know what the decision makers want to do, then you won't get the sale.*

Today, sellers increasingly need to develop the softer skills. This is the ability to:

- *Build rapport and trust*
- *Understand business risk*
- *Read people's motivations*
- *Understand impact of emotions*
- *Apply active listening*
- *Make people feel valued*
- *Develop humility*
- *Be compassionate*
- *Increase awareness of people's drivers*

It is possible, of course, that you will find the need to reposition your business and its solutions as market conditions, the competitive environment, and your company change. Take BP, for example—the epitome of fossil fuel suppliers has, in the new atmosphere of ecoactivism, repositioned itself as a leader in sustainable energy. If that aggressive young market entrant that you once were has become a billion-dollar market leader and your innovative technologies that were favored only by corporate early adopters have "crossed the chasm (*ibid*)" and now constitute the mainstream solution, then things are now different for you. Success in repositioning must come from outside thinking, as Jack Trout says in "Repositioning: Marketing in the Era of Competition, Change and Crisis." That's where the market is. You will need to examine what are the newly appropriate attributes for your brand, preferably without having to consider changing your core values, brand name, or visual identity. Your company and product positioning will alter and your messages will follow suit. General Motors took a big gamble on repositioning itself as a supplier of "economy" cars by rebadging basic, functional, and charisma-free Daewoo vehicles as Chevrolets in the United States. This was a spectacular sales and marketing failure, simply because they tried to change perceptions of a brand with 90 percent awareness, built up over decades: a supplier of large, comfortable, high-spec, powerful, American-made vehicles.

Effective repositioning is based on readjusting perceptions, not contradicting them. Human beings have a deeper impression of what we already know than what we are told is new or different. Brands are symbols around which companies, suppliers, supplementary organizations, the public, and your customer's customers construct identities. Reveal them to be flimsy or false at your peril. GM's massive PR campaign to support the launch of their "new" range of vehicles was so diametrically opposed to their brand identity and their image in the minds of their existing and potential customers that it was ridiculed. It appears that GM's staff and its dealers were simply embarrassed suddenly to alter all of the messages that they had been imparting to customers for years. There's a reminder there, too, to ensure that you bring along the hearts and minds of your GTM partners with you at all times. More on that in Chapter 4.

Another frequent example of getting repositioning wrong is the belief that a change of company name and logo will do it. The jury is out on what this has meant for Meta (still often referred to as Facebook), Hermes (the parcel delivery company, now EvRi), and Standard Life Aberdeen (the building society, now ABRDN). Each of these has made the rebranding move in an attempt to wipe away reputations tainted by highly visible arrogance and reputational disaster or abysmal customer service. The last of these three has made a bad start by attracting universal ridicule over its vowel-free new name, and EvRi has been seen as arrogant by taking out full-page ads describing its wonderful services that will be even better under a new name, without acknowledging or apologizing to the tens of thousands of disappointed and furious customers whose parcels did not arrive satisfactorily. Branding is about you, but it's for your customers.

A good *positioning statement* identifies who you are, what you do, for whom, what benefits you deliver for the client, and why you are different from competitors. A strong positioning statement is highly relevant for any size of business. You can develop the pithy, short "elevator pitch" as a subset of this, but you'll probably want a couple of paragraphs to contain all that you need to say. That statement should then be what your people, your partners, and your promotional material repeat consistently. Get some expert help to write one for you. Your tagline or strapline (see later) can be made up of select words from that statement. Your positioning statement adds another dimension to the brand and includes references to the target audience, the competitive environment within which you are judged, the benefits, your competitive differentiation, and the personality of the company.

For example: "*For* growing technology businesses seeking rapid new revenues from Europe, ABC Outsourcing *is* a multi-skilled corporate services organization *that delivers* structured, proven, and comprehensive programs *to* facilitate growth and expand companies into new territories.

Unlike single-specialty or general-service outsourcers, ABC Outsourcing and its certified partners apply exceptional sales, marketing, legal, financial, technical, and operational expertise to establish companies and accelerate revenues in Europe."

Product Positioning

Product positioning follows on from all of your brand positioning work. According to Philip Kotler, the development of effective benefit-centered positioning involves three things. First, you have to understand the primary benefits your potential customers are seeking. Second, your competitor research must give you a clear picture of the extent to which the products with which yours are competing—claim to provide the benefits sought by consumers. Third, you need to know what is actually being bought. Just as you did with your corporate positioning work, the first step is to look at the core values—this time, those of your products or services. A feature list comes first, which you will no doubt already be familiar with. The next step is to be clear about the functions that those features perform and what benefits they provide to your target audience. For this, you need to know that audience. As before, your sales team will know what has attracted existing customers and what specific benefits offered by the product were the ones that beat the competition to the sale. For new prospects, the results of your segmentation strategy (see Chapter 1) will have provided a target customer profile that includes their industry sector, their size, and their likely budget for your offering, the specific problem they are trying to solve, the level of skills that they possess to evaluate and use the product as you intend, and the way they prefer to buy it. Knowing all of this, you can then rank the features of your product or service according to their likely importance to the prospective buyer. Even at this early stage, your research and analysis should have identified the path that your R&D group should be following to take your products to the next level, as defined by the typical target customer's future ambitions and needs.

Paradoxically, the more successful is your corporate positioning as being the ideal supplier, the more pressure is on your product positioning strategy to match up to the prospect's expectations. You cannot assume the leadership position in your industry if your products and services are not also seen as leaders in their field. In the world of constant information availability (see Chapter 4, Figure 4.2), you will be dealing with a well-informed buyer, well versed in the standards of the products that you are selling. If your salesperson has to spend an inordinate amount of time convincing the buyer merely that your products meet the current general standards that he or she expects, then something is wrong with your product positioning or the way it has been communicated.

This includes the price factor. We examine the value-based selling (VBS) approach in Chapter 5, where business benefits and outcomes dominate the proposition, but, at the naked product level, you still have to be competitive. That doesn't necessarily mean being the cheapest, but if you are not so, then there must be product features or potential benefits that clearly justify a premium. Hopefully, your branding work will be helping you in this situation, communicating proven quality and reliability to support your product benefits.

Pricing strategy is worth every moment spent on it. PwC recently found from a survey of CFOs that their top priority for maintaining or increasing margins in 2022 was to revisit their pricing strategy.

Is this a branding and positioning topic? Yes; the price of your product or solution is the clearest indication to your target market of how much you perceive it to be worth—to you, to the prospect, and compared to the competition. It's a positioning statement of its own. You are trying to find the sweet spot that conveys the fair value in relation to their budget and to the other options that your buyer is looking for. Whether you are selling a $10, £100, or €10,000 product, you will know instinctively, and from your earlier research and segmentation strategy, what that means for its position in the market. Does your branding convey the message that you are a top-end, high-quality supplier? Then, your product pricing will reflect this. Is your key branding proposition that you will supply the world with your kind of product at a price level that has never before been available? Again, your pricing must reflect this. It is remarkable the number of companies that have promoted themselves as the ones who will bring product X or service Y to the world at an "affordable" price for the first time, only to be seen to be using what has come to be known as "stealth" pricing, where the promoted price level is a fantasy and the real cost to the user is no better than is offered by current suppliers. Their brand positioning promise does not match up with what they deliver to the market and they go out of business, fast.

Profitwell emphasizes the importance of establishing your "value metric." Before setting a dollar value, you need to decide what you are setting that value *on*. Is it per item, per visit, per square foot, per seat (software license), or per capacity unit (e.g. GB/therm/hour) used? This appears obvious, but reflects the value that your customer gets from you in the most fundamental way. Clear value metrics increase willingness to purchase (WTP), whereas complex pricing does the opposite. If by buying more, they clearly receive more of that value, your brand attribute of being a value-providing supplier increases as well. It is then easier to price and sell your added value, your services, your time, or whatever it is that can help your profitable value-based selling (VBS) strategy (see Chapter 5). Again, your segmentation work will have informed you how and why your target customers buy (see Chapter 4). You will know what value metric they understand and upon which they are comfortable to evaluate your proposal. VBS extends pricing strategy into the realm of calculated risk-taking on the realization of promised and projected business outcomes, which must be carefully handled, but can be a winning competitive pricing strategy.

Using "free" as a pricing strategy for mass customer acquisition has become very popular, that is, giving away an initial product in order to get customer engagement and set up a platform for moving to the paid-for product. This is not so much a pricing strategy as a customer acquisition one, often referred to as "freemium." With digital platforms and products, such as selling software or information provision over the Internet, this can lower customer acquisition cost, but can also delay true product purchase. Judging the amount of your full product that you use as the enticement for the customer to engage with you and then devising effective conversion tactics is not a simple task. Studies have shown, however, that willingness to buy is increased by using this method.

My experience with Prevx, the cybersecurity software firm I founded, is an example of the kind of "strategic pivot" that I feel makes the difference between moderate and outstanding business success. We needed to find the barely-visible early adopter community for our product; traditional sales and marketing approaches weren't cutting it. We invested major effort in some new development, then risked the "freemium" approach, allowing free downloads. Self-qualifying, the early adopters reached out to us, and Prevx went viral, which created extensive global press coverage. Our cost of sales was reduced dramatically and our growth was super-charged.

Nick Ray, CEO, Director, Founder,
NXD of Software & Technology Firms,
United Kingdom

In this same context, the science of pricing subscriptions and access by the month, on an annual basis, per download, per user, per device, and so on is one that is sufficiently well established for you to find expert help with. Note that geographic and cultural differences do exist in the acceptability of such pricing models, so do not assume that what is right for your home country is necessarily right for every other, and, in some geographies, even small variations in price can have major effects on WTP and your revenues.

For a physical product, many companies use the simple cost-plus pricing method. You look at your gross production cost and add a percentage that can allow for quantity and negotiated discounts, but the result is a price that still meets your profitability targets. If your cost base is low, you may well still be offering a competitive price compared to your competition. You might make that price as low as you feel able, in order to penetrate a market. That can work well, but bear in mind that a high-volume, low-cost competitor can match it. Your customer will also not be happy or may switch if (probably when) you have to raise your price as your costs increase, or you do not get the volume of sales that your economy pricing was expected to deliver. You will also have made a tacit positioning statement about your product: you are the economy version, with all that says about perceived quality.

At the other end of the scale is the strategy of *price skimming*, where you charge a premium price to attract the top end or early adopter of the target market who is willing to tolerate it. That may be because they want to get something new, to get it first, to be seen to buy the best, or if you are the only supplier at that time (see the earlier discussion in this chapter on differentiation). If you take this approach, your financial plan needs to incorporate the gradual lowering of your price premium, which will inevitably be necessary as your competitors catch up with your technology or marketing and sales efforts into that sector (see Chapter 1 on the technology adoption life cycle). Having established yourself, you may also deliberately lower your sights and reduce price to target companies in the mainstream and to increase volume. In a number of industries, supply, political, environmental, social, and other factors make pricing a dynamic exercise. Pricing then requires a full-time team to monitor it, with the need for constant revaluation and adjustment of the norm. Examples of this are the energy industry, large-scale freight and transport, and health care, where pricing agility is a necessary corporate skill.

Pricing strategy may be a to-do item on your boardroom agenda that you can tick off when you've done it, but is a topic that should be regularly revisited as you progress into your market.

Brand Image—You've Got It Together; Now Get It Across

You have developed your brand identity to your own satisfaction, developed from solid company values. It's underpinned by the attributes that differentiate the best of your company and the solution you offer. You have your pricing and positioning sorted out and your differentiation is clear. Now there's a need to communicate this powerful identity to your prospective market. Your *brand image*—the projection of that brand identity—is the way in which people perceive or imagine your brand. It is a *receiver* concept and may or may not be the same as the identity of the brand that you have so carefully crafted. The identity messages need decoding by the audience. Your brand identity may be communicated in an inadequate or misleading way or someone else's opinion—or a deliberate filter from a strong competitor—may change the way the target audience perceives the image. It's that brand identity—the total notion of what you are all about—that you as the brand owner, or even business owner, are trying to communicate. You have to do it well in everything that the audience sees—and they see it all.

Your corporate *tagline* (or strapline), mentioned earlier, is important. This is not simply a promotional whim. A tagline is a phrase that permanently accompanies your brand name to communicate quickly your business positioning and brand identity into a single line that means something to your marketplace. A tagline is meant to provide potential buyers with an indication of your brand identity and its market position in just a few memorable words. Those words will ideally come from within your positioning statement. You are looking for impact, accuracy, and memorability. Smaller companies who get this right can magnify their presence beyond their comparative size in the market.

Set a communication objective and devise your strapline to meet it. It may be explaining what the company does and must be consistent with the other messages you use. It is very often the case, unfortunately, that a few catchy words are thrown together and are not seen as too important in this context. Be more judicious in your choice than that! Most visible in advertising and promotion, it will help to define your business, prompt positive recollection, and secure your brand in your prospective customer's mind. Consistency in this short but highly visible corporate message enhances the credibility of the brand and helps to firm up its identity. As a guide, think of the B2C ones you know that define brands that you admire. Many have become part of our culture, defining a business for millions. Think of "The Best a Man Can Get" (Gillette), "It Does What It Says on the Tin" (Ronseal), "The Happiest Place on Earth" (Disneyland), "Just Do It" (Nike), "Finger-lickin' Good" (KFC), and "The Ultimate Driving Machine" (BMW).

When writing your tagline, consider these criteria:

- It should be short. Great taglines often have as few as 10 syllables so that they're quick to recite and easy to tuck in alongside logos.
- It has to be simple and memorable. You hear it, memorize it quickly, and repeat it with ease.
- It should make clear your brand's market position and key benefits. This is particularly important if the brand name doesn't, on its own, quickly communicate the brand's offerings and distinctions.
- It has to differentiate your business from all others. In fact, a great tagline is unique and doesn't work when linked to a competitor's brand name. This is a good test!
- It reflects the brand's identity, character, promise, and personality. It also needs to be believable and original.

That's quite a set of demands upon a few words! A tagline is about the business itself and should be immutable, standing the test of time. Taglines are emotive—they represent the tone and feeling you want for your products or services. And referring back to visual identity, a tagline will usually form part of your regular company graphic. But, despite all of this, it is not compulsory. If it adds no further meaning or positive benefit to the brand identity or positioning, it is probably best left out.

A *slogan* is not the same thing. Larger companies will usually have one tagline (e.g., Disney's tagline is "The happiest place on earth") and many slogans (Disney's slogans are "Where dreams come true," "I'm going to Disneyland," "Where the magic began," and more). A slogan is designed for more flexible use and is less likely to outlast a single promotional campaign. It may be used for a longer period, but usually for only a single product line.

For further high-profile use, any tagline must meet the communication objective:

- Explain what the company does—Schott: "Nobody knows more about glass."
- Communicate leadership—Oracle: "Enabling the information age through network computing."
- Mold customer expectations by making a promise—Cathay Pacific: "Arrive in better shape."
- Communicate a vision—ICI: "We're making the future."
- State a strong product-oriented benefit for the target audience—Canva: "Online design made easy."

Marketing messages are at the sharp end of communicating the results of all of this hard work in developing your brand. These are the words and phrases that contain the key benefits and positioning statements for the brand and communicate its key attributes. Consistency in corporate messages enhances the credibility of the brand and helps to firm up its identity. We will deal with promotion and messaging in more depth in Chapter 4.

Your brand image is communicated by putting all of your good work into your core content and repurposing it extensively and judiciously, as we have discussed, but the *visual identity* that you adopt in your promotional activities and materials will be the trigger for calling up your brand image in your target's mind. Make sure that your "look"—designs, colors, and your logo—is consistent with the personality of the firm and aids instant recall of all of your attributes, enhancing your brand identity. Visual identity is the interrelated approach to graphic design, style, shape, and color in everything that promotes the brand identity and represents the brand image.

There are four basic components in a visual identity:

- Company name
- Logo or symbol
- Typeface
- Color scheme

The end result should aid recognition, enhance the brand identity, and evoke other attributes of the company and its brand. There is a reason that you recognize the world's top brands by their logos. Think back to our Kodak example and to MacDonald's. They have been designed to be:

- Striking; noticeably distinctive
- Subtly exciting but reassuring
- Simple but effective
- Easy to replicate and use; be practical for marketing purposes
- Supportive of the brand personality

Make no mistake: there is a science to this, and you should get expert help with it. Design triggers emotions, and you need those emotions around your brand to be the ones that you intend. Obsessive consistency is a must. This is what will help to get you the brand image that you want into the minds of your target market and to keep it there.

Summary

The upstream marketing work described in this chapter takes time, effort, and expertise. Why is it worth it? There are proven major business benefits. Your marketing and sales people—whether you have one or one hundred of them—will be able to focus on their objectives and have clear guidance as to what every message from your business is expected to convey. Your customers travel through the crowded world of continuous information. They seek to manage their own businesses and choose the best strategic suppliers and partnerships. Those vendors with the strongest corporate brands and clearest price, product, and competitive positioning will be the ones who shine through the fog. Your prospect is looking for certainty—reassurance that his or her chosen supplier will be the right choice from the myriad of those available. Use your brand to make it easy for them. Make them proud to be your customer!

There is much that you can do, today, to begin to reap the rewards from good branding practice. First, take a hard look at your business model, product and service offerings, your target markets and audiences, and the competition. Find out what everyone thinks of you right now. Use CSR and customer experience surveys (now often labeled as VOC—voice of customer) on a regular basis to help you with this, as discussed in Chapter 8. Yes, more research, but vital. Are you happy with the answer? Take action, if you are not.

Every communication you make will be visible to all of your audiences—existing and prospective clients, staff, media, investors, potential acquirers, and so on. So even if messages are deliberately different for each of these, your branding must be established first, then be consistent throughout. The potentially confusing world of social media marketing, as important as it is, can best be controlled by having that core content nailed down. It has to be aligned with all of the brand messages that you want to convey, to each of your audiences. The fast-moving nature of this part of your communications means that a mistake or contradiction travels the airwaves fast and is difficult to retract. Get it right the first time.

The many different elements and terminologies of branding get thrown around somewhat randomly. This chapter has attempted to explain what each of them mean and how they contribute to the final result. You must be clear-minded about what you want your brand to represent. The core values of the company, as discussed earlier, and the benefits of being your client, customer, or partner must shine through in everything you say, to everyone.

The Takeaways and Lessons Learned From Chapter 2	Do	Don't
Branding	Get expert help to develop your brand Use the core values of your business to establish your brand identity. Your brand should represent what you truly are Ensure that all of your employees understand, empathize with, and can represent your brand to the world Constantly seek market feedback to measure and evaluate your brand image Be obsessively consistent in all aspects of your branding	Don't think short term. The best brands are built to last a lifetime, and longer Don't underestimate the power of your brand to drive up WTP in your target market Don't assume that the brand image in the market's mind is exactly what you intended it to be: go find out, regularly
Positioning	Spend the time to develop a market positioning that will serve you for the duration of your long-term business plan A good *positioning statement* identifies who you are, what you do, for whom, what benefits you deliver for the client, and why you are different from competitors. It forms the basis for the messages that your sales and marketing activity takes to the market Social media marketing is a discipline that you must embrace. You must be as good at it as your competition; preferably, better. Maintain your branding throughout	Don't be a follower Differentiation is your winning play Don't be unrealistic. Your positioning must be credible and supportable Don't be complacent; be agile. Markets are dynamic; your positioning should be, too, if circumstances change Don't just pretend to be an expert in social media marketing. Acquire the skills Don't treat social media as a sales channel; it's there to promote your brand and develop relationships

CHAPTER 3

Prospect Qualification and Competitive Analysis

Overview

In Chapters 1 and 2, the marketing team found and identified the most lucrative market segments and the target businesses operating within them. They built a compelling message to help establish your brand. In this chapter, we will investigate how your sales team can now work closely with marketing to analyze and understand the prospective customers' business dynamics, how those prospects buy, and with whom you are competing to get the business.

Why is this important? In the previous chapter, we worked on establishing our brand identity and positioning to make our business the most attractive and relevant supplier to our target market. Now we investigate that market further, identifying the specific target prospects most susceptible to our proposition. By taking the time to qualify your prospects and understand your competitors, you will more quickly produce and maintain a realistic and healthy sales pipeline and reduce the length of your sales cycle. Senior practitioners will discuss the lessons they have learned in the field that touch on this area of work.

Prospect Qualification—Analyzing Who We're Dealing With

Just as you work hard to develop a seamless selling process, your prospective customer will be making an effort to have an equivalent buying process. First of all, you must know who does what. A single name on your prospect list will almost certainly not tell the whole story—you will need to dig deeper. You will probably have been introduced to the company by a single individual with whom you had your initial conversations. You need to quickly compile a knowledge base of the business's structure and the individuals within it. If it's a large company, this can be daunting, but an understanding of their bureaucracy is essential. How is the firm managed? Where are issues relevant to you discussed, and between whom? Is there a rigid timetable and procurement procedure for what you are selling? Who influences the final decisions and who makes them?

No two B2B sales are identical. You may be confronted by a formal purchasing committee—made up of product specialists, budget holders, and users—with its own rigid acquisition system and timetable. In that case, you have to be aware of their procedures, their budget, and the real user needs within the business. Alternatively, there may be a single management individual to whom all responsibility has been devolved for the purchase of your kind of solution. You need to know how, when, and through whom that company is buying. In Chapter 1, we examined the ways in which marketing and sales together can effectively tackle the prospecting—sales-pipeline-filling—task. Now, they can work together further to analyze what needs to be done to secure business from each of those prospective customers.

> *Working with companies on statistically precise sales funnel management—focusing on ensuring a healthy pipeline—I found that marketing and sales teams had to be reminded that customers join their sales funnel at different points of their buying journey. Sometimes, estimates of the length of the prospect sales cycle of three months turned out to be nearer twenty-four months or greater! Getting this wrong can have a huge impact on revenue forecasting and, therefore, business stability.*
>
> Charles Besondy, President and Author,
> Besondy Publishing LLC; Founder, Besondy
> Consulting & Interim Management Inc., Texas

Defining the Buying Process

The most important piece of intelligence you can gather on your prospective customers is their buying behavior and process. There will almost certainly be a multilevel approval process and formal sign-off points for the stages of acceptance, including the budget, of course. Every deal is different, no matter how specialized you have become in your target segment, so always recognize that it is the customer *buying cycle* that is dominant in terms of time factor, not what you might regard as your own typical sales cycle. By eliminating the communication with those who have no influence in the purchase decision, you can save yourself considerable wasted time, energy, and unproductive marketing and sales spend. Once you know who the actual buyers are, you can focus on them alone. The B2B large-scale buying and selling process is complex (more on this in Chapter 4). Large buying groups make for additional complexity. A number of our senior interviewees in this book attest to this. Research from The Challenger Group found that the average number of decision makers in a B2B buying group has risen from 6.2 stakeholders to over 10, and it's still growing. I've even seen estimates as high as 15! The result for the seller and his or her team is that every deal is different, being driven by multiple different individual and collective mindsets. The lead buyer is not your enemy. He or she has the difficult job of building consensus between a number of people in a reasonable amount of time and avoiding the inevitable drift toward a preference for the status quo. The structuring of small and agile sales project teams from within your company is one that requires skill and C-suite influence. Should the lead come from your CMO or your head of sales? Choose whoever is best at structuring focused, adaptable, and collaborative working among all of the relevant disciplines in your firm, to match each of your prospect's buying teams. If, as a smaller firm, you cannot do this, then try to ensure that the individual leading the project is sufficiently multiskilled to interact with each of the customer's people.

Again, it's remarkable how many of our interviewees emphasize this approach and talk of its success in their own careers.

Andy Heyes in Conversation With Michael Grant

Harvey Nash is a fast-growing global integrated technology and talent provider with currently 2,500 employees.

Andy Heyes is the Managing Director for London and the Southeast of the United Kingdom. He has been with the company for over 24 years, having started as a "resourcer" and previously as a City of

London money broker. Andy leads a team of over 100 recruitment consultants.

Andy, you lead a large and successful team from the City of London. Your team 'sells' probably the most import 'commodity' of all-people and their careers. Tell us about your strategy for making them successful.

Sales Strategy

Input from all staff levels goes into the development of the HN Sales Strategy in order that everyone buys into it and feels a part of it. This is initially developed at global level and must be strong enough to cope with both constant change and growth. This global strategy is then boiled down to local country and regional needs. Even in the UK, I've developed seven "locally" implemented strategies as the micro economies can change significantly between the City of London and Newcastle (a major city in the north of the UK). Each local strategy is presented to the senior national management team with a local SWOT analysis. The agreed strategy is then communicated to the local sales/consultancy teams through "Sales Kick-Offs," making it "theirs" through empowerment and ownership.

Half yearly reviews are done on the strategy against local performance, so that everyone knows who is doing what and the current market situation. The teams share their success stories on reaching deals.

Building a Successful Sales Team

What makes an individual successful at Harvey Nash is all about finding the right sales person with the right abundant skills. It's all about attracting the very best people as your recruitment sales consultants. The attributes that we seek consistently across the board are attitude, resilience, commercialism, good communication skills and a passion to succeed.

With these skills you can build a great business across everyone, and the managers have to meet the same blueprint.

People are complex. One day they can be nice and next week become the devil's child. Your sales team must be able to cope with this fact.

Our sales consultants have to be able to survive cyclical changes. During the COVID-19 pandemic, no one was hiring, but everyone would take a phone, Zoom or Teams call. The relationships were therefore current when the tide turned.

A whole generation of talent disappeared during COVID and left the recruitment industry. In this business, it takes longer than in other professions to recruit and to get up to scratch. It's not simply learning about recruitment, but also learning and understanding a lot about your market.

Practical Advice

- *In my early recruitment days, if someone had mentioned IBM, I would have asked what that meant! I learnt by failure in those days. You need to know exactly what is happening in your market to gain any credibility.*
- *You must know that what your client is requesting is doable. Never over-promise and under-deliver. Better to turn work away than let a client down.*
- *Work out who you are and what you want to be known for in your company. I wanted bigger clients, better relationships and to be transparent in how I am operating.*
- *Sales wins are all about having great relationships, so when change happens you automatically gain the business. Be memorable.*
- *The secret is always being with your client on site, always available, always going the extra mile, and your client believing that they are at the center of your life!*
- *Getting to know the right person at the right level is vital. In the City of London, it is not always what you know, but who you know.*
- *Longevity in a client relationship can be super-wonderful. Someone you know at the bottom may reach the top; when they move jobs, you can gain a new client.*
- *Be sociable. Go to everything; constantly network; enjoy meeting people. Be a positive and happy person, while working long hours; work hard, and graft.*
- *The best sales people love their work and immerse themselves in it, while having fun. Clients need to like you and find you trustworthy.*

Sales Success Stories

I knew someone in a global investment bank who was moving offices within London. I had only ever spoken to them over the phone. I finally went to meet them in person seeking an exclusive deal. They hired 90 IT specialists in that year. I went to meet them twice a week and met in the pub every Friday. Each time they not only gave me more assignments, but even suggested likely candidates to fill the roles.

A global bank in the City had been tied into a competitive recruitment supplier list through a tight purchasing department process. The prospective client suggested writing a "Statement of Work" which proved a real challenge with a colleague over the weekend—I would probably be embarrassed by its quality today! I took this down to the client on Monday morning and the following day we found ourselves on the approved supplier list. From then on, we placed 14 IT specialists per week until the top four floors of their skyscraper were entirely filled with our candidates.

Recently, a deal with a globally famous social media platform was won. Over the past years we had courted a Canadian partner of theirs whenever they were in the UK, showing off our new London offices and hosting dinners. Time well spent, as they handed the introduction in the USA right into our hands, with massive potential!

Through my love of sport—both football (soccer) and cricket—my wife discovered a potential client for us at a local match one day. It turned out to be a major national bookmaker with whom we placed 187 candidates within 18 months. It's all about the networking!

After making a weekly call to the CIO at a famous children's hospital for an entire year, out of the blue came a call apologizing for never responding to my calls, accompanied by an immediate requirement for four IT engineers. Both resilience and persistence do pay off!

But *why* do they buy solutions like yours? Almost certainly, there will be a careful internal evaluation of the business benefits that will accrue by dealing with you. Certainly, there is widespread concern in some industries that investment in major technology projects, for example, is not providing value for money. Whether you are selling technology, office facilities, or services of some kind, your buyer will have to justify the spending of company resources to his or her board, on the basis of the benefits to the firm. The buyers will be focused on their business objectives; if they are not, you should help guide them in that direction. If you can *jointly* plan to achieve measurable improvements—helping your buyer to specify and quantify clear expected benefits—you become part of the solution. It is not wise to overestimate the positive impact of what you are proposing, but internal reviews of your solution will benefit from your providing a clearly calculated and reasonable forecast of positive effects. By having properly investigated the workings of the business you are selling into, you will have a clear idea of both the immediate and the incremental changes that will come about if you make that sale. Don't leave anything to supposition. State these clearly. Encourage your buyers and recommenders to ensure that the users of the proposed solution are committed to the project, are involved throughout, and are sufficiently trained and prepared. Most failed business projects are ones where this does not happen. Help your buyer to understand (and communicate to them) how their own job might change because of this new initiative. Better to do this early on in the process, rather than have the customer's fear of change cause you problems later. You need as many cheerleaders and internal advocates as possible.

When I was working for a large international consulting firm, I was always fascinated by the way our Paris office used to structure its bid team. They engaged in some very specific research on the chief client in order to find out which "grande école" (a Grande École is like a superior business school that runs parallel to universities) they had attended. They would then find a member of staff who had been to the same graduate school in that select group and, whatever that person's position in the organization and, frankly, whatever relevant expertise that person might or might not have, get him (and in those days it usually was "him") to front the bid, while wearing a recognizable tie... Did it work? Well, enough times that they tried it on multiple occasions...

The research done by the same Paris office was occasionally flawed. I recall a presentation to the head of manufacturing (in Paris) who was leading a pan-European project to select and implement new sales,

(*Continued*)

(*Continues*)

> *manufacturing and distribution systems. The client spoke perfect English, of course, but I had presented for 15 minutes in French before getting stuck over some arcane technical expression. At that point he put me out of my misery, and gently also explained that "I am, in fact, German...."*
>
> Kimball Bailey

Let's look at an example of user-purchasing influence. We mentioned the health care industry in Chapter 1. Focused, specialized vendors of, for example, computer networks into this segment, like 3Com and Cisco, have had success in supplying high-speed connections within and between hospitals. Many of these systems have been sold on the basis that they met the need for connecting the different centers of expertise that are vital to the operating theater. They have made it possible for a surgeon in the United States to operate on a patient who is suffering from a complex or rare condition about which the surgeon is not the most expert. With real-time online guidance from the world expert in that particular procedure, he or she can perform that operation successfully, even if the world expert is 3,000 miles away in Germany! Systems integrators who successfully sold one of these systems for 3Com focused on the clinical need that their prospect research had uncovered. But it wasn't the ability to connect the hospital systems across the world that closed the sale. Yes, the technical capabilities had to be good enough; yes, the buyer had to be convinced that the installation and support provided was world class. But it was the vendor's recognition of an altogether higher level of need that sealed the partnership: *the need to save lives.* The sale was to the hospital IT team and the budget holders, but it was the higher purpose of the users—the clinicians themselves—that had been understood and catered to. The vendor ensured that the life-saving users—the surgeons—were introduced to this large-scale investment and made comfortable that it would aid them in their vital work. They were encouraged to participate in the trial process (we look further into trial and evaluation management in Chapter 6). The most advanced of those systems now can even make it possible for the remote surgeon to perform the operation himself or herself, using networked mechanical arms, and the network system vendor continues to reap add-on sales rewards.

Beware of being drawn in to "customizing" your solution beyond what is achievable, to secure the deal. The experienced buyer will know that the further the solution moves from a standard package, the higher the risk of failure, but will still want as personalized a version of what you normally sell as he or she can get. The packaged solution should always be the preferred option; any requirements for a purpose-built customization or adaptation should only be agreed to if they are truly deliverable. Are the adaptations to your standard offering critical to achieving the business benefits that the purchaser is seeking or just unnecessary embellishments? Don't be tempted to get the deal only to discover that you've promised—and been contracted to deliver— the undeliverable. The buyer will use the contract as his or her risk management insurance policy against promised but actually unavailable products or customizations.

There is another element that your prospect analysis should seek to discover. Can you see a team within the customer's organization that will manage the installed project properly? Having one is what can lead to a successful and long-term relationship with your solution and your firm. Your buyer may be the senior sponsor to support the program objectives, but does he or she see the need for, say, a business manager responsible for delivering the business benefits and an experienced project manager to manage the technical parts? It is tempting to underplay the need to recommend the allocation of customer resources to make your solution work, because it looks like a major addition to the prospect's workload. But you are looking for a partnership, not a "cut-and-run" sale that has a high chance of failure, further down the line. In the final analysis, it will be the customer organization itself that delivers the business benefits, not you. More on this in Chapter 7.

If your go-to-market strategy involves solution delivery via expert VARs or consultants, then it comes down to you to ensure that those partners also appreciate the importance of the multiple relationships that help ensure success. If you are handing on some of that responsibility, then make sure that you and your third-party partner are of one mind about what is required.

Interview With Greg Adams by Tom Cairns

Greg Adams currently serves as a partner/principal with a global professional services firm focused on marketing, sales, and service transformation programs for large cross-industry organizations. He previously spent over 25 years leading information technology sales teams, including time at both Salesforce and IBM. He has led teams in the United States, Europe (including four years based in London), and globally; has led as many as 400 sellers; and had revenue responsibility up to U.S.$700m. He holds a BA in marketing from Adrian College and an MBA from Eastern Michigan University. He and his family currently reside near Chicago (USA).

TC: As technology becomes more and more advanced, with AI and machine learning being applied in the sales process, are salespeople becoming less good at what they do?

GA: I like to think of selling as a profession balanced between "art and science." As someone who now spends a lot of time working with large organizations focused on implementing technology to support marketing, selling, and servicing customers, I see a lot of organizations very focused on the science of selling. We need to balance that with the art of selling, namely those things that are tougher to automate.

Sellers in many organizations spend a lot of time talking to people who work for their same company (forecast reviews, cadence reviews, big deal reviews, etc.). Technology (like CRM) should enable sellers to spend more time with their clients and allow for them to be smarter and more responsive to client demands. The focus should always be the customer or client. Forward looking metrics are important (in fact, very important), but they are not the end goal. Metrics should drive focus and give sales leaders early insights to risks and opportunities in their business.

Top sellers still understand their win themes, know the decision makers and influencers across their client's organization, and deeply understand their client's buying process. They also understand the business problem their solution solves and have a clear and concise value proposition for their client.

So, no, I don't think salespeople are less good at what they do. There are still a lot of world-class sales teams doing great work enabled by technology.

Our world moves fast these days. Technology helps sellers stay on top of their business.

TC: Looking at the three linked disciplines in this book, what would you say is your key expertise area?

GA: I've worked in all three disciplines (marketing, sales, and account management), all of which I see as being highly related. I spent over twenty years as a sales manager or upline sales leader, so have a lot of personal experience around what works and what doesn't. That said, one of the great things about selling is that you're always learning.

TC: Is it the quality of the process that matters most? What was pivotal? What was it that turned the deal in your favor, so that you won the deal or lost the deal? What were the lessons learned?

GA: It does start with having the right solution for the customer. In the tech industry particularly, we've seen example after example where the best technical solution does not necessarily win the market. That said, your solution needs to be viable, and it helps a lot if it's top tier. A good solution with a great sales team will tend to beat a great solution with a poor sales team. I've usually been fortunate to have both in my favor.

An example I like to reference is a large deal I led with a multi billion-dollar distribution client in the US. As we went through the sales process, we learned that the CIO really preferred our competitor. We spent months trying to move him to at least being neutral on the selection, but ultimately were unsuccessful in changing his mind. Throughout the sales process, we worked to cultivate a relationship with his boss and peers on the executive team. By the time the decision was made, most of the rest of the leadership at the account preferred our solution.

TC: Who were the decision makers? Who signed the order?

GA: In this case, it really was a committee recommendation. The committee was made up of the CIO, COO, and the head of strategy. We determined that the head of strategy was highly influential to the overall growth plan for the company, and was a trusted adviser to the CEO. We spent a lot of time with this executive, but also the rest of the leadership team.

We had the advantage of objectively being the better technical solution, but that alone was not going to win us this business. We took a very direct approach to our value and our competitor's deficiencies, and made the decision personal. We surrounded our detractor with supporters. When it was time for the recommendation, the executives that supported us asked the CIO if he was so confident in his preference for our competitor that he'd "bet his job" on the outcome (with our competitor). We made his support of our competitor a personal risk for him, and he surrendered to the rest of the team's decision in our favor.

Ultimately, the CEO signed the order. This executive never became a supporter of ours, but we were successful both in winning the deal and, most importantly, delivering a successful project with our technology.

TC: What were the lessons learned?

GA: There are so many lessons here that I'd categorize under the "art" of selling. Know your client and why they have undertaken an initiative. What outcomes do they desire, and how do they measure success? Don't be single threaded in the deal. It's critical to understand the org structure, and who are influencers and who are decision makers. Be objective about your relationships, where you have gaps or risks, and where you can establish advocates. Don't be shy about asking for support, and when you have the better solution for the client, make that known and both qualify and quantify those benefits. You also need to know your competitor—objectively. In this case, we were technically superior, but that is not always so clear.

Sales campaigns like this one are always complex, and the decision making is multi faceted. You must think about BOTH the selling process and your client's buying process. Think about the client's end-to-end process and align to support that. Ultimately, position yourself to be the better and less risky decision. I've had so many wins where the client says "you just knew us and understood our objective better." This is all the "art" of selling. You can't automate this, but you can use technology to drive alignment and momentum within your team to support this kind of sales cycle.

TC: Do you have other examples of well-run sales cycles?

GA: I had a rep on an account we had been trying to open for years, with little success to show for our efforts. We put a new rep on the account who was known for being unconventional, and it worked. The rep was able to get a meeting with a senior leader and invited me to go along. When I asked for the call plan, his response was something like "just follow my lead." I must have been having a busy day because I went with it as asked.

After pleasantries were exchanged, the rep said, "I've spent a lot of time studying your company, and frankly you're really messed up in this area." I was slightly horrified with how he opened the discussion, and assumed the call would be over quickly (thinking to myself, "well, at least there is no existing business lost here"). To his credit, the executive responded with "tell me more, how do you think you can help?" That started a multi month sales cycle that opened a lot of doors with this prospect.

TC: What was the lesson learned here?

GA*: The seller did his homework and developed a thoughtful and insightful point of view on an important area of this client's business that was underperforming. He was confident enough in his assessment and our solution to challenge the client to think beyond the status quo. If he had not taken this approach, I'm not sure we would have engaged with the client. He knew he had to create some noise to start a dialogue, which he did, and it worked.*

The client later told me that he almost threw us out of his office, but decided that the feedback was sincere and probably accurate. We also caught him on a good day, so yes, there may be a little luck involved here too. The rep's homework and sincerity opened the door and kept us engaged, and created an opportunity that the client didn't even know they wanted before this call.

Within a year, we closed a multi million-dollar transaction with this client, and the client won several high-profile industry accolades for the solution built with our technology. It has been one of their most successful IT programs.

Canny buyers will be keen to develop a high-level relationship with their strategic suppliers. They will have done their own analysis of your company; they will know your hierarchy and senior people. Involve those senior people—if the size of the deal justifies it—in the process. Where appropriate, perhaps your senior management team could meet the customer's board members to help secure the relationship at the highest level. If your buyer has set up a cross-functional procurement team, then it is possible that you will encounter during the sales cycle one member of that team who is not on your side—possibly having a different, preferred supplier. It is good general sales advice to avoid confrontational relationships which benefit neither side. Get to the bottom of that individual's objections and try to handle them in a factual, unemotional way. If there is simply no getting them on your side, then recognize the things you have to do with your internal supporters to marginalize that objector as much as is possible. Never show personal negativity or animosity or try to belittle the input, no matter how negative. It's easy to get defensive in that situation. Put your ego aside. If you listen with an open mind, you may well learn more about how to close that deal from the objector than from the supporter or neutral! Don't forget that you are likely to be selling the idea of an ongoing relationship as well as a product or solution. If their objections to your proposal come from an affinity with your competitor, that does present a challenge, but it means that they could be your best source of competitive intelligence (see the next section).

In the latter stages of the sales cycle, your buyer is likely to insist on demonstrable evidence and documented proof that your performance claims for your solution are true. Is this particular prospect in the habit of asking for a trial period or doing a detailed competitive evaluation? You need to know this as early in the sales cycle as possible. If your company's branding and positioning work has been strong enough (see Chapter 2), your credentials will shine through and bolster your chances of closing the deal. Skilled buyers know that their choice of a capable and reliable supplier—no matter what the product—is likely to be a critical factor in the success of any project in the short and the longer term. Your job is to pay attention to getting the evaluation and trial part of the selling process right, even if it is not you personally that is hands-on in that process. More on this in Chapter 6.

Competitive Analysis—Who Do We Have to Beat?

Your marketing efforts do not exist in a vacuum. Prospect research and analysis must include competitive analysis. All the while that your prospect is receiving your sales messages, he or she will also be receiving those of your competitors. As we will see in examining the world of information in which your buyer operates (see Figure 4.3), the customer will also be on high alert for newly available information—from anywhere—concerning the type of purchase that is currently under consideration. You will have made it your business to have found out early in your customer contact process whether you are in a competitive situation and with whom; that's vital. Your approach can be refined and made more effective by understanding what alternatives are being given to the intended purchaser or acquisition team.

These are the things you need to know:

- Are you in a competitive situation? If so, with what company, or companies? Your prospect will not usually be shy about telling you that you are part of a competitive bid for business, so just ask. He or she has the best interests of his or her own firm at heart and will want to see potential suppliers doing their best to compete in offering the best value. If the answer is not forthcoming, get the essential details of the competitive offer. If you know your market sufficiently well, you will then probably be able to figure out who you are competing against.

- Do you know them? Have you competed with them for a sale before this one? Did your company win or lose the deal? In either case, why? Speak to the salespeople who were involved in that prior contact with this company. There will be much to be learned from their success or failure.

- What are their strengths and weaknesses, relative to your company? It could be that you are competing with an industry giant or a minnow—either way, you need to know. Even the smallest competitor can be a serious threat if you don't understand why they would be considered as a viable supplier in this deal. Perhaps they are an innovative start-up which has a technological or expertise advantage; you need to understand this in order to compete effectively. And that doesn't mean denigrating or insulting them or their salespeople directly. You can be forthright and direct in pointing out your relative strengths, so that the buyer can discern the competition's weaknesses, but don't make it into a fight or a slanging match. That will lose you the deal.

- Is the prospect a potentially new customer for the competitor or an existing one? If they are an incumbent supplier, does that affect your proposition? Will you have to be compatible in some way with what has gone before? Have they got this customer so immersed in their solution that your efforts are likely to fail no matter what you do? (See Chapter 7's discussion on value-based selling.) If that is the case, it is a sign of good business judgment, not weakness, to walk away and find a better prospect. You can probably learn from the experience. You may see how to do things differently and beat that competitor next time, and even proactively seek out and attack their user base, if you utilize the information that you gather about them. Make sure that your marketing team hears the details; there may be some useful adaptations that they can make to their communications to help you the next time that you as a salesperson are in that same competitive situation. If your company has done a good branding and positioning job (see Chapter 2), it is very unlikely that there will be any need to re-examine the core values of the business, but tweaking the marketing messages to facilitate the competitive sales approach is a piece of business agility that can help to attract prospects and to close sales in a competitive market.

In *Outsmart! How to Do What Your Competitors Can't*, Jim Champy—echoing Peter Drucker from decades earlier—sees the opportunity that can come from chaos. In the tumultuous times for business that we operate in today, global and localized financial, political, and cultural upheaval presents enormous challenges. Businesses that can streamline their marketing and sales processes and sharpen their people's efforts by "simplifying complexity" for themselves and their customers can open up new opportunities for growth and competitive advantage. There is a school of thought that holds management thinking time too precious to be used on examining competitive activity—the thinking being that your own management team can always come up with the best strategy. Possibly true, but thinking outside the bubble tends to be far more focused and productive if that team can see what competitors are doing, right or wrong, and what results they are achieving in your own target segment. Being open to learning from others will trump ego (or complacency) every time.

> *Learn from the mistakes of others. You can never live long enough to make them all yourself.*
>
> Groucho Marx

Take the competitor analysis piece by piece. We'll use Figure 3.1, to do this.

Examine their company's financial statistics. It's easy to discover the size of the company, but get your CFO to give you an analysis of their financial health, their growth (or decline), their financial and people resources, and their market share, with respect to the segment that you are competing in. If the competitor has a set of brand values that they are proud of, you will be able to find those out as well. In their corporate content, you will find their positioning statement and an indication of how they see themselves. What does the market think of them, though? Try to go beyond their own customer endorsements and find out from analysts, commentators, and others how they are perceived. Is their brand image what they would like it to be, or is there any level of dissatisfaction with them? Do they have a good corporate reputation? Perhaps you know something about one of their existing customers, or one of your sales team may have had contact with them. Use that knowledge to your advantage.

You will have a good feel for your own company's visibility in the marketplace, but is your competitor more or less visible than you? Is their presence making it easier for them to stay front-of-mind in your prospect's company? Your marketing people will be aware of the competitor's promotional strategy and the messages that they give out. Is this prospect for whom you are competing likely to be attracted by what they are saying, and is that message the same as or different from your own? Is it better, more powerful, or convincing in some way? As we will look at in Chapter 4, the quality of their *content*—used across all of the communication channels—is a key factor. Your objective is to be the most authoritative voice in your industry, about your kind of solutions. You will want to be certain that your website, your downloadable pdfs, e-books, videos, and promotional materials are all superior—or at least equal—to those of this competitor, as decision-supporting input for the prospective customer. Let's aim high and go for superior!

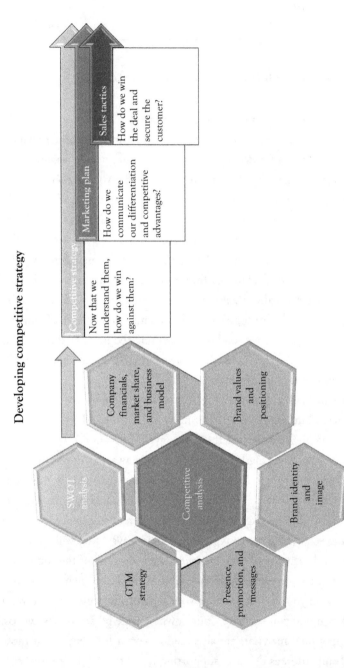

Figure 3.1 Investigate and analyze your competition, then plan how to beat them

Your competitor's GTM strategy may be different from your own. Find out how the buyer would be expected to buy from them. That may be direct or indirect selling. If it's a direct sales model, make sure you understand the degree to which they rely on face to face interaction as opposed to digital means. Don't assume that the customer prefers salespeople to be physically present in his or her office; that may not be the case, so find out. Relative to the size and importance of the deal that you are pursuing, find out and compare how your competitor structures the sale approach. They might be very good at involving their own senior management to sell at the highest level, supporting the efforts of the sales team. If their CEO is selling to the prospect's CEO while your sales manager is selling to the project manager, you will lose the fight. A diktat will come from board level to go with your competitor's offering. If there is an indirect route to the sale, say via a systems integrator, consultant, distributor, or dealer, the picture for you as a vendor changes. You will want to provide all of the relevant support that your third party requires. Being an SME doesn't change the principle: your chosen partner will need the best backup that you can provide. Aim high.

If you are that third party, the level of your supplier's involvement is one that you must judge for your best advantage. The endorsement and visible support of the original equipment manufacturer (OEM) could be your winning card, but only if this is important to the prospective customer. There is no point in putting a huge emphasis on the OEM's global presence if the customer will never have ambitions for it outside of Idaho, and your main advantage is that you are a local supplier. What we are doing now is comparing the practical application of your *company positioning* with that of your competitor; have confidence that you have that right.

Once you have gathered your competitor data, turn that into actionable knowledge by going through a conclusive SWOT (strengths, weaknesses, opportunities, and threats) analysis with your team and from that, devise your competitive strategy. You must conclude how you will win against them, by forming a coherent marketing plan and a set of sales tactics to do so. This is good marketing and sales practice, giving you the best possible chance of closing the sale and gaining a new and profitable customer.

Competitive Strategy—Winning Battles to Win the War

What does a competitive strategy look like? As we discuss in the next chapter, the selling and buying processes are iterative and moving along in parallel, though not necessarily in a coordinated way. No matter where you are in your journey to the sale, your competitor or competitors are doing the same as you—they are directing large amounts of information at their contacts in the prospective account. So, what should your competitive strategy and sales and marketing tactics look like?

1. *Marketing.* Flooding the prospect with more data than you have been is not the way to react to a competitive information flow. You should get more refined marketing material: better targeted and easier and more concise to read and assimilate. You should be out to inform better, not to drown out the competition. Find out what they are doing to compete with you.
   - If they send a 50-page research report that includes praise for their solution, then send the person you know to be the best recipient a Three-minute video of your very best reference account, saying in their particular shared industry language that they are totally satisfied with you as a supplier.
   - If they send an enormously detailed technical document to the techie on the buying team, send him or her a single-page performance comparison between your solution and the others in the market.
   - If they send the CFO a favorable price comparison, get in touch with him or her and ask if he or she would like to see a detailed ROI analysis between your solution and that of the competitor.
   Do the information filtering work for them, rather than adding to the size of their task of doing it themselves.
2. *Sales.* You discover that your competitor has arranged a presentation to the customer buying team of their overall proposal.
   - Arrange to have your own CEO have an informal chat with the prospect's CEO about the state of the industry that they

understand and rely on for business or operate in, respectively. Try to make that before the competitor's presentation.

- Offer the senior procurement manager a crib sheet of carefully prepared questions for his or her use at the presentation.
- Using your website and your social media interactions with influencers in the account (see more on this in Chapter 4), offer the chance to attend a short, sharp webinar about the area that is relevant to your sale, with at least one "must see" participant—an industry maven or respected commentator.

The message here is to pre-empt, outthink, outflank, outmaneuver, and be even more visible but even more relevant to the job in hand. Be bold, be aggressive within reason, and win the small battles to win the war.

And in the Final Analysis …

If, when you have thoroughly assessed your competitor, understood their strategy and tactics, and realized what it takes to win against them, you realize that it's just too difficult, well, you can walk away. That takes suppression of the sales ego and some personal conviction that you are right to do so, but if there is simply too much time, effort, and drain on resources involved to make it worthwhile, then do it: walk away. As Steven Lockwood says in his interview in Chapter 2, one of the three key principles for sales success as he sees it is: "Understanding that not all projects are good projects, and qualification is key to finding those deals you can win versus those you cannot." Your competitor might have too strong a product, too aggressive a price, too much sales resource to put into it, or simply too good a hold on the account at every level for you to win. Make a cool-headed assessment and communicate your decision to your own people. Learn from the experience and be more ready to win next time.

You *can* walk away.

Summary

Are prospect qualification and competitive analysis critical elements of a successful marketing and sales cycle? Many CMOs believe that better data, analytics, and insights are very important to winning and retaining customers. The trends in marketing spend (discussed in Chapter 4) continue to show that they are using part of their budget to improve their capabilities in this area. The simple message is this: *know your prospect.* Close cooperation between marketing and sales is essential here, as we have said before, and this is undeniably an objective that both functions will share. As well as the nature of their business, the complexities (or if you're lucky, the simplicity!) of the prospect's buying process must not remain a mystery as your sales process gets under way. Many marketers currently talk about *prospect profiles*, that is, a set of characteristics of the business, its people, and processes that defines their personality, just like your own company's finely honed brand personality (see Chapter 2). Many hours of wasted effort can be avoided if your approach is guided by this level of understanding of how the business is motivated to make the final decision and ultimately a purchase. And don't overlook individual's personal motivations and the emotions at work that will affect the buying process. AI-driven marketing automation can help with this, but it is the prospect's interaction with your sales and marketing people that will produce the most useful results.

You will have seen a repetition of the mantra that you do not sell in a vacuum. There are competitors out there with a fierce belief that they are better at finding, contacting, and selling to the same target businesses as you. Try to be as familiar with those competitors as you are with your own company, understanding their strengths and weaknesses. Be sufficiently well prepared so as never to be outmaneuvered or surprised by a competitive move. Put yourself in the best position you can with the prospect, to communicate to them that it is your firm that is the better choice as their supplier, with the better solution. Not doing so will lower your effectiveness as a sales organization and make your targets harder to achieve.

In difficult times, when all markets are buffeted by external influences beyond their control and firms are forced to be conservative in their cost management or even to cut back drastically, it can be the status quo that is your most stubborn competitor. You cannot inject ambition into a business that lacks it. You can hone your business value proposition still further to show any prospect that your solution can help them meet their objectives, whether those are for rapid growth or for cost containment or reduction. Use your competition analysis techniques to discover exactly what you are up against and how to sell against lethargy or indifference to the possibilities you can offer.

The Takeaways and Lessons Learned From Chapter 3	Do	Don't
Prospect analysis and qualification	Use the best CRM and BAM systems, but don't be satisfied with merely listing details. Investigate each one as if you were a potential investor: you will be investing your time and effort in selling to them, so make sure it's worthwhile Use every contact as an information-gathering opportunity. You haven't qualified a prospect until you've made contact and asked some direct questions	Don't assume that every business in your selected segment works in precisely the same way Don't ignore the importance of the WTB (where they buy) aspect Make sure that you know who is involved in delivering the solution
Competitive analysis	Do this in a structured way, taking into account all of the elements Do an in-depth SWOT analysis in order to develop a practical competitive strategy. It will be reusable every time you meet that competitor	Don't ignore the importance of this Don't leave this even to the smartest of sales and marketing teams; involve all of the expertise in your company Don't be afraid to ask the prospect for competitive info, including their opinion of the competitor's strengths and weaknesses in that deal Don't insult or denigrate the competitor: just outsell them

The Takeaways and Lessons Learned From Chapter 3	Do	Don't
Competitive strategy	This is a continuous process: you will have to amend and adapt your strategy as you meet differing competition Remember that your prospect's doing nothing—remaining with the status quo—is one of your competitors, too	Don't mistake the effect of quantity over quality. Be a filter for the best info for your prospect, not the one who provides the most
And finally....	You *can* qualify out!	Don't let size, name, glamor, or potential spend overawe you. It's about whether you can close the deal in a timescale and on terms that make it worthwhile

CHAPTER 4

Promotion, Go-To-Market Strategy, and the Sales Process

Overview

In this chapter, we discuss how to inform, influence, motivate, and sell: the very core of the marketing and sales process. How do you move the prospect that we identified and analyzed in depth in the previous chapter's work, from awareness, through positive opinion, to consideration, leading on to trial or evaluation and to the point of purchase? This is the important set of collective actions that—carried out well—will lead to successful sales. In the previous three chapters, we have established our universe of logical prospects, in our chosen market segments, who have the need and ability to buy what we are offering. We have removed the guesswork; we know who to communicate with and what we need to say. We now have to inform them that we are there, that we are credible, that we truly understand their issues and needs, and that we have the relevant solutions. The process is not a linear one, with the buyer drawing in market and competitive information, rethinking, re-evaluating, and making continual new demands on the seller. Senior practitioners will discuss their perspective on this and comment on the lessons they have learned.

Inform, Influence, and Motivate

CMOs are—as they have always been—under pressure to show respectable ROI on their spend (Figure 4.1). When "the marketing budget" is discussed, it's usually primarily a discussion about how to allocate an always-limited promotional budget. Gartner found that marketing budgets have been cut by as much as 15 percent over the last few years. Marketing funds have always been the first of the enterprise budgets to be cut and the last to be restored, and this is as unwise now as it has ever been. The business changes

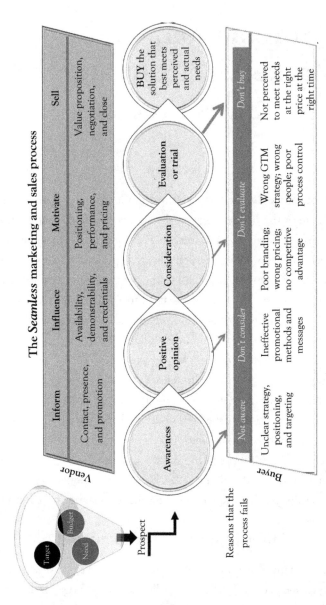

Figure 4.1 A seamless process is needed to avoid losing prospective sales

brought about by the COVID-19 pandemic have led CFOs to become comfortable with the lower cost base that spending cuts have yielded in marketing, alongside savings on real estate and travel costs. By doing a good job with their planning, CMOs proved that they could do more with less, curbing spending on events, agencies, and ad budgets in the face of a crisis. Unfortunately, the impact of near-term marketing budget cuts on brand awareness and consideration is often not immediately appreciated by marketing's stakeholders in the enterprise. CMOs need to demonstrate in their next budgeting cycle that the illusion of savings today presents a significant risk to tomorrow, as brands lose customer relevance, share of voice, and the ability to reach customers with targeted and timely messages.

That said, a direct reduction in enterprise expenditures for marketing-owned activity is not the only reason for these results. The volatility associated with a rapid digitization of commercial activity, along with renewed commitments to customer centricity, can also induce organizations to shift budget for such activity outside the control of a CMO. For example, CEOs are saying the top focus points for their newly appointed chief digital officers (CDOs)—those responsible for pushing and guiding the company to go truly digital—now include customer experience and e-commerce. As these capabilities move to be enterprise-wide digital business initiatives, a CMO's accountability and budget authority may give way to mere supporting roles. CMOs must therefore not only focus on how to reclaim the resources needed to achieve their objectives, but also continuously justify their ownership of both budget and delivery of critical business priorities. Recent data from various sources show that they are doing this. In their study "Marketing Manager Mindset," Livestorm discovered that most marketing budgets, which remained moderate in relation to turnover, either increased or stayed the same between 2021 and 2022. More B2B firms increased their marketing budgets than did B2C.

Across the board, marketers are most focused on using the marketing budget for increasing brand awareness, followed by establishing brand authority and sales. There is a clear emphasis on broad, top-of-funnel, positioning-related tactics. B2C firms and nonprofits care the most about customer engagement, while B2B companies are the most invested in retention. This recognizes, as we discuss in Chapter 8, that B2B customers often have a higher lifetime value, but take more work to acquire and are worth retaining. Most marketers are intent on drawing attention to their company credentials and branding by using major investment in core content, showing a strong top-of-funnel focus. Consideration of conversions, and whether people are engaging, lags far behind reach and traffic, in those particular findings. A few non profit and government marketing teams are spending on referral, affiliate, and account-based marketing (see Chapter 8), but they are the least popular spending areas for those precious marketing dollars, pounds, or euros. The question has to be asked—particularly by the sales teams—of whether this is the best strategy to drive sales. To support the approach described, marketers (perhaps because they've already seen great results from their strategy) are making search engine optimization (SEO) a priority. This has reduced the spend on the more traditional—although increasingly digital and automated—direct mail.

Increased investment in new marketing channels has been heavily driven by the sometimes-devastating effect of the COVID-19 pandemic, as well as its impact on other aspects of nearly everyone's marketing strategy. Only 12 percent of marketers said it didn't change their decisions at all, but different industry sectors were affected differently. Unsurprisingly, some of the sectors most badly hit, like construction, amusement and recreation, and hospitality, leisure, and tourism saw some of the most dramatic budget decreases. Science and technology, chemicals and pharmaceuticals, and entertainment saw no budget decreases, while health care and manufacturing saw the most increases.

Regardless of industry sector, building brand awareness, followed by establishing authority in the chosen segment, is still the top priority. Generating sales seems to have been the lowest priority in marketing, judging by where the money was spent. This makes sense, since content marketing is considered to be a long-term strategy, with a heavy top-of-funnel focus. Video and blogs have been the most popular forms of content. In spend terms, these have dwarfed everything else; nearly twice as many marketers are now working with video and blog content compared to the next runner-up, online courses. The conclusion must be that other options, like podcasts and interactive tools, have not been getting the desired ROI on that marketing spend. As Mike Ames says (see his interview in Chapter 1), social media is now critical to identify targets, to find out information about them, to build credibility, and to promote one's own services.

As Livestorm says, "Even though it wasn't a close race, it's still interesting—and surprising—that online courses came in third. This is despite the fact that, for the most part, marketers didn't call out audience education as a significant goal." There must be some payback going on with them. All of these data are useful in helping you to see what is happening in the wider world of sales and marketing and the many options that you have. We'll look at the challenge of choosing where the marketing budget—large or small—is spent, later in this chapter.

Go-To-Market Strategy—Reaching Your Buyer

Whether your sales process is largely face to face, digital, via Zoom, Teams, and the like, or purely online, the basic principles will apply. During your research, segmentation, and strategy work, you will have investigated your target customers' preferred buying methods. In some cases, this will be directly from the manufacturer, producer, developer, or service provider; in others, there will be an accepted or preferred intermediary between the originator and the user. This will determine your go-to-market strategy. You may be that intermediary yourself, tailoring a product or service from your own supplier to your customers' needs. As the original developer, let's say, of a software product, you must decide if you are best positioned as the procurer and supporter of sufficient prospects to meet your targets. Or are you at your best as the supplier, trainer, and supporter of a far smaller number of expert value-added resellers (VARs) or systems integrators (SIs) and consultants? Many a company has been undone in believing it can maintain profits by doing everything, when its expertise is in producing and developing the product, not in delivering and supporting it in the way that its target market requires or even insists upon. Partnering with channels that have industry knowledge and solution capability is the way to go.

> *It is noticeable everywhere that greater emphasis is being put upon the management of the channel, in recognition of the fact that around 75 percent of all global trade goes through some variant of it. We see "Channel Chiefs" being appointed who can recruit expert PAMs (Partner Account Managers) who see a real career in the role, and the head of go-to-market strategy is now being invited to the C-Suite.*
>
> Jacqui Rand, Founder and Director,
> The Channel Consultants Ltd., United Kingdom

Your decision whether to sell direct or indirect through partners will be guided by a number of key factors. Let's look at some of these.

- Resources, skills, and expertise: do you have enough of them to sell to and support your prospects and customers? If your business model includes the provision of sufficient sales and marketing resource to attack your chosen market, then you can go for the direct supplier route. If not, unless you are in a true "blue ocean" (*ibid*) situation, there will almost certainly be third-party vendors who have the knowledge and skills to do the job for you. A smaller business can amplify its marketplace effects considerably by the judicious choice and management of third-party partners.
- Financial model: much depends on where you plan to find your growth and profitability. If your product margins are high, you may be tempted to retain them entirely by direct selling, but those margins can also be a good reason to use a third-party partnering route to market. That's because you will have the opportunity to provide worthwhile margin opportunities for resellers. Your calculation should be on the benefits of having an expanded sales force and a first-line support network at minimal cost. Doing those things internally is an expensive exercise. To take a simplistic example, getting one hundred direct customers each spending $10,000 of which you retain 50 percent product margin might sound great, but they may cost you another 25 percent to find, sell to, and support. A 100-strong partner network may get you a thousand of those same customers by your giving up 33 percent of your product margin to equip them to do the selling and supporting work for you (trained by you, of course). Do the sums, then decide.

Remember, however, that it is the added value to their own businesses that your potential partners are looking for, and they are aware that your ambitions for segment specialization and optimized support costs, along with your own geographic ambitions, are likely to be best served by working with them.

There has been a power shift: the manufacturer or developer is no longer able to dictate terms to the dealers, distributors, resellers and consultants, as they used to do. The "third party"—who is very aware that they own the customer relationship—is looking for a supplier who can show strong branding and differentiation in their target market. They prefer a firm that is easy to do business with, that can demonstrate expert marketing, sales, financial and technical support.

Jacqui Rand, Founder and Director,
The Channel Consultants Ltd., United Kingdom

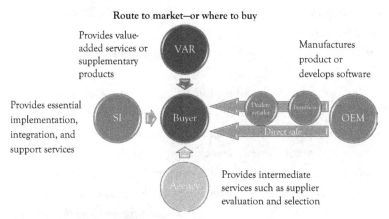

Figure 4.2 Your buyer's preferred purchasing point must guide your choice of route to market

Carlo Tortora Brayda di Belvedere in Conversation With Michael Grant

Carlo is the founder and CEO of the Gorilla Corporation, based in San Francisco and France. Gorilla is a global leader in Partner Co-Marketing through Channel Marketing Automation (CMA). They have worked with technology manufacturers over decades to improve their channel strategy and go-to-market execution, enabling indirect sales growth at a worldwide level. They support vendors on pre-IPO scale-up and post-IPO channel optimization.

Carlo, putting one's trust in 'third parties' to achieve most of the sales for a company may on the surface appear risky. You have proven that this works. Can you please share with us your methods and the lessons that you have learned during your career in Channel Management?

Everything we do is totally based upon increasing sales as an outsourced agency. We create channel sales programs and orchestrate a sales process where we sell alongside their sales partners. We develop software called a "matching tool" which works out the most appropriate targets with whom to form strategic alliances. We facilitate that relationship development and drive the relationship building, as partnerships only work if driven hard. Most companies don't have the rigor to do this themselves using a conventional assignment of tasks, and relationships easily flake. We tend to crack the whip and maintain the discipline. Our marketing team then generates sales opportunities through combined programs and provides a sales pipeline to co-sell with VARs.

All our clients are technology companies, but we sell into both vertical and horizontal markets for them. We cover the Federal government, education, finance and banking, and assisted living, among others. Cybersecurity is currently an important horizontal target for us. We focus on the SMB, mid-market and low enterprises. We can avoid much of the channel conflict areas by targeting "the smaller of the large;" say, the Fortune 1200 companies.

We generated $500m for a major global software company over ten years of new revenue which was not on their "radar."

I was told by one middle manager—a potential major client in Europe— that all of my services were already done to perfection "in house" and that they would never have any need of my company. A previous happy client in the USA changed his job, and I kept on at him. He introduced me globally to that same skeptical company and, overnight, "changed the world"!

Most of our business is US-based, but strongly supplemented by business in Western Europe. In order of preference for us are Germany (along with Austria and Switzerland), the UK, France, Spain and Italy. Of these, the most important prize for us is Germany, which has experienced the greatest growth, but whose market—culturally—is so hard and difficult for those of us in the US. Germany is the starting point now for most US-based organizations. To conduct German projects out of Germany is essential, and we have lost business in the past by trying to do this out of the UK. Everyone's dream here at present is to establish themselves in the

German market. We now operate offices in Munich, and Rotterdam for the Benelux countries.

I haven't always been lucky in my career, and have learned many lessons that might help others to avoid mistakes and wrong turns.

It is important to understand the decision-making ecosystem of the customer. Never assume that your contact is the only one able to make the buying decision. Always get a true appreciation of the customer ecosystem, a vital sales rule often overlooked! It might be that the decision process lies outside the company, and could be the supplier of a product adjacent to yours. You also need to cover off the "influencers" in some both small and global operations.

Face to face relationships can never be replaced by a virtual one based on Zoom or Teams. You might succeed on your first deal, but you are rarely generating a lasting relationship. Our first deal with a global systems company was achieved through a conference call. It was a seven-digit deal at the time. The price point and value proposition were all perfect, but misunderstandings soon set in over changes in planning by the customer. You are suddenly on the back foot in the relationship. The moment we invested heavily in face to face time, everything changed. It was almost a spiritual thing when I entered his personal space and could become a real partner. Sure enough, the project soon got back on track.

We wanted to create a very strong networking community with CIOs, CISOs and channel partners. We recognized that we needed the right kind of thought leadership role to draw them in, and just how well private/public partnerships can work if hosted in the right forum. We set out on a "think-tank" venture with a third party not for profit organization, of which I am now the Executive Chairman and which is known as the Tortora Brayda Institute. This provides a great forum with the right kind of round table dialogues. In the US, government would normally only talk with the biggest companies, while the rest of the industry became disassociated.

Cybersecurity knows no borders, especially in turbulent times, such as with the invasion of Ukraine by Russia. Extending your field of view outside the US borders has become critical. We intend to become part of the solution to address national interests. We already participate in global NATO conferences, and have grown both respected and closer to our prospects, but more importantly can become a force for good alongside them. The Institute has both wide and senior membership influencers, which brings with it "door openers" that we might otherwise never have discovered.

Should you decide that a direct sales approach is the one that best serves your business model, you then face the changes that have occurred in all businesses, as a result of the increased acceptance of WFH (working from home) culture or hybrid working. This is when staff spend part of the time in an office location and part working from home or a location remote from the corporate hub. It's no longer simply the case—on the sales side—of sending in the sales team to meet the customer's buying team on any working day. Selling via a combination of face to face, video calls, and telephone interaction is now the reality. I hear many stories of all of these happening simultaneously, to get all of the relevant people together at the same time! This needs a new set of sales skills and increased attention to detail in managing today's busy sales diaries for optimum effectiveness.

If yours is a business that can be run with purely online sales, then the pressure on the sales function is a different one, but no less intense for that. For those sales managers who worry that the human element will be much reduced or disappear altogether as a result of digital marketing and sales technology, I believe that although "digital selling" will increase, B2B vendors will, in effect, seek to slow down that process by inserting a contact with a "live" salesperson as part of the sales process. This will put their salespeople in a stronger and even more important role, as they become even more the personification of the business's brand and an even greater influence on the differentiation that a strong brand identity can convey. Marketing has already become a heavily digital function; sales will remain more of a hybrid one. The global pandemic having dramatically driven the acceleration of the working from home model, with the resulting limitations on face to face selling, virtual selling becomes a vital skill. It is true that since face to face sales have long been the norm, many salespeople are uncomfortable with distance or remote selling. Not so with buyers, who have adapted fast to a virtual sales approach.

Virtual Selling

It wasn't long ago that the idea of buying vehicles—as an example— online, sight unseen, was thought ridiculous. Now, the majority of consumer car sales are made this way and B2B is following suit. Jeb Blount (*ibid*) relates that one major U.S. truck-reselling firm makes more than

90 percent of its sales virtually. These vehicles cost between $20,000 and $200,000. Customers receive photos and videos. They don't do test drives; they don't kick the tires. Nevertheless, this firm successfully closes "tens of thousands" of used-truck deals, annually. The customers are happy and the vendor's costs are much reduced. But companies that operate virtually must stick to the sales basics as well as using digital means.

> *If you fail to rapidly adopt and assimilate omnichannel virtual selling into your business development, sales and account management processes, you will either become extinct or be replaced by a robot. That's a brutal and absolute fact.*
>
> Jeb Blount, "Virtual Selling"

That core content we have discussed becomes even more important, as does personalized contact with prospects. You still have to recruit the best marketing and sales professionals, then train and coach them well. Most reservations about virtual selling come from salespeople, not prospects. So long as there remains a formal selling process, and the introduction of virtual selling doesn't dilute this, a hybrid selling approach will still get you to the successful sale.

Forbes research indicates that more than six out of 10 executives believe video calls offer better communication than telephone calls. Video calls display people's faces, of course, so you can still read their expressions. Video enables salespeople to establish "emotional connections" with prospects—something you can't do well with text or e-mail. Oddly, for people who spend their lives in conversation with others, many salespeople are uncomfortable being "on camera." Sales training now must include instruction on how to be comfortable, professional, empathetic, and persuasive through a screen, rather than face to face across a desk.

This new sales reality is here to stay, so top salespeople will work on transferring the techniques they already know about successful sales calls to the video situation.

If you are the indirect sales partner of a significant manufacturer or developer, the virtual selling environment is ideal for allowing you to get beyond what would normally be the limits of sales support from your supplier. Have a senior supplier person commit to a few minutes of participation in your sales call. They can add the strategic dimension to your sales pitch. Don't let them dominate, but provide the participant with a concise brief of what you need and expect from them, before the call. The level of commitment they have to make is minimal and their travel time from anywhere in the world is nil!

Face to face selling will not go away. As the pandemic's restrictions ease, all over the world, more of what was previously the norm in sales will happen again. But it will be different—it will be a hybrid of local and virtual—and will be ever more demanding. We look in more depth at managing the sales pitch in all its forms in Chapter 5.

Is It Possible to Operate With a Mixture of Direct and Indirect Sales?

Yes. But just as either approach requires discipline and clarity, that is compounded when both are in play. There are many examples of companies deciding, for example, to carve out a specific group of high-value customers or a specific segment to keep to itself, while using channels to sell to the remainder of their target market. Is it not likely that your channel partners will also recognize how lucrative those selected accounts could be? They may want to (or may already) be selling to them. Having engaged a network of third-party suppliers, you must have a very clear demarcation between their "territory" and your own, however that is defined. Perhaps there will even be some sharing between you, that is, you make the sale and manage the account; they do the technical support. Or there may be an arrangement where the channel partner finds the account and hands product supply and management over to you, keeping lucrative support for itself. It can get tricky, despite the best intentions. The customer will have his or her own best interests at heart and so will favor whatever arrangement best suits him or her; this can generate conflict between you and your channels, where everyone loses. The best decider on the issue is the customer: how do they want to be sold to and supported? Think of your audience as the center of a universe that you need to navigate. You orbit their world, operating in their time zone, not vice versa. As Gartner puts it, "Think about the customer eco-system, not your own ego-system." Take that as your prime guidance in selecting how and where you make your solution available to them.

Promotion and the Marketing Mix

In his book *Basic Marketing. A Managerial Approach*, E. Jerome McCarthy originally devised and published "The 7Ps" marketing model. Earlier, "The 4Ps" marketing mix—product, promotion, price, and place—was focused on product, rather than services marketing or a combination of the two. The three additional elements were the "service mix Ps": people, physical evidence, and processes, reflecting a realization that customer service was an important element of the mix.

As the scope of marketing continues to develop, so does the marketing mix. Since 2007, Larry Londre's "9Ps of Marketing ©2007" has included:

- Planning, process, or marketing process
- People/prospects/potential purchasers/purchasers (target market)
- Product
- Price/pricing
- Place/distribution
- Promotion
- Partners/strategic alliances
- Presentation

Put simply, this is a framework that organizations of all sizes can use for the consideration of all of those ingredients that form a comprehensive recipe for a marketing strategy. The message it sends, above all, is that your marketing strategy must serve the company business plan and be in line with its corporate objectives. Many marketing tools and services built around this framework are available.

After developing the marketing strategy that best serves the company business plan, the next major task for the CMO is to construct a budget that allocates the marketing resources most effectively to do the same. The "marketing mix" that the budget has to cover includes all forms of content, promotion, and the skills to implement the marketing plan, as mentioned above. The first step is to be very, very clear about the objectives. A total of 40 percent of CMOs said that one of their key objectives in the allocation of budgets was to improve brand awareness—vital, as we described in Chapter 2, for the sales process. Agencies' share of the total budget (23 percent) has declined a little, year over year. Respondents to

Gartner's recent CMO study[1], who were from a wide range of industries across several countries, reported that 29 percent of work previously carried out by agencies has moved in-house in the last 12 months. The top three external agency capabilities that companies are moving in-house are *brand strategy, innovation and technology,* and *marketing strategy development.* This reflects, I believe, the fact that upstream marketing is being increasingly recognized as a vital core skill with brand value for the enterprise that is best developed and executed by the business itself. There is much talk of data and analytics in CMO circles, but this and other investigations seem to indicate that big data and automated analytics have failed to live up to marketing's expectations. By contrast, Gartner also contends that the opt-out rate from mobile app tracking—a major source of that data—will decline from 85 percent to 60 percent as both B2B and B2C users realize that untargeted ads increase their exposure to low-quality content.

In his 2020 research on future B2B marketing and artificial intelligence (AI), one of Koldyshev Maxim Vladimirovich's conclusions was that his case studies of large companies indicated that three main problems were being solved by integrating AI into their marketing and sales systems. These are the elimination of incomplete, outdated, and inaccurate data; the need for rapid decision making from the complications of large-scale big data accumulation; and the lack of cooperation between sales, marketing, and service functions (that is referred to repeatedly throughout this book). I personally remain skeptical about the ability of the majority of firms to achieve that level of success in this highly technical area.

More than ever, the skills and experience that a CMO needs to be successful are a mixture of business acumen, strategic thinking, people skills (including the art of effective collaboration), marketing experience, and financial control, along with sufficient technical understanding to integrate the ever-evolving strengths of digital marketing effectively.

---

[1] Gartner Inc. and/or its affiliates. 2021. "The State of Marketing Budgets 2021—Insights From Gartner's Annual CMO Spend Survey." Research conducted online from March through May 2021 among 400 respondents in the United States (49 percent), Canada (1 percent), France (12 percent), Germany (11 percent) and the United Kingdom (27 percent) across any company sizes and industries.

The move in B2B marketing promotion away from "traditional" to online media has continued. The role of the media buyer has been supplanted by the social media and digital marketing agency. Marketing

> *In my 30-year executive search career, I have seen the role and person profiles of senior marketing and sales roles in B2B businesses change considerably. Many new skill sets and enlightened attitudes are required. Newly developed and refined marketing tools and practices such as social media need someone with a mix of technical savvy and customer empathy to manage a team that can successfully utilize them. The WFH or hybrid working model (which is here to stay) has affected both ends of the buying and selling equation. Companies are looking for senior managers who have already adapted to online and digital methods of marketing and selling, including the less obvious challenges to their teams of work/life balance, motivation and productivity.*
>
> Steve Lavelle, Managing Partner, NGS Global, United Kingdom

budgets (Gartner, *ibid*) as a proportion of revenue were down from 11 percent in 2020 to 6.4 percent in 2021, with 72 percent of that investment being in digital. This includes spending on websites, e-mail marketing, mobile, digital ads, social media, and SEO. Driven by the effects of the COVID-19 pandemic, the budget for live events has disappeared. The marketing spend to support partners constitutes only 9.4 percent of the average marketing budget. We will discuss the growing importance of partner support later.

Interestingly, in an era when many companies are striving to take a high-minded view of their brand identity (see Chapter 2) and to promote their environmental, social, and governance (ESG) credentials, spending on *PR* is not one of the top 10 categories for today's CMOs. It could be argued that *sponsorship*—which does rank more highly, attracting 9.6 percent of budgets—*could* be ranked as PR activity and is, indeed, often managed by an external PR company. Press and public relations—to expand to its full title—can be an enormously powerful promotional tool, when handled well. My own experience is that a good PR company, liaising with and managed by a senior internal marketer, can assist in awareness generation, brand building, and exposure to the target market very cost effectively. But they need senior executive cooperation and the right core content to work with. Choose your PR firm with a keen eye on that second part of their function: public relations. Don't hire a company that will be attempting to forge relationships in your target segments for the first time. You need them to have already established contacts in the places—in newspapers, industry periodicals, online blogs, and information services—where you want to be seen. The old adage of "There's no such thing as bad PR" is just nonsense. Even the megabrand of IBM ("No one ever got fired for buying IBM" was a common phrase that showed its strength) became "It's Being Mended," when the unacceptable degree of its computing equipment failures began to appear in the press. Get control of the way you are reported upon, avoid negative commentary, and learn how to use the media to your advantage. Even the smallest firm can do this effectively, as Nick Ray points out in his comments about Prevx in Chapter 2, where carefully managed word of mouth among those in a specialist market got extensive press coverage.

To repeat an important point: all marketing budgets are, of course, limited to some degree, no matter the size of the company. You cannot be everywhere and do everything. Follow your strategic priorities to choose your budget allocation. "Omnichannel marketing" is a term that is being commonly used, but "omni" means "all" where what you need is "best"— the most appropriate to get in front of your intended audience. As ever, it is not only the marketing team that can help to get this right. Your salespeople and your customer support people can provide valuable insights into how your prospects and customers gather information. Use digital tools to measure your results against the most relevant KPIs: conversion rates and keyword rankings on your SEO results; website traffic and click-through rates; open rates on your e-mails; cost-per-click on your paid advertising, and so on. Be ruthless in excising any marketing channel that is not giving you the ROI that you need.

Focus on Core Content Development and ROI

What possibly sets the top performers apart most crucially at this point is that they are four times more likely than the less successful to spend at least half their marketing budget on content marketing. We discussed the importance to the whole organization of high-quality content in

Chapter 2. Content marketing—its development, usage, distribution, and communication—is certainly a hot topic and attracting an ever-growing portion of that precious marketing cash. Interestingly, supporting the contention that content marketing development must be driven by customer needs, the proportion of the budget allocated to content marketing is significantly higher in North America than in Germany, for example.

Although the majority in, for example, German-speaking countries are not willing to devote even 15 percent of their marketing budget to content marketing, the proportions in the Gartner CMI study (*ibid*) reveal a significant upward trend. The most frequently mentioned budget share in North America lies in the range from 10 to 24 percent, closely followed by a share of up to 50 percent. More than one-fifth go as far as to invest more than half of their marketing budget in content marketing. In the digital marketing pot, after content marketing in importance comes e-mail marketing software, followed by online advertising. This includes search engine ads, advertising banners on specialized portals, and other platforms for videos and animations on the Internet.

The trend study also shows that the pandemic has acted as an amplifier of the digital transformation—especially for two out of three B2B—companies. It is very clear that the respondents have tackled a large number of projects—for instance, by adapting their websites, editorial and topic calendars, and their products and services—but they have also shifted resources to social media and community management. Within this, however, is what the report calls the "sleeping giant" of content marketing, the basis for all of the words, pictures, and video being used everywhere.

So, what is "content"? Videos for social media came out at the top of the list. Video is so important for effective social media content that this ranking shouldn't be surprising. Social was followed by video ads, which again have been proven very effective compared to static image or plain-text options. Short-form videos were more popular than longer ones, unsurprisingly, since short-form video currently rules the Internet. It's worth looking, as you consider your own most appropriate use of media marketing, exactly where this essential investment in video content should be seen.

Basic content consists of (usually) free information that will be highly of interest to your target market, supporting those all-important brand values. These are not pages of promotional messages, but a display of your expertise, experience, and attitudes, offering a new form of value to your market. Develop sophisticated content for the long game, recognizing that B2B sales cycles are long and that you may have to keep audiences

> *The incoming data on the influence of video on buying behaviors is incontrovertible. Three quarters of buyers state that they made a buying decision after watching a video.*
>
> Jeb Blount

engaged for quite some time. Your main objective is to deepen their relationship with your brand throughout the marketing and sales cycle and to display your expertise. "Following the customer journey" is a phrase often used in marketing, now, to emphasize how critical timing is, when applied to distribution or availability of content.

Statista's *Content Marketing Compass, 2022* advises:

> *A scalable, successful, and nuanced content marketing strategy will help you create and manage digital content more easily, make it usable at the right time, and measure success. A strong strategy can be evaluated in terms of how well it enables everyone in the front line (sales, customer care, managers, and even accounting and legal departments) to tell their stories. And this will best be achieved if your customers and consumers retell and even embellish your stories in a way that benefits you.*

Although not a new technology, digital asset management (DAM) systems are increasingly being seen by CMOs as an essential element in their quest for effective content management. Forrester's report, by Nick Barber, "Digital Asset Management for Customer Experience, Q1 2022," provides a good summary of what is available. The increasing integration of AI into these systems is allowing them to be not just library-like repositories of corporate content, but proactive aids to its development and distribution to the right places, to enhance the customer experience. As mentioned earlier, however, there has been a lot of criticism of the current use of AI from the recipients of it, for example, those using chatbots to interact with their vendors. Many feel that the technology could be renamed "artificial interference," as it seems intent on distancing them from the vendor! In their 2022 paper on the subject, "Implementing Artificial Intelligence in Traditional B2B Marketing Practices," Keegan, Dennehy, and Naudé examined how 18 companies tried to use AI in a variety of activities. They suggest that AI is not yet fit for managing the complexities that are inherent in the B2B buying process, as it is a role that is heavily reliant on human intervention. AI in B2B is claimed to be exceptional at predicting future trends from analysis of past events but unable to adapt to the rapid changes in business scenarios. In the context of managing core content, this agility is essential for the marketing personalization that we focused on in Chapter 1.

If your *GTM strategy* is to use third parties to get your product or solution to market (see earlier), your content development plan must take this into account. Much of the core content that you produce will be immediately useful to and usable by your channel partners. They will, however, have their own materials of all kinds as well. It will be doing a different job to your own, promoting *their* brand and the services that *they* offer. Provide adaptable pieces of content that they can use and incorporate into their own. Use links, on both your own website and theirs, to cross-refer to and make the most of their strengths. This can be tricky, because although making the sales and supporting a continuingly purchasing customer is an objective they share with you, they will be doing it differently. Be sensitive to what they need and write that into your content strategy.

What Forms of Content Can You Usefully Develop?

- *White papers* are the format that saw by far the highest usage growth in B2B, from 20 percent to 55 percent usage in firms, year over year. Plans seem to indicate that white papers will continue their great popularity in the future, especially in B2B, with 42 percent of companies saying their use will expand.
- *PowerPoint presentations*, though hardly new, are still an important component of content. Providing a downloadable

and editable one that, as well as getting across the message that you intend, can be plagiarized and used in whole or in part by the recipient is a common and useful tactic.

- *Business comment and news pieces* provide some of that top-level, industry-specific data that your prospect finds difficult to source for themselves. It is the seller's advantage (see Chapter 5) to be constantly talking to different players in an industry segment and learning from each of them. Your prospect will be unlikely to have the time or the means to do the same, so you can provide valuable data in this regard. Research data—either primary or public domain—are also often included.

- *Product.* There has been an enormous increase in the number of software companies providing downloadable pieces or self-running demo versions of their products. The boom in mobile app technology has greatly increased this. Equally, research companies, marketing companies, and consultancies provide enticing taster pieces of what they sell. Guides, checklists, business tools, and so on put something useful in the prospect's hands and get visibility for the brand. This is more about content than a "freemium" pricing strategy, that being where the whole product is given away in the hope of enticing purchases of more, later. See Chapter 2 for the example of Nick Ray and Prevx.

- *Video.* As discussed, this is the booming area of content. Standards are now very high; so in B2B, professional levels of filming, editing, and production are necessary. As you see, some of our interviewees (like Mike Ames, in Chapter 1) say how video content is essential to the promotion of their businesses. And there are several subsets of videos to consider:
  - *Webinars* continue to attract a lot of marketing money and good attendances. Best used for demonstrations of expertise in your particular discipline. A popular format is to have multiple guest speakers with a concluding shared discussion. Follow-up to registered viewers is the payoff. Use the incentive of presentations from the webinar or a

link to a recording of it to secure contact details. Don't confuse a webinar with an online course.

○ *Online courses.* Costly in time, money, and effort to produce to what is now the required high standard. Be clear about your objective for offering these. Again, follow-up is the payoff. If this is, in effect, a free version of your regular product, make that clear.

○ *Short-form face-to-camera presentations.* Increasingly popular. Choose your topic and follow-up objectives carefully; make sure your presenter is well trained and keep it short. Far more acceptable when voice only, rather than with shared visuals.

○ *Short-form promos.* Essentially advertising by another name, just using your own or free space. Don't irritate by making them compulsory for access to more content. Think of the slightly helpful "skip ads" or annoying "video will play after ads" prompts that you hate.

○ *Case studies.* This is where those satisfied customers—your reference accounts—come to the fore (see Chapter 8 for further discussion). This is powerful content that can enhance your brand and get you more business—when done properly. Get the professionals in for this. Your handheld mobile phone video of your customer behind his or her desk will not suffice! You need a cameraman, a scriptwriter, a producer, and the complete cooperation of the customer's marketing team to make this work. Set your objectives first. Be clear to the customer about what will be required of him or her and how the finished product—which you should guarantee they will see and have the chance to approve before it goes public—will be used.

If your resources are limited, you can still use the power of video. It can be done relatively inexpensively with a good iPhone, the relevant video and postproduction software, and a bit of personal training. As ever, careful preparation is the key to success. And of course, it might just be the case that a large customer—for the case study example—will have video production facilities that they will allow you to use. If you can't make a good-quality job of it, just don't do it.

It is easy for your enthusiasm for content to result in an explosion of the sheer quantity of data that you are able to produce about your products, solutions, company, and the industry in which you have chosen to operate. What you need to be focused on is specific, differentiated, high-quality, customer-needs-driven information that supports every stage of your sales and marketing process. As Figure 4.3 attempts to show, there is a continuous flow of information coming into the customer's buying cycle at every stage. Your content must be what is needed at a specific time and be easy to digest, no matter how it is delivered. This timing and relevance equation should drive your choice of content delivery channel, whether it be free social media, paid media, direct mail, or the face to face sales visit. In practice, multiple ones are typically used (see later), to get the right mix of the nature, timing, and target for that content. As has always been the case with traditional marketing media, spreading the marketing investment too thinly across too many of the options in a massively noisy environment—an easy mistake to make—will result in a loss of impact rather than increased effectiveness. Spending on paid social media is increasing, as marketers see the benefits of controlling the placement and timing of the messages they deliver, rather than allow it to be more random, as with free social media usage. Paid advertising and sponsored posts on LinkedIn currently attract the biggest share of those budgets. Your digital marketing agency (if you have the budget to retain one) will have the tools to help guide your choices and to do that important continuous assessment of ROI. One of the major benefits that marketing automation brings is that ability to measure precisely and consistently and to make changes quickly. Choosing the right agency to work with requires care and experience, particularly now that many agencies have decided to specialize, in, for example, search engine optimization (SEO) or content marketing design and delivery. For many years, e-mail marketing has been a key component of the B2B sales process; there are specialists in enhanced digitization of that promotional method. As ever, my recommendation is that not a dollar is spent without there having been a cool and critical evaluation of what pieces of the exciting digital marketing process support the brand of the business, as discussed in Chapter 2.

All of the techniques and tools are irrelevant if there is a fractious or piecemeal relationship between them. Coordination and locked-in consistent thinking are essential to make the most of your branding and communications—and your sales work. There is no substitute for *business insight*, running throughout your marketing, sales, and customer support people or teams. There is much said in this book about establishing customer relationships, but the customer only wants those relationships with sellers who understand his or her business and can help them to achieve their vision and success. As you have read from some of our contributors, you need to train or hire the people who truly empathize with the aims and attitudes of those to whom they are communicating, selling, and later, supporting.

Social listening is the latest phrase that seeks to encompass the need to establish a direct relationship with the audience. This is used very differently by B2B, compared to B2C, firms. Facebook and Instagram (mostly used by B2C but gaining B2B acceptance) still rule most marketers' social strategy. In the former, the targeting is much sharper, looking at job titles and responsibilities in industry segments relevant to their targeting, rather than going for huge consumer numbers. TikTok's rising popularity, Meta's wavering stock price, and LinkedIn's grip on B2B all show how dynamic the landscape is; marketers need to be in constant touch with these trends. There is much discussion about the shortage of outstanding digital marketing talent. Your own company needs a strategy and a proactive plan to ensure that your marketing department contains the right skills. Most B2B firms use between three and five social media channels. Meta remains the most popular, followed by Instagram and then YouTube. This is possibly because there has not been more critical assessment of Meta's established effectiveness, and its dominance is just because of its solid, first-mover advantage under its previous brand of Facebook that has given it a relatively immovable prominence for so long. Remember, ROI is what you're after, based on your own KPIs. The buzz and inherently frantic nature of social media marketing means that you do have to maintain a constant watching—or rather, listening—brief on your customers' and prospects' preferences for their sources of information (see Figure 4.2) in a world of information overload. And keep an eye on your competition! YouTube is riding high on marketers' list, right now, but trends are pointing clearly at TikTok being the next big video channel, B2B reckoned to follow B2C in this regard. LinkedIn has become the most important for B2B marketers, finally overtaking Facebook. Twitter drops in prominence here, but otherwise, YouTube and Instagram round out the top spots, just like we saw in prior rankings from Gartner, Forrester, HubSpot, and others surveying the activity.

In the activity blur that all of this can induce, it's important to remember that the majority of first online interactions now take place on a *mobile device*, not a desk-based one. Although most web apps either originate on or take account of smartphone use, it is wise to check just how good your splendid content looks on a very small screen. Ease of access and navigation, clarity, touch-screen compatibility, and the avoidance of excessive scrolling required for reading define the experience that billions of smartphone users expect. Beware of the auto-cut-down software that can reduce your precious desktop website and content to bare bones that do not do your brand justice.

As we discussed earlier, brand awareness, engagement, and community building are the key goals of social media marketing, but in a company where everyone can be a frontline resource, sales or customer experience and support (rather than marketing teams) can be the prime movers behind social media-focused content. As ever, tune all that effort to the needs of the customer, using your team members who know them the best. Statista's advice is, therefore, "A strategic content marketing operation isn't the storyteller of the business. It enables everyone else to be the storytellers. Remember: it's your story—don't forget that you need everyone to tell it well."

Looking at the way the buying and selling process now works as a continuous exchange of messages and information from both sides (see Figure 4.3), we can see that the marketing/sales/buying process can no longer be looked at as a linear one, from either the buyer or seller perspective. As the buyer moves from the realization of the business problem and the need to solve it, through the various stages toward buying, there is constant revisiting of each prior stage. This coincides with bringing in more from the world of information available to support or check the conclusions already reached.

The seller, meanwhile, is simultaneously bringing to that world of information its own messages, as it tries to move the buyer from awareness

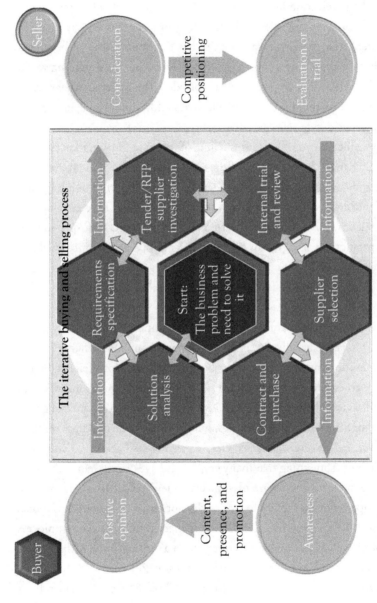

Figure 4.3 The process is characterized by constant information flow and revisions

of its presence to serious consideration of its suitability as a competitive supplier. There is no longer a simple "handover" from marketing to sales in this regard. The buyer's persistent need for iterative information requires, more than ever, cohesion and consistency between highly focused branding, all content, and sales and marketing messages, as we discussed in Chapter 2. In effect, the canny seller has the opportunity to become a conduit for the sifting and analysis of the otherwise overwhelming world of information that the buyer must consider. This is yet another way of becoming a partner in the task of effectively addressing the business problem by considering relevant data.

Imagine that your business is selling office space. That market has seen radical changes from the work-from-home revolution, brought about by the pandemic. Not only has the demand for monolithic buildings full of bland floor space been affected, but office workers have developed a new relationship with their pattern and place of work. Cash-per-square-foot promotions and photos of shiny desks in open-plan offices will not attract eyeballs any more. After the two years of COVID-19 ravaging the workplace, companies have increasingly called their employees back to in-person work, at least for part of the week. "Hybrid" work style is the new buzzword, with workers working from home for the majority of the week. Managers usually cite easier collaboration and maintenance of vital work culture as reasons to return, but because many of their colleagues on any given day will be absent from the office, Zoom or Teams meetings are still a central aspect of the day. It's frustrating to participate in a group video meeting with colleagues calling in from the same building, on their own screens, as often happens. Gearing their lives back up to an office-based one is something that many employees have proven reluctant to do. Be responsive to and aware of your customers' problems in this regard. As a supplier of the facility to work, why not change your business model and provide a series of localized, interconnected hubs, so that employees do not have to face the longer commute to a central space, with all of its costs in terms of travel, parking, time, and stress?

Despite companies like J.P. Morgan Chase & Co., Alphabet Inc.'s Google, and Apple Inc. having brought employees back to the office, many Americans and others prefer remote work. A recent survey from management consultancy Advanced Workplace Associates showed that only three percent of white-collar employees prefer to work in the office five days a week, and 86 percent want to work from home at least two days a week. U.S. office occupancy is currently at about 39.5 percent, according to Kastle Systems, which provides security services for commercial office spaces. In this example, you could provide your office space customers with all of the best current discussion on this topic and be the moderator of it, bringing them conclusions and a solution to the problem. You could go even further and become the provider of prepackaged work at home kits to set up those who will spend a lot of time there with the most appropriate and effective furniture and technology kit with which to do that. Your value-added proposition could include a complete specification, delivery, setup, and maintenance service for remote workers, on behalf of your customer. People have spent the last two years proving they can be productive for their firms by working from home, though some studies dispute this. You could be the business partner that steps up to secure that business benefit for your customer during what will be a protracted adjustment period. Companies are still figuring out how best to continue using pandemic-era technology that's made some aspects of work easier, while also encouraging real-life interactions; their employees are demanding at least hybrid and often completely remote ways of working.

Managers of workers like these want to read about the new hybrid working environment and how to manage it. How do they onboard new employees with a new kind of contract of employment? There are suddenly different expectations of what part their jobs will play in their calculation of work/life balance. The number of people leaving firms that will not meet those new demands is so large that it has been called "The Great Resignation." In a tight labor market, skilled workers are dictating terms. "Company culture"—is there really such a thing? (Yes!); new location philosophies—do cities still wear the crown? (No!); business technology—is the hybrid, mobile, hot-desking workforce asking for the same level and type of technology they always did? (No!) Develop content that discusses these issues, while showing that your business is at the heart of them, cares about them, and understands how your solutions can help. You need a library of such consistent content—always kept updated—that you can use to form the heart of your digital marketing strategy. Select and use the keywords (an important digital marketing skill to develop) that reflect the online searches that your prospects make.

SEO is a marketing tool that bows to the might of Google, the most popular search engine, which is something of a law to itself. Google's frequently changing algorithms are a constant challenge for marketers seeking to get their websites and all of this content that we are discussing onto a search engine results page (SERP). It is a hard fact that the first Google SERP is where you need to be, and that 75 percent of all click-throughs from that page are from the top three positions. Google's algorithms also favor sites that are easy to use and offer a good user experience. The "Core Web Vitals" are three metrics included in Google's page experience signals that quantify the user experience of interacting with a page. Core Web Vitals measure how quickly a page is visible, how long it takes before a user can interact with the page, and the visual stability of the elements on the page. Therefore, a site with fast response speeds and good mobile usability, for example, will rank higher than one that does not have these attributes. This is an area where competitive analysis again becomes important. By analyzing what industry keywords are producing those top results and to what extent your main competitors are appearing on a high level of SERPs, you can be more scientific in tailoring your own SEO efforts.

As a business that is concerned to place your brand in the position of market leadership and credible industry commentator (see Chapter 2), you will find it highly instructive to find out what the current search trends are in your sphere of business. By knowing the current hot topics, you can tailor your content with the right keywords, topics, type of user experience, and backlinks. Effective keywords, for example, may not be the obvious ones, like "HGVs," if you sell trucks. It may be more about process than product, like "transport logistics" or "fleet management." An analysis of what is getting the SERPs will help to guide you on this and to help you to generate differentiated but effective keywords from your competition. The most favored user experience might not be a hotlink to a standard page on your site, but rather to a video, a blog post, or a downloadable pdf or e-book. If your prime competitor is providing stimulating and informative written or video content and you are not, their influence on your target market's thinking about their next supplier will be the greater. And backlinks are essentially referrals and links back to your site from the websites or other postings by associated businesses or commentators. This last issue is one of amplification. If you can get backlinks to your own site and content from highly visible influencers in your target segment, not only will your website attract more visitors, but they will also be arriving there with the tacit "recommendation" of, say (to continue the example above), Logistics UK (formerly the Freight Transport Association). Having done your analysis of who is important and being googled by your target market, you can draw up a list of those external businesses and associations that you can then approach. You will have to convince them that your content is of interest to their users and that you deserve a link on their site.

But your finely crafted content is an asset with multiple uses. You can offer parts of it as attractive, subtly promotional but valuable pieces through your e-mail marketing, for example. Building an opt-in list of prospects can take time, but once signed up, anyone on that list is going to expect material from you that is high quality and compatible with the messages that first attracted them. You want your e-mails to arrive with an expectation that they will be of value and to deliver that value. When you judge that it is time for a promotional approach or sales call to that prospect, you want it to be warmly received by a potential buyer who knows what you are all about.

Digital Marketing and Social Media—
The Essential Tools

Overall, it appears that *social media channels*, regarded by many as the driving force in digital marketing, now have the same importance for content marketing as a company's website: a finding that applies to both B2B and B2C. Let us define "digital marketing" simply as any marketing campaign that appears on a mobile phone, tablet, computer, or other such device. The attractions are obvious: properly managed, you can personalize your communication to a greater extent, get more of a connection, and generate a conversation between you and your prospects or customers. Your reach is immediately global and, despite that advantage, costs are lower than most traditional methods and results more quantifiable. New apps and other technologies to help in every aspect of this are becoming available every day. In their "Content Marketing Compass," Statista's sample group of businesses relates some of the challenges of *marketing automation*. Let's look at those challenges.

What majority of B2B marketers primarily understand by a marketing automation system is that it includes the automated execution of marketing campaigns across multiple channels and an effective information and technical support system. CMOs have usually been the most avid supporters of introducing it, but seem now not to be universally happy with what they wished for. A total of 44 percent report a lack of interfaces to other systems such as CRM, website, social media, and the online store, if there is one. Those who have not made the move to digital marketing cite the lack of in-house skills as the main obstacle to their doing so. Those who have already implemented some level of marketing automation cite the lack of an overall strategy and clear goals as the main obstacle to their seeing major benefits from it. Tellingly, "lack of support from the IT group" also makes an appearance as an obstacle. Those achieving a high level of success are those who are establishing specific KPIs and measuring performance against them. For the majority of B2B marketers in companies who have made successful digital transitions, webinars and the maintenance and delivery of hyper-personalized *content* are the most significant benefits.

Social media marketing has been very much the preserve of B2C, as far as marketing is concerned, but it is fast gaining ground in the B2B space, too. Essentially, your business takes on the role of a partner in discussion with a wide range of prospects. As before, this must be managed carefully to match precisely the brand personality that you want to project. Random posts or responses—or worse still, ill-judged or emotional ones—are ill-advised. From the beginning, your marketing and sales strategy should dictate the kind of interactions that are best suited to you and your intended audience. Equally, the medium that you choose has a profile, so using the ones that appeal mainly to hyperactive teenagers, for example, even though you may not intend to converse with them, probably does not reflect an appropriate channel for your business. The fact that you can see a constant measurement of what is happening—clicks, comments, shares, and so on—is obviously a bonus, but it is possible to be overwhelmed with interaction that is not useful. It needs to be managed carefully.

Meta and LinkedIn are the main communication resources for the 77 percent of B2B marketers who use *paid social* (as opposed to free posts): 75 percent use paid media on LinkedIn and 69 percent on Meta. Instagram takes third place. LinkedIn (used to communicate professional messages and professionalism per se) was regarded as twice as productive as Meta (used more for emotions). As discussed earlier, setting KPIs for the technology used and measuring performance against them is vital. Currently, as mentioned earlier, it is website traffic and engagement numbers, along with social media analytics, that dominate the measured results that B2B companies are looking at.

There is also a role within the scope of digital marketing for direct advertising. Huge amounts of marketing spend goes on Internet banner ads, again, more in B2C than B2B, but the B2B sector share of spend is growing. EMarketer magazine forecasted that 10 percent of digital ad spend by 2024 will be on connected TV—digital streaming platforms like Netflix, Prime, Roku, and Apple TV—which will take share directly from traditional free-to-air channels. Design, placement, and the monitoring of results are essential in this area, as statistics for "eyeballs" can get very confusing and be misleading. You are interested only in how many click-throughs to the destination of your choice that you get. "Visibility" on the Internet is a vacuous concept without precise detail. Pay-per-click marketing (PPC) is also very popular, but very unpredictable. You post an ad on a platform and get charged every time someone clicks on it. This is ostensibly more measurable for results than the advance payment banner ads approach, but the various factors involved can again make it unpredictable. You are at the mercy of Google algorithms, which prioritize the appearance of your ad according to its "quality" (no one knows what that really means!), the keyword relevance, the quality of your landing page (where a click sends the clicker), and the amount that you "bid" for the ad. This is another area where hiring or contracting out to people who understand these concepts and how to manipulate them effectively is essential. The ability to measure response and effectiveness in digital marketing and social media engagement is revolutionizing the marketing function.

Summary

Many of our interviewees stress the complexities of today's B2B buying and selling processes. But complex does not mean unfathomable or out of control. This whole process must be as seamless as you can make it, or your sales pipeline will be overly optimistic and the deals will not materialize. The successful sellers will always be the ones who understand the successful buyers. Match your sales process and all of its supporting activity to what you will have discovered is the buying process of your target market and its individual prospects. Match your selling team to their buying team, each time you structure a sales deal. The message to the head of sales is: marketing is your best buddy; and vice versa.

The contemporary CMO has a multifaceted role. The job is seen as the center of the customer experience, the control point for the many elements of digital marketing—including the holding and deployment of big data—and the place where the highly scrutinized job of marketing ROI measurement is done—and of course, where branding, creativity, and core content creation happen. Increasingly, and rightly, there is a greater focus on *outcomes* than on *output*. Developing and executing a broad marketing mix is no longer the single function of the job: it has to be an activity that is going to produce measurable results and give highly collaborative support to the frontline sales team. It's a big job.

That sales team needs an inspirational and highly skilled leader, too: someone—as many of our interviewees in this book have said—who is completely on top of the newest selling tools and techniques and is able to deploy them through a carefully selected, well-trained, and highly motivated team of salespeople and others from the firm, to meet challenging customer acquisition and revenue targets. He or she "owns the number" and commits to the company's sales targets. It's a big job.

In a small firm, these two roles might be held by the same individual. Although that makes any conflict unlikely, the challenge then becomes striking a balance in the functional demands. Stick with the principles outlined here; stick with your strategy and targeting and prioritize high-quality work over high quantity. It can be done; those ambitious growth targets can be met!

Go-to-market strategy is worth spending quality time on. Work from the customer's preferences and a realistic view of your own capabilities. A strong partner network, well drilled and supported, is the biggest form of amplifier you can have for your brand and your market scope. If you are the third-party partner to the OEM, learn quickly how to best work with them and to be important to them. More support will come your way if your firm is a star partner. Your GTM strategy will also dictate the best form of your core content and how it gets used. Be consistent with it, but adaptable to circumstance and the needs of the sales team. It is never finished: refresh, refresh, refresh.

In an accelerated digital business world, it is easy to overestimate the power of digital marketing and social media as a means to achieve your goals. Remember that customer relationships are the key to your future, not SEO ratings and followers on LinkedIn. Adhere to your segmentation strategy and go deep, rather than broad, guided by the needs of your target market.

The Takeaways and Lessons Learned From Chapter 4	Do	Don't
Promotion	Take care to match your marketing mix to your business plan and your target market. Focus on outcomes not output Be realistic about your skills. Use agencies when you lack them in the team. As a general guideline: own upstream; outsource downstream marketing	Don't neglect to set KPIs and ROI measurement for each part of your spend There are many promo options: don't make the mistake of diluting your impact by spreading the budget thinly over too many activities, digital or otherwise Don't ignore PR. It's still a powerful tool
Sales	Be clear who owns the targets and is committed to achieving them Pay by results, not by activity	Don't hire in haste. Get the right people the first time Don't assume that the great salesperson automatically becomes the great sales manager or that the best hunter is the best account manager. Match skills and personalities to the task

The Takeaways and Lessons Learned From Chapter 4	Do	Don't
GTM strategy	Be driven by the prospects' choices. Be available where they choose to buy Face to face selling is still vital, but train your salesforce to be the best at virtual selling, too	Don't sign a partner deal and walk away. Manage them just as you do your internal team Don't tolerate channel conflict: fix it fast
Core content	Core content is your corporate marketing lifeblood. Spend sufficient time, money, and effort on getting it right and then keeping it fresh. The marketing function manages it, but the whole company contributes Consider using a DAM system to avoid being overwhelmed with the storage and distribution of your content assets	Don't try to do everything. Find out what works and is well accepted by the target customers, then do that well
Digital marketing and social media	Whether your business is pushing overall digital transformation or not, marketing must embrace and master digital Be SEO maestros, using an agency if you feel the need Social media is a set of communication tools and channels, not a strategy in itself. Be selective, stay in control, and monitor ROI continuously. The power of measurement is a digital marketing strength	Don't get left behind. The new hybrid working model needs digital marketing both from you and to your markets Don't follow trends; follow your marketing strategy. Social media is just a part of your communications delivery system

CHAPTER 5

The Pitch—Proposal, Tender, and Presentation

Overview

In the previous chapters, we have researched, analyzed, segmented, strategized, branded, positioned, promoted, and then implemented actions to get us (or our partners) and our products or services in front of the prospective customer. The critical point in this fifth chapter is that what we now say and do determines the success or failure of the sale.

In this chapter, we will look at how and when to put together that vital sales proposal or tender and what it might contain. Now we have to make our case—our pitch—to be the right supplier, in the most professional way we can. Why is this important? It's far too easy for busy salespeople, under pressure to reach quotas, to undervalue this vital communication to the prospective buyer. Conversely, it can be overdone, with a surfeit of information that confuses, rather than convinces. We examine the importance of value-based selling (VBS), getting your timing right in this part of the sales process, and how your proposal should be presented to the target audience. Highly experienced businesspeople will discuss the lessons they learned in the field, and we will draw some conclusions on how you can approach this vital part of the sales process.

The First Sales Call

Whether that first sales call is virtual, via video, or face to face, it is critically important to the salesperson as he or she begins the customer relationship. You will have arrived at this point via your prospecting activity. That could mean that this meeting has been preceded by telephone, e-mail or social media contact, or a combination thereof. Some qualification has obviously taken place: by the buyer, of you and what you offer; and by you, of the buyer and his or her ability and need to buy. You may well have preceded this call with the sending of some specific information about your company and your solution. This will determine each participant's expectations for the meeting.

Depending on the situation and the time available, the salesperson at this point in the sale process has some key objectives: to establish rapport and an initial level of trust; to ask open questions and listen to the answers; and, assuming that your initial assessment concludes that this is a real prospect for you, to ensure that a follow-up is confirmed on a likely sales cycle that you now understand. That next step may be a demonstration, a meeting with others in your team and/or others in the prospective buyer's team, or more information exchange to move further along the selling process and to motivate the prospect to buy from you. Salespeople have always been trained to do this, but maybe not via a screen. The technique is different, though the principles remain the same.

Video Sales Call Tips

- Don't cut down your preparation time or schedule immediately back-to-back video calls. Do what you would normally do: prepare properly—a face-to-camera rehearsal can do wonders for your confidence, for example. Read and properly prepare your sales material before the meeting; get comfortable with the screen sharing function, and make sure that those documents that you will want to share are available on your desktop. Don't skimp on setting an agreed agenda and sticking to it. The courtesy you would show to your prospective customer by not overstaying your welcome in their office must still apply to occupying their screentime.

- Make sure that your environment is right. An advantage you have with a video sales call is that you are in control of it, on your home ground. Get your video, audio, lighting, and background settings right—try them out, before the call! Virtual backgrounds or the blur function are useful, but keep them simple—use your company logo, for example—but remember the "disappearance effect" if you move out of optimal camera range. Keep still! If you are in a home or shared office space, ensure your privacy and quiet for the duration of the call. If there is unavoidable background noise, use the "noise suppression" function.

- Check your camera position to place you in the center of the screen, level with your face and—though close enough to see your features clearly—not so close that you appear to dominate the screen.

- It is easy to slip into permanent "Big Brother" broadcast mode when you are interacting through a screen—or not interacting at all! Again, as you would instinctively if you were a few feet away from your audience, allow them to speak, responding to what you are saying and asking questions. Beware cordial greetings, introductions, and small talk taking up too much time.

- Allow the prospect to share material, too. Be as patient with their enthusiasm to show you whatever they want (within reason: do maintain agenda control) as you would be if you were across the desk from them. If they are unfamiliar with the video software, help them out, patiently, and lead them an instruction at a time to achieve what they are trying to do. Remember to stop screen sharing and return to speaker or gallery view, when appropriate.

- In many instances, there might not be just two of you. You might be speaking to multiple people, physically present in one location, or to multiple remote locations. Or to a combination of both! Make certain you know the details of attendees before you begin—again, just as you would do before a physical meeting. Remember, you also have the power to bring in expert help on your own side. You will be optimizing your colleagues' time, rather than asking them to take a slice of their day to travel to and attend the meeting, and they can participate from anywhere in the world. Include their participation in your agenda, with their purpose and credentials, so as not to surprise your audience.

- Conclude the meeting and establish next steps as you would normally do. With virtual signing software, you can even easily take the order during the call, when appropriate. Confirmatory diary bookings can be made in real time, while you are still on the call, to ensure commitment. All of your normal closing techniques still apply in the virtual world.

> *Today's salesperson is not the door-kicker of yesterday. He or she has to develop sufficient expertise to become a trusted adviser; to be recognised as part of that particular industry; to "be somebody" whose opinions and recommendations are both expert and actionable.*
>
> Juan Pablo Pazos, President and CEO, XmarteK, Miami

It may take only that first call or (more likely) more contact in other ways, but a key part of the knowledge that you must "bank" is the timing and the process to which your buyer is working. Refer back to Chapter 4, Figure 4.2: your buyer is moving through his or her process as you are trying to drive yours forward. Get a firm grip on what has already happened, the likely timing of what will happen, and the points of intersection where you can help that buying team reach their satisfactory conclusion. Delivering everything you have, in every available form, up front, is not the answer! There will be a right time to deliver your proposal, your executive summary, and your presentation into the mix for optimum effect (Figure 5.1).

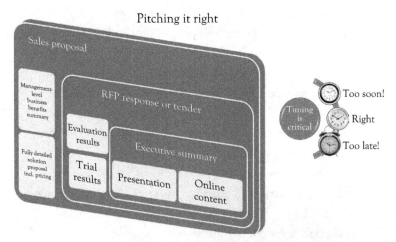

Figure 5.1 The essential parts of your sales pitch must be well coordinated

The Proposal

Having convinced your prospect that you might have what they want, this stage of the selling process will involve you in presenting in great detail the value proposition that you can offer. VBS can boost margins and competitiveness, but correctly pitching the details of where the value in your proposition lies requires care and skill. VBS is based on demonstrating and documenting the monetary worth of the economic, technical, service, and social benefits a specific customer receives in exchange for the price being paid. This is a powerful marketing approach because, ultimately, B2B customers purchase goods and services to reduce their costs or boost their own revenues. In their *MIT Sloan Management Review* article in 2021, Joona Keränen, and Antti Saurama defined three key types of VBS. Based on extensive interviews with more than 70 companies, the authors discovered a wide spectrum of readiness and ability to engage in VBS. Their findings suggest that vendors can adopt either a *product-centric, customer process-centric,* or *performance-centric* VBS approach. As we discussed in Chapter 3, B2B customers make any purchase of goods and services to achieve specific business benefits, for the price that they pay. This will form the essential core of the proposition that you, as the vendor, will present to the prospect (see Chapter 5). Without a profound understanding of a customer's business model (see Chapter 3), it is difficult for the vendor to pick out the impactful value drivers on which to focus. The value proposition must also be compelling, both in comparison with the option of doing nothing and with the pitch that the prospect is getting from your competitor. If you are promising to deliver real business value, your prospect will expect to see some proof of your ability to do this. This is where your best customer references (see Chapter 7) become invaluable in providing a degree of certainty and risk reduction to the buyer. Post-sale, this value proposition will be the one upon which your implemented solution will be judged (also Chapter 7). The authors of the MIT Sloan article found that it was all too easy for vendors to fall back to a purely price-led approach, and thereby lose out to a value-based competitive pitch. Picking the right approach is one that requires careful thought.

> *It is very tempting for salespeople to fall back on price lists or standardised rate cards for the product or service they are selling. Day-rate consulting services are an example of this, where it is the commitment to renewal or extension (more time or more users) that is the more worthwhile measure for our business.*
>
> Mark Robinson, entrepreneur

Selling on the product-centric value proposition does not involve underplaying the specific benefits of your precious product—far from it. The focus simply shifts to an emphasis on the value that the product brings to the customer—the industrial paint that dries faster than that from the competition and allows for quicker repaints, cutting on-site time; the bearings that self-lubricate (when the competitors' ones do not) and require less maintenance, cutting service costs; and so on. The customer remains responsible for the actual value creation, but you are providing the tools to decrease the total cost of ownership (TCO) of the product. Your competitors will not long allow you that advantage, so you will find yourself committed to an R&D race on the product front to maintain your product value differentiation. Consequently, successful product-centric VBS relies on purchasing managers who really "get" the concept of TCO, looking beyond the benefits to the purchasing department. It also relies on ensuring that your sales and marketing reach includes the other stakeholders in the acquisition of your products. Chapter 3 included guidance on identifying and involving everyone in the customer's multi-function buying team.

In customer process-centric VBS, value is *cocreated* by seller and customer: the seller actively facilitates value creation through consultative work. The MIT report uses the example of Hilti, the power-tool manufacturer. That company shifted its value proposition from selling premium tools to launching its Tool Fleet Management program to optimize customers' overall tool ownership costs. This was the area where the biggest impact on their productivity was felt. Caterpillar's and Volvo's truck fleet analysis and consultations are another, similarly quoted example, where the vendor's role is education and facilitation around the supply and optimum use of the products themselves. That approach allows premium pricing of their product, because it is an enabler of valuable process improvements. This also raises the barrier to competition. Your competitor will have to compete with the deeper customer relationship that you will have established with your demonstration of expertise.

Performance-centric VBS is where

pricing logic is usually tied to results such as improved productivity, efficiency, or availability, or decreased TCO. This can sometimes include complex gain-sharing (or pain-sharing) arrangements, where predetermined incentives and penalties are applied if vendors overperform or underperform. Customers may find it attractive to tie payments to business outcomes, since it reduces risk and aligns buyers' and sellers' goals. (ibid)

This is a more complex arrangement, attempting to provide the ultimate in shared business benefits. Both vendor and customer have to have or create infrastructure and management processes to ensure its success, so it's not for everyone.

At Clarity International, one of my consulting businesses, we recognised the intangibility of our strategy consulting product. We recognised that our time was our precious raw material, but did not price our services conventionally by the hour or day. Rather, after detailed joint assessment of the customer's needs and the solution we could provide, we set a project price. Part of this was a success fee dependent upon achieving the agreed, measurable results we could achieve for the client by helping to implement the solution—demonstrating, by taking a share of the risk, our belief in and commitment to the project's success.

Nick Ray, CEO, Director, Founder,
NXD of Software & Technology Firms,
United Kingdom

In practice, not all of your customers will be responsive to or prepared for VBS. It requires expertise in buying and process control by the customer and a clear, thoroughly thought-through proposition from you, the vendor, who has to ensure understanding and control of all the key

variables that can affect value realization. Without this, you bear unnecessary risks in guaranteeing outcomes you cannot control. Hence, to facilitate the adoption of customer-centric VBS, vendors (those large enough
to have the luxury of so doing, at least) often recruit key individuals
directly from their customer industries. This is to gain deeper understanding of customer goals and processes, and of that industry, as we looked
at with segmentation strategy in Chapter 1. For example, to strengthen
its capabilities to sell complex and high-value technology and business
services, IBM acquired the whole consulting arm of PricewaterhouseC-
oopers. It's up to you to discover when and with whom the approach will
be mutually beneficial.

Typically, performance-centric VBS is very challenging, and only a
few companies have been able to master it. Rolls-Royce's Power-by-the-
Hour agreements—started in the 1990s—for jet and ship engines are
a well-known example of this and are seen as a major prompt for the
"subscription economy" that is so prevalent now, wherein the commitment to performance is both manageable and profitable. Rolls-Royce
realized that the airlines didn't want to be in the jet engine business;
they wanted to focus on flying passengers from point A to point B.
An unexpected engine failure could cost the airlines millions in engine
replacement costs, lost flight revenue, need to reschedule stranded passengers, need for back-up aircraft, buffer engine inventory, crew over-
time, and so on. When an airliner's engine was nearing the end of its life
(based on flight hours) or failed abruptly, the airlines would purchase a
replacement engine from vendors like Rolls-Royce, install it, and maintain it. But in a typically varied fleet, there were multiple engine models to monitor. Airline service departments were simply not qualified
or equipped to maximize the life of their jet engines, often replacing
them prematurely or letting them run until they failed unexpectedly. So
Rolls-Royce developed a new subscription model called "Power-by-the-
Hour." Really, it was engine-as-a-service (EaaS)! For a flat hourly rate
per engine, Rolls-Royce would handle installations, check-ups, maintenance, and decommissioning. The airline finance departments loved the
predictability of the subscription payments, as opposed to the unpre-
dictability of engine purchases and overhauls. The cost of paying Rolls-
Royce handsomely for this was balanced against not having to spend

resources on engine inventory, repair facilities, technicians, and engine liability insurance. The advantage for Rolls-Royce was economy of scale. Since they were now managing the lifecycle of hundreds or thousands of aircraft engines, they could invest heavily into studying how engines performed, how to detect potential failure points, and what types of preventative maintenance were most effective. Rolls-Royce became the expert not only in designing and building jet engines but also in operating and repairing them.

You can see how both buyer and seller can benefit greatly in this way, and competitors have a hard time breaking the bond of trust and understanding between you and your customer that this can create. For vendors, successful performance-centric VBS depends on their ability to assess and mitigate potential risk. They need confidence in their ability to realize the targeted value outcomes. A key challenge is ensuring that you as a vendor can understand and control all the key variables that can affect value realization. Otherwise, there is an obvious danger in bearing unnecessary risks in guaranteeing outcomes that you cannot control. If you decide to take this approach, the commitments to it will need to be in your detailed proposal and you will need confidence in your own ability to present them and to take detailed questions on them. Don't make it too good to be true!

Mark Robinson in Conversation With Kimball Bailey

Mark Robinson cofounded Kimble Applications, the international professional services automation (PSA) software company in 2010. Kimble helps professional services organizations run their end-to-end processes: sales management, recruitment and resourcing, time management, delivery and project management, forecasting, performance management, and billing. Kimble is a SaaS application built on the Salesforce platform.

Prior to Kimble, Mark worked in consulting with software giant Oracle before founding and growing two IT consulting companies, which he successfully sold.

What made Mark recognize the size of the gap in the market that Kimble could address?

Every professional services company that grows in line with its success, says Mark, *will, sooner or later, have to change the way in which it sells, markets and delivers its services.*

The actual number of staff will vary, maybe 70 to 100 is pretty much normal, but it all becomes too much for the founder, the person with the pixie dust, to remain personally involved in all the important sales or pre-sales and in delivering projects—something has to give. So, what happens? He or she hires a head of sales or a head of marketing, and this brings its own stresses and difficulties, so that very often the "square peg in the round hole" winds up leaving—or being fired. But the fact that it didn't work out isn't always the fault of the new sales director! If the owner-manager wants to change the business model into an ongoing "sales engine," both the new process and the change to achieve it need to be managed well. He or she still needs to be involved in the important sales, but you need to bring rigor and discipline into the whole sales process to build a professional sales organization. That represents a significant challenge—so it's the way you go about it that becomes critical.

Introducing an effective sales process isn't about waving a magic wand. It's about common sense. There are hundreds of sales methods and consulting firms selling their own sales processes and techniques. The best, in my experience, was one many years ago that focused on the "touchy-feely" aspects of sales, from behavior and relationship-building to NLP techniques such as eye contact. The problem is that rational sales methodologies are not necessarily followed by—or used to sell to—rational people. Sales courses tend to assume, for example, that people aren't just lying through their teeth!

So how does Mark apply this?

The key word is "value." This means different things to different people and different organizations. But "value-selling" is critical.

I have a real interest in pricing structures, and how to use pricing to win. You need to know what a piece of work is going to cost you, in terms of days and daily rate, but the value of the solution may be far in excess of that. A quick software tweak may represent many thousands of pounds worth of business benefit. It takes a strong relationship with the client to enable both parties to recognize that perception of value. Is the business case compelling for the buyer as well as the seller? Too many salespeople hide behind a pricing structure.

*So, in this context, you must have real clarity in terms of understanding the people to whom you are selling. Closing the deal is very much subject to the relationship with a specific individual. This is why we always carry out "win analysis," which we often find to be much more important than loss analysis; so why we won a deal as well as why we may have lost it. Sure, we might lose—and do so—because we were talking to the wrong person, or our perception of client value may have been wrong, or we weren't sufficiently differentiated, or they hated the salesperson, or because the incumbent had a better existing relationship. But we learn so much from a win too. One incredibly valuable piece of wisdom to pick up from a win is to find out "how did we **nearly** blow it?" and to learn from that—it positions you well in terms of understanding your strengths.*

And, of course, while it is always easier to sell the second piece of work or product to a client than it is to sell the first, that assumes an ongoing relationship. A framework agreement—that some organizations mistakenly see as a cash cow—is often managed by both parties to exclude relationship building. What a waste!

And what about selling Kimble as a product?

Again, very much about relationship. Especially in the US, the clients loved to talk about the founders' own story, because that resonated with the problems that they themselves were facing. They recognized that the forward-looking stuff, looking through the windscreen not the rear-view mirror—managing pipeline, managing resources and so on—were all critical. Because we had had the same pain points, we were able to help the client put the fire out before it had actually started.

And because we understood the way in which the client's business operated, we could talk knowledgeably about their behavior, and introduce a product that we believed in and that we knew matched the requirements of any organization in their position.

Our unique selling point was around best practice process, and we had many conversations with clients about what we called "software-enabled business change." Our software matched good business processes, and it was far more practical—not to mention far less expensive—for a client to change its business processes to match our best practice. Don't spend *money customizing a product to replicate existing processes (or, worse, systems) if it doesn't add any value to do so; that is where projects start to go wrong. Think about the business outcome, not the current process. It's not as if aligning business process gives a client a differentiated competitive advantage per se—the competitive advantage comes from using the software effectively, to take **out** complexity and to mature and streamline business processes, so we become an enabler of business transformation. Real differentiation will come from client-facing processes ... Of course, I'm not saying we don't configure the software, that is part of our USP, I'm saying that we don't bespoke it for no evident client benefit.*

So, a key message to both buyer and seller is that the software is only as good as the behaviors it drives. If either side doesn't get that, the relationship will be permanently on the back foot. It is the quality and consistency of the new business process that means that the client can get benefit across its entire structure. Enable the client transformation through focusing on the business outcome—not pandering to the "we've always done it this way" brigade. So, the seller has to find out what is important to the client, and be seen to deliver that value.

However you structure it, now that you are being seriously considered as a supplier to the prospective customer, you have to solidify what has been discussed in your sales calls. You need a compelling presentation of what your company and solution can provide for that business. This may not be the endgame in your sales process, but it is certainly a critical point. It is also where you can most often be eliminated from the competitive process. A written proposal may come before a presentation, be the conclusion to one, or follow it up. The nature of the document should reflect which of these it is being used for. Timing is critical. The most important thing to remember, in any case, is that this is a sales document. That may sound obvious, but so many proposals—the result of many hours of costly and painstaking work—are highly descriptive and detailed books that don't entice the reader to move beyond the first page. Or worse, they compel him or her to flick briefly through it and move to the price. If that happens, you've probably lost the deal. This is a document that, independently, has to sell as well as you would, if you were sitting in front of that buyer or evaluator.

First, let's take the example of the proposal that forms the basis of a visual presentation. Some salespeople like to hand out the document to the audience at the beginning and then refer to it as they go through the presentation. This *can* work, but you will have, however, worked hard on getting the opportunity to get face to face with the management team, so it's almost certainly better to use that opportunity to have them watch and listen to you, rather than be distracted by pages of information on the desk in front of them. Put yourself in their shoes. It can be annoying for the listener to be told that a presentation slide is necessarily a summary "and the full details are in the proposal" that they don't yet have, as you are holding it back until the end. This is where your skills as a presenter come into their own. Managing the audience's expectations when the meeting is first called, then again at the beginning, it is essential to describe what they are going to see and hear from you before the detailed proposal is in their hands. This will give you the leeway to defer the need for those more finite details until you are ready to provide them. And you may discover something during the presentation interactions, which means the proposal needs to be changed!

Focus on the "A-ha!"

A very wise man once explained—over 35 years ago, and I have never forgotten it—that, when you are presenting or writing a proposal, there are only three things—maybe four—that you need to think about:

*"**A-ha!**" Yes, these people know what they are talking about. Yes, they can deliver a credible solution that meets my outcomes and ticks the boxes in terms of the benefits I am looking for. Yes, this makes me want to work with them. A-ha! Maximize these and focus on them.*

*"**Oh-oh…**" Effectively the reverse of an "a-ha," because the solution has critical gaps, or won't meet the client outcomes, for whatever reason. This is likely to be an issue for every bidder, so it depends on what the "oh-ohs" actually are in the context of delivery and of competition. You have three choices:*

- *Recognize that this bid is not for you and step aside gracefully (but even with a couple of "known knowns" your bid, however flawed, may still be the best).*

(Continued)

(*Continues*)

- *Address them, minimize them, explain why they are less of an issue than might be thought, and make sure that the negative impact is outweighed by the "a-has."*
- *More cynically, try and hide them and hope for the best. It would be fair to say that this is likely to end in tears.*

*"**Ho-hum.**" How many proposals and presentations have we seen full of verbal or PowerPoint diarrhea about the seller company—a pet hate being its geographical reach where that is not relevant to the client? Find out what the client's priorities are (a good client will have set these out anyway in an "agenda" for presentation) and focus on them. Turn a feature into an advantage into a benefit, the "ho-hums" into "a-has." "We have offices in 33 countries" can become "We can support implementation on a global basis," but it is better if it becomes "You need direct local support across Western Europe, and we have offices in Paris, Munich and Amsterdam that will provide that."*

*The fourth point, and a slightly riskier one, is the **Ghost**. This is to raise doubts about your competition in a number of potential contexts. It could be to minimize an "oh-oh": "We can't do X, but we will work with you to deliver that next year, we can do Y in the meantime, and we know none of our competitors can do X either." It could be to maximize the benefit associated with an "a-ha": "We are small and focused, and we prefer to keep our costs down, rather than spending client fees on decorating the atrium in our new City HQ"…*

Kimball Bailey

It could be that you do not get that presentation opportunity, and the proposal has to be delivered into your prospective buyers' hands for them to read and consider when you are not there. In that case, two essential things need to happen. One is that you need to make it clear that you are freely available to take questions about the proposal, in any way that the buyer requires: by telephone, by video call, or in person. Scatter a reminder of this throughout the document, making plain the contact details. And be available, of course! The second is to include an *executive summary* that is so outstandingly good that it alone could secure the deal! When the proposal is asked to stand alone and remote like this, you will know from the earlier stages of your sales process (see Chapter 3) that it needed to be addressed to all of the critical buyers and recommenders. You will not have control over exactly where it goes within that organization when it leaves your hands. Other reviews and opinions may be sought that you did not anticipate, from people who have not had the benefit of all of your previous communications. That means that the executive summary *has* to present the whole story: who you are, why your company is the ideal supplier in this case, and why the business benefits of what you are proposing are simply outstanding. In a succinct and compelling way, your solution must be positioned as beyond the capabilities of the competition. It is a very important document!

Pugh and Bacon, in *Powerful Proposals: How to Give Your Business the Winning Edge*, emphasize the importance of the executive summary and give guidance on how to prepare a document that can stand alone as a convincer for any one member of your audience. The point is made that the summary can often be distributed far more widely than the full proposal document. This means it will be read by experts and nonexperts in your solution and by higher and lower levels of management in the prospective customer's business. It needs visual impact to support its winning details, so that even those who merely skim through its few pages gain a favorable impression from it—that brand image you've worked so hard to develop. Ensure that the electronic format is as easy to use as the printed one. There is software out there to help you with this. It is tempting to produce this document before the main proposal. Mark Robinson, interviewed for this book, favors doing just that; others believe that this can lead to problems. Whatever you decide, it should be a powerful summary derived from your detailed document, not a separate one. Ideally, reading the summary should prompt further interest in getting into the details, so the links to the core proposal should be clear and obvious. In an electronic version, make sure that any imbedded links all work. This will also help you to ensure that your key selling points are to the fore in the proposal. To repeat the point: both are sales documents, not background items to be filed away!

Selling Is a Team Sport

Good salespeople develop the habit of surrounding themselves with people smarter in some skills than they are. The best way to produce the compelling proposal that we have described, and to use it to succeed, is by making its production into a team effort. Who is on your team? As Sir Kenneth Olisa says in his foreword to this book, the professional discipline of the sales (and marketing) professional should be recognized as being as hard won and as extensive as those of the other recognized business disciplines. Yes, ultimately, this might involve a forceful approach to reaching an agreement to sign a contract or sales order, but it is also about the ability to muster all of the strengths of the company's brand, reputation, products, and people into an unbeatable team to win the deal.

Your sales team will usually consist of people in your company, but consider the potential of including your reference customers and others in your industry. You should have the objective to develop those relationships before you need them. At the last minute, when something goes wrong, or the day before an important sales meeting is not the time to be contacting a person you have never met and to be asking for their help.

You can build the strength of your team even further by having others in your company—if you have them, of course—also develop relationships. Bringing others into the account broadens the conversations and allows for more learning. The strength of an account manager's relationship with his or her customer is seen when they are the first to be told about new business opportunities. The account manager who finds out about new opportunities at the same time as their competitor cannot be said to have a strong relationship with the account. Constructing your sales team for a particular deal is similar to recruiting your employees for any business venture, but with greater focus. As in the latter case, the leader has to admit to not knowing everything there is to know! Your industry, your solution, and your prospective buyer's equivalent team will dictate who you choose. Who can you add to your team? What relationships do you need to work on? Certainly, this is a point where the sales and marketing functions in your own firm need to be working in perfect synchronization. The CMO or marketing team—as owners of the core content on which your sales materials are based—must constantly get real-time customer feedback from frontline salespeople. They need that feedback to allow them to provide the prospect-specific additions to the core content that you are already using.

> *It is so important for the sales and marketing people to have a shared world view. Conflict between the two functions can eliminate all other business efficiencies and hold back both customer acquisition and business growth.*
>
> Charles Besondy, President and Author,
> Besondy Publishing LLC; Founder, Besondy Consulting and
> Interim Management Inc., Texas

When do you bring in the "techies"? Well, whatever the nature of your business, you are likely to have people who best understand the very fundamentals of your solution, whether that be building materials, jet engines, factory production-line robotics, business solutions, or software. Gauge this carefully for the optimum effect: pitch the right person to the right person or group, at the right time. The same applies to customer support, finance, R&D, or any other source of your credentials. Especially your reference accounts—those customers who have agreed to act as your enthusiastic salespeople from a position of experience with your company. It's about who is on the team, how you will use them, and when.

The Presentation

> *In an orator, the acuteness of the logician, the wisdom of a philosopher, the language nearly of poetry, the memory of the lawyer, the voice of a tragedian, the gesture almost of the best actor is required. Nothing therefore is more rarely found among mankind than a consummate orator.*
>
> Cicero, in *On Oratory*, 55 BC

Marcus Tullius Cicero was a Roman statesman, scholar, and philosopher who had a reputation as a powerfully persuasive speaker. He was not shy about proclaiming himself as the "rarely found" great orator. Often, those who consider themselves to be pitch-perfect are confusing bravado and self-assurance with effective presentation skills. You may have made many sales or other presentations yourself, and seen as many more. Have you rated any of these as perfect, as having got a memorable message across and helped to achieve its objective? That objective may have been to educate, to launch a product or service, or to sell your company's or your own credentials as part of an overall sales process. And that's a key point: is now the time for the all-singing-all-dancing presentation? It depends where you are in the sales cycle. If you are at an early stage, where serious competitors are still in the mix, it may fall to you to present your company and personal credentials, prior to being able to define and prepare the details of a proposal. You are through the awareness and initial introductions stage, but you need to turn that awareness into a positive opinion that gets you on the consideration path.

Who is the audience? If you have a room full of evaluators, looking for product specs and performance that match their needs, then make sure that the most senior of them is present on the customer side and that your most technically capable individual is there on your side—that may even be you, of course! If it's a highly technical pitch, don't be afraid to come up a level and do at least a basic company brand and positioning piece, first. Then move onto the benefits statements about what dealing with you and using those particular solutions will mean for the company. Even the techie guys with the pocket pen-and-pencil holders in their short-sleeved shirts want to know who and what they are dealing with before examining your widgets!

Iebe Ypma in Conversation With Peter Bayley

Iebe Ypma—a Dutch national, born in Japan and educated in Germany and South Africa before coming to work at Unilever in the United Kingdom in the late 1970s—has managed the procurement of business services and IT since the early days of his career. Now a director of Alastor Consulting, he has been a strategic advisory consultant for nearly 40 years (including long spells at A.T. Kearney and EY), where he has advised clients on many procurements in a range of sectors and across multiple geographies. He has run training programs for the Chartered Institute of Procurement & Supply and developed procurement guidelines for a best practice group covering both the public and private sectors. He is a former Chair of the Association of MBAs.

What makes a procurement successful?

Well, this may sound trite, but it is taking a "win-win" approach, ensuring that the buyer has negotiated value for money and left enough "on the table" to ensure the vendor's viability and long-term commitment.

So, what are the biggest mistakes that you see happening? Or the most common? Or both?

Are you ready for a long list? Let me give a few examples based on the procurement of IT software, though the issues and principles apply just as much to other products or services:

- *Embarking on a procurement without understanding the key needs.*
- *Running the procurement as a "tick box" exercise.*
- *Simply replicating the current services, systems and processes (often resulting in a more expensive and complex solution)—after all, if you are simply reproducing your current system and associated business processes, why go through a costly change and procurement exercise?*
- *Specifying in detail how you want the solution to look, not what it is that the solution has to deliver.*
- *Selecting the preferred supplier based on a scoring sheet, without getting "under the bonnet" to truly understand the supplier capability, and the functionality of the proposed solution—remember, you don't get any benefit from implementing software, you get benefit from how you chose to deploy and exploit it.*
- *Managing the procurement process with the suppliers on an adversarial basis.*

  All of these are significant mistakes made by the buyer when the procurement is—hopefully—intended to result in a long-term relationship with a supplier that will be delivering key services and benefits to your organization.

  There is a better way.

So, what needs to happen differently?

Elsewhere in this book we have seen Mark Robinson of Kimble describing how an organization can apply the processes embedded in best practice software to change its own business for the better. And I have already stressed how critical it is that a buyer should set out its requirements in terms of what is required, not how it has to be delivered.

Let's assume an intelligent buyer procuring a software package (to continue the example) has a good reason to change, in terms of clear and defined business outcomes. Sadly, too often that is not the case! And let's also assume that the buyer is prepared to invest time and effort into defining its priority requirements clearly and exploring the ability of the supplier to deliver those. It sounds simple, doesn't it: ask the right questions to establish that the supplier capability and solution functionality match your specific needs and requirements. And set up a framework to help the vendor to respond clearly and measurably and demonstrate that it can meet business requirements and deliver anticipated benefit.

So, the buyer needs to ask the right questions about itself and about its own requirements. For example:

- *What is it that makes your organization different from its competitors? Is it functional? Geographic? Complex? Time-critical?*
- *What is it, for example, about your internal processes, regulatory environment, customer service relationship and delivery, that are key to the continuity of your organization and its ongoing success?*
- *What goes wrong with your current systems—in terms of functionality or technical capability—that you would seek to improve upon?*
- *What are the outcomes that you are seeking from this procurement?*
- *What benefits are you looking to deliver as part of this procurement?*

Focusing on these key requirements and differentiators will enable the relevant capability of the supplier and functionality of the solution to be evaluated.

So, once the buyer has thought about this, how does the supplier demonstrate capability against the requirements?

What I have always encouraged is setting out these requirements in an "Agenda" (hence I call the procurement process Agenda Based Selection), focusing on the priorities we have already considered. This differs considerably from an all-embracing boilerplate "Request for Proposal" or "Invitation to Tender." The purpose of the agenda is to assess supplier understanding of the needs and assess how the solution meets those needs.

This Agenda should be built around a number of anonymized "real life" scenarios and data covering the key requirements. These scenarios are then used to evaluate the supplier, the proposed solution, and any potential alternatives. One of the key issues is to base the evaluation only on demonstrated capability—as any promise of future capabilities may be motivated by the desire to land the sale.

Applied effectively, this process forms a sound foundation for a supplier and solution evaluation, focused on outcomes and expected benefits. The absolute "a-ha!" moment when a supplier demonstrates that it can easily address long-standing business process problems should not be underestimated.

Developing the Agenda will provide the procurement with a clear sense of purpose, speeding the final supplier and solution ranking and the selection process.

And so, you have identified a supplier with a good fit—do you not then need to trial it?

Yes—but again, a lazy buyer may just demand a trial version of the software to consider over an undefined timescale in an unstructured manner. I think it is worth the time and effort to build a test pack to evaluate the software—again, using real data, and utilizing staff who will use the solution in the future. This should be more than a "side of desk" activity for the evaluating team, and the time spent in the evaluation will not be wasted. Again, this enables the buying team to reconfirm the business needs and how the associated business benefits will be realized, without being shackled by the restrictions of the current system. The team will also develop an understanding of how business processes can be changed to take advantage of best practice within the new solution.

> *This Agenda-based approach is fully compatible with the conventional RFI (Request for Information), RFP (Request for Proposal), ITT (Invitation to Tender) and similar procurement processes—it just improves upon them. And of course, no contracts will be signed until both parties are happy with the implications of the implementation.*
>
> *And the key thing is that we have a win-win scenario here for both parties. What is good for the buyer is equally good for a vendor that can structure its response around a clear process, focus on delivering business benefit, and showcase its solution the most effectively against the requirements that really matter.*

You will already have made it your business to understand the prospect's buying process (see Chapter 3), so you will know what the next step will be after everyone has left the room. If the presentation is a closing one, rather than an early one, the stage is set differently. In that case, you will have needed to ensure that you have decision makers in the room. Sometimes recommenders will be there, too, but don't waste your closing firepower on a roomful of people powerless to get your deal signed. If the senior players cannot be there, then you should not be there. Be hardnosed about the setup of attendees or you will waste a lot of time. You will be the best judge of the mood (see later in this section), but be bold enough to state from the outset that you expect to get the decision on this day, in this room. In order to make that a reality, whatever needed to go before has had to have happened. That is part of your preparation prior to the meeting, ensuring that the documents that everyone should have seen have actually been seen. Again, change the date of any such closing presentation meeting which looks like it will be too early for information and objections to have been covered beforehand. A delay is better than a debacle. You really do not want to hear words like "I can't possibly endorse a go-ahead on this when I haven't seen the final specs and pricing." This just destroys your best efforts to get pens to paper. Make sure this guy *has* seen the papers he (quite rightly) needs to see, in order to do his job properly.

Remember the power of your customer champions and advocates. That senior woman who is convinced that your solution is the right one: why not give her a short speaking slot in your presentation to say so?

I have even seen a major, successful, board-level closing presentation where the salesperson merely introduced and closed the session, which was three pitches by the internal recommenders, as to why they thought this deal was the one that their company should go for.

It's easy to conclude that, in a presentation, content is everything, whether you design it to entertain, to motivate, to sell, to inform, or to instruct. Often, many of these elements have to be combined to create the desired effect and to produce the result that is needed. Almost certainly, you will have spent most of the time on the content. This is understandable, but can lead to there simply being too much of it. Any audience's capacity to retain information is limited; your main points need to have the space to breathe. If there are more than three main points, look again and reconsider how much you are surrounding them with. Basic presentation technique can be formally taught and is a good use of your time, even as a refresher for the most experienced presenters. There are no shortcuts to getting it right and yes, though it sounds like a cliché, preparation is everything. The multiple-award-winning British actor, Sir Michael Caine, has frequently said—in answer to how he manages to appear so relaxed in his screen roles—that the preparation is the work and the performance is his relaxation. He is so well prepared that he can concentrate purely on the delivery. That can work for you, too.

It can happen that you are called upon to do something impromptu or to step into someone else's shoes, either to use presentation materials that are not your own or to improvise. That's often tricky, but rarely daunting or undoable for someone experienced in putting across a message.

There are always the same key elements:

- What outcome or effect are you looking for?
- What is the nature of the audience and its expectations?
- What level of detail and duration is designated or appropriate?
- What are the medium and the materials?
- What are the location, atmosphere, and level of speaker facilities?
- If this is a sales presentation, what part of the sales cycle are you at and what do you need to concentrate on?
- What should happen next?

It was the champion golfer Gary Player who said, when told that he seemed to be a lucky player, "Yes, the harder I practise, the luckier I seem to get." Always practise. Sometimes that might be on the way to the event. Make that not immediately before—you will find a short period of reflective calm beneficial—but do run it through in as close a real-life state as possible. Persist: go through the whole thing half a dozen times as you prepare. Get comfortable with it. Get to the stage, desk, table, or lectern—or at least the room—before the event kicks off. There is nothing worse than a stumbling, bumbling opening in front of the audience, looking for a remote control, flicking through notes, or the like. Seeing others do that so often must have irritated you as much as it has me; you will have seen an instant loss of at least some level of credibility—and that's not good.

And back up: never forget it. I would go so far as to say never, ever, go into a presentation without a printed copy (with clearly marked page numbering) and without being ready to make the presentation with nothing more than a whiteboard or flip-chart and a marker. Always have a second copy of an electronic presentation in a separate file on your device and another on a memory stick. Over the years, every one of those safety precautions has come to my aid at one time or another.

Scripting is also a consideration. Sometimes, the content and timing will dictate careful wording that can't be improvised from bullet points. That's when you need a script. This needs reading and re-reading, not just for flow and continuity but for tone and timing. And by reading, I recommend speaking it out loud. Improvization is easy if you have a script to spring from and to come back to—but potentially disastrous if not. Even the most skilled presenter will tell you that some improvization and ad-libbing can naturalize and enhance a pitch. Enthusiasm to improvise something, however, though a positive aspect of a good presentation, can equally be an enemy of it. It can potentially take you wildly off-course, giving out too many words that will dilute the core message and ruin your timing. I am sure that you will have seen speakers rushing to complete a presentation, having overrun their allotted time. And often, the key points and most memorable messages have been saved until the end and are deserving of clear, calm delivery, not a race to the finish.

It may sound a little fussy, but I believe in the correct physical aspect of presentation technique, too. Give yourself the personal benefit of ascending into a state of complete calm before major outings in front of an audience. Never drink alcohol beforehand; eat only lightly, if at all. Margaret Thatcher, the United Kingdom's first female prime minister, said that "one should always be a little cold and a little hungry" to be in the right condition for a major presentation. Try consciously to move slowly and deliberately; no hesitation but no rushing; no sweating. Always stand to speak—no matter what the venue or location of the speaking position—and without holding notes if you can avoid it. If a remote control or a pointer is needed, insist either on using your own, familiar device or on trying out beforehand the one offered by the venue. We all wince when seeing presenters fiddling with papers or remotes, complete with mumbled apologies or excuses. The presentation content, so carefully crafted, will be forgotten: the fumbles will always be remembered.

Begin with something arresting but nonessential or even trivial. Most audiences will be mentally (if not physically) settling down for the first couple of minutes. Grabbing and holding their attention is then the key. Hit a big message after the joke or story intro; then have a series of new points, high points, or surprises throughout. There is no point in cramming in lots of messages or holding back for a big finale if the audience is no longer listening. Deliberately combat the natural waves of inattention and distraction with waves of attention-grabbing. Carefully crafted content can do it, but so can movement and your style of delivery. Read the room and respond!

Wherever possible, subtly leave the presentation position—particularly with larger audiences—to address faces more directly, often to the sides of the stage or the room. This has to coincide with making a particular point or asking a rhetorical question, or it looks staged and overly theatrical. To disagree somewhat with Cicero from our introductory quote, don't try to be Mick Jagger, the flamboyant rock singer, or Laurence Olivier, the great Shakespearean stage and screen actor. Learn not to overdo the stage movements and thereby make it look like nervous wandering or overacting. Remember, too, that you will have left behind a static microphone, if that is what you were using. And of course, it is essential to get back to any notes at the lectern in time to move on to your next point. This all needs practice. An audience that is widely distributed, physically, needs to be addressed equally widely, so as to make them feel included and to elicit nodded support for what is being said. It will also make you feel less remote from them and help you to relax. Eye contact is great where it is possible, of course, even if that is with only the first couple of rows or with the people nearest you in the room. And again, watch out for that double-edged sword of enthusiasm: raising the pitch of your voice and speaking too quickly when you're excited is a common trap for presenters. A consistently low, well-paced, and measured Timbre is an asset. Pauses for emphasis or thought are OK, too. It's not a race.

If conducting a Q&A, be precise on how many questions you will take from the outset or for how long you will take them. Any "question" by an audience member that shows signs of being a miniature monolog must be quickly shut down, as politely as you can. Of course, some questions need to be deferred or deflected, and all should be repeated in summary if there is a possibility that the audience had not heard them properly. In a large auditorium, get a good audience mike and a competent handler to make that less necessary.

What about your appearance? Well, only immaculate will do, of course! But seriously, do dress appropriately. If you don't already have a handle on the accepted dress code, find it out beforehand. "Mirror your audience" is the conventional wisdom. "Meet the audience's expectations" is a far better maxim: if they expect someone completely different from themselves, then don't hesitate to provide that person. A room full of programmers and data scientists will not expect you to be like them if you are plainly not, so why pretend in any way? If you always wear a business suit, then stick with it. Give them what might be the senior management perspective they anticipated, tailoring sufficient technical detail to what they want. Any audience expects to be satisfied, not patronized.

Your intention every time should be to project your own personality; elicit some empathy; provoke real interest in what you are presenting; use a little drama to engender anticipation; use a little humor to keep it as light as seems right; and leave a lasting and clear impression of your company's brand personality and positioning, as appropriate for that audience. Making a sales presentation to strangers or those with whom you are more familiar is always a challenge, whether to an audience of five or 50.

If that audience is of a considerably larger scale—say, 500 plus—and the objective is less about making the sale than putting over a specific set of messages about your company, for example, the basic principles remain as important, but the dynamics (as described earlier) require practice and experience. It can become a challenge that you will learn to love and to plan as a strong, major part of your sales cycle. Make the work the diligent preparation; use the presentation as the welcome relaxation.

The Tender or RFP

Most salespeople who sell into government will tell you that the biggest challenge with responding to a tender (where they are most often used) is that it has probably been written with the preferred or incumbent supplier in mind.

Obliged as they often are to "go to the market", continually for large contractual sales, most government and similar organizations prefer to avoid disruptive change and, therefore, to maintain the status quo. Though this does not stop them from negotiating what they would call an improved price, the procurement officer will usually draft any tender in such a way as to facilitate an easy response from the incumbent supplier—assuming that their previous work has been satisfactory. This can lead to that provider's gaining another year's contract, but sometimes with a depleted profit margin. We talk more about this in Chapter 8. So, how can the ambitious new vendor break through this protectionist barrier? The answer—inevitably—is through some hard work.

The UK government's website, as an example, is very helpful in briefing SMEs, specifically, on where to find tender opportunities and how to produce an effective bid.

They even have guidance on points of grammar in the writing of it! Though the proportion of, for example, consultancy contracts awarded annually to SMEs by the UK public sector has remained fairly stable since 2016 at around 20 percent, that is a one-fifth share of a lucrative £2.5B total market that has grown from just £0.7B over that same period. An example, therefore, of a target segment that an ambitious and competitively well-positioned SME can go after. Tussell, in their report on UK local government procurement with Tech SMEs, cites the growth in that area from 16 percent to 23 percent. So SMEs have increased their market share by nearly 50 percent! In that same report, their research suggests that, by 2023, over 700 local government IT contracts held by SMEs, valued at £147M, will expire. This only serves to emphasize the opportunity. We can perhaps assume that other countries are similar. Though it might be easier (than with the central government) to make direct contact with those in local government who are responsible for procurement and the budget, there will still be regulations, guidelines, and quirks that make selling into the segment demanding for the vendor. Maintain the integrity of your sales process and—as always—qualify the deal ruthlessly.

Points to watch out for include:

- The required level of compatibility with existing products, systems, or services
- The degree to which delivery, installation, or operational dates are geared to any pretesting, trialing, or evaluation processes
- The process of purchase expenditure approval or budget compliance and how much upward referral is required to central government, and any political influences over the deal
- The price paid previously and how that was justified internally

Let's look at each of these important points in reverse order. Let's first look at price. If the net potential value of the order or contract is very large, it will always be tempting to meet or beat the prior price. If you're lucky or thorough enough to find it out, you may know the competing bid. Don't be tempted to undercut it to get the deal. Keep in mind the need for this to be profitable for your own firm. Resist the temptation to skew your approach because of the potentially prestigious addition to the customer list and the big top-line number! The price of underquoting can be a damaging, long-term hit to your company; big customers and big sales demand big levels of support commitment. It is likely that you will be entering a long-term relationship on the premise of being a trusted supplier. More on this in Chapters 7 and 8. It's not worth struggling to afford to support a customer and ruin your reputation by being unable so to do. The benefits of that relationship must be mutual, or it will fail. Also, it is notoriously difficult—if not contractually impossible—to raise prices or charge that customer more for anything after the contract is signed. You are more likely to be under pressure to reduce your prices, at contract renewal time if not before, even while your own costs are rising. Begin as you mean to continue—by offering the best value that you can both for you and for the user.

As previously discussed in Chapter 1, knowing the buying process of the potential customer is *essential.*

In government circles, particularly, this can be confusing at best and labyrinthine at worst. If, for example, tenders are regularly issued in the defense sector in April, then the salesperson should be examining the prior, winning tender at the beginning of the year. Governments generally have a desire to do the right thing for their suppliers as well as their users, making opportunities for every business to sell to them. Research shows, however, that the same few major suppliers become very well practiced in tenders of a particular type for a particular sector and appear regularly on the supplier list. This list is usually open to public scrutiny in most major economies, so ensure that you get a look at it to see with which incumbents you will be competing. One of the elements with which those experienced suppliers will be familiar—and adept at manipulating—is the process of budget allocation and spending approval for whichever department in the government of the country they are dealing with. Again, this takes some work, but the relevant timetables and deadlines will usually be available to you because of the requirement for public scrutiny. It is often more difficult to communicate personally with the decision makers at any level in public sector sales, so influencing and motivating activities need to be highly focused on providing extensive informational support for their decision making. As we discussed in Chapter 2, you will need to tailor specific parts of your marketing content to appeal to those decision makers; your marketing department has to work with sales to get it in front of them.

The trial and evaluation stage (see Chapter 6), though not always part of a sale, is one that you will most often encounter in the public sector. The high level of government and public scrutiny over any expenditure necessitates this. You will need to be prepared for timescales that may be both long and inflexible. Or sometimes, flexible or vague to the point of frustration! You may well find your product or solution being evaluated in a competitive situation. Getting close enough to the process to maintain some level of control can be challenging; your team members often having to sign nondisclosure agreements to be allowed to gain access to public sector premises and systems.

Last in this list comes that challenge of unseating or working closely with an incumbent supplier. You may have to consider product or methodology modifications, either to offer a bespoke solution or to be compatible with existing systems and methods. An incumbent supplier will have these to hand and have that advantage. You, meanwhile, have to sell relentlessly on the value and unique benefits of your proposal, as the earlier part of this chapter describes. Public sector buyers and their teams have an insatiable appetite for information on which to base and by which to justify their decisions, so make sure that you are providing it. In the public sector, there is a particular focus on the social value as part of whatever taxpayers' money is used for. Look beyond even the longer-term value proposition that you might well be selling to identify what social value is to be gained by the use of what you are proposing. But don't fake it—authenticity is important. Your own ESG stance and purpose statement (see Chapter 2) may allow you to differentiate your tender input from your competition and fit in with what the public sector customer has to be seen to provide to its citizens. Use this element as an additional lever in your sales process, rather than view it as a barrier.

> *In public sector sales, thorough research is key. Salespeople must know not only when upcoming tenders and RFPs are happening, but precisely what they are for and who is involved. Usually, the head of procurement will emphasise the framework that any sales team must work with, setting the rules for pricing, delivery, and the transparency of ongoing support costs. Meanwhile, in my experience, it is often the case that budget holders and influential users will be frustrated by these constraints. To secure the sale, the salesperson must develop a rapport and common language with all of those stakeholders.*
>
> Nichola Thurston-Smith, former Head of Public Sector
> Strategic Accounts, Microsoft

Tender bids that fail are those that do not answer the specific questions in sufficient detail, do not "prove"—as far as is possible—the proposer's skills and competence in the relevant area, or simply don't show that they are eligible to bid. And if you cannot provide compelling pricing in this very cost-sensitive environment, that will certainly kill your chances of a win. Those organizations that require a tender are usually unshakeable on that process, so there is no way around it and you will have to prepare one according to their guidelines if you want to win that contract. If you do not, and you feel the process was not a fair one, you can challenge the award decision. This appears to be happening with greater frequency, despite the fact that it can, however, be a long and protracted effort. You may find out some useful information that will improve your efforts the next time around, but reversals of the original decision are rare. Your time is probably better spent in simply asking what you could have done better, leaving any relationship that you may have formed on a positive note (it's always ultimately down to relationships), then moving on and looking at other prospects.

Summary

Qualification, preparation, astute timing, and consistency will be the watchwords for this stage of the sales process, for organizations of all sizes. Get these elements wrong and the list of lost, not-closed, nearly closed, and not-sure prospective sales will get unacceptably long and your target revenues will suffer. As we discussed in Chapter 3, qualifying your prospect is a basic skill, but going further to qualify the deal is yet another. You probably have expertise outside of sales and marketing in your firm that can help you to do that, as they help you to sell. Your finance, marketing, R&D, and other functions can be brought into the negotiations to help you and your customer to reach the right conclusion.

The sales call is not an excuse for a blustering tirade of company selling points to be thrown at your prospect. It is a point in the sales cycle that needs preparation and management. And there will be more than one during the process as you seek to raise awareness, inform and convince your prospect that their decision to deal both with you and your firm is a low-risk and wise one. The purchasing budget will always be high on the agenda. Use refined VBS techniques to transform the sales pitch into a mutually productive conversation between businesspeople seeking to do the best for each other and for each other's companies, over the long term.

Handling tenders, RFPs, and proposals is a vital skill to master. Content is important in each case, but so is timing: keep your resources in check until the time is right to use them to optimum effect. It's tempting to go for the big bang of a celebrity-laden presentation as early as possible, but that can be wasteful and counterproductive. Better to be in a near-closing position first, with most if not all objections countered in earlier meetings and with just the final confidence vote to be given by your signatory.

The very best practitioners of all of this will be those who most quickly and effectively move to the next stage: closing the deal and opening a new customer relationship.

The Takeaways and Lessons Learned From Chapter 5	Do	Don't
The first sales call	Prepare, prepare, prepare Confirm, confirm, confirm Know who is in the room Be respectful of time constraints Talk less; listen more Assume nothing, investigate, and discover everything Sell on value and business benefits, not price	Don't do any less if it's a virtual, video call than if it were face to face Don't leave without knowing where you stand and having got a commitment to the next step Don't close the door in a negative way. Leave the possibility of a return open
The proposal	Timing is critical. Make certain that they are ready for your proposal Customize and personalize Include a detailed business benefits summary Include pricing. Be specific for the proposal; don't hide behind a rate card	Don't use a standardized boiler-plate format. That's not good enough. Hold back on the full detail of your solution, but make it clear and digestible

The Takeaways and Lessons Learned From Chapter 5	Do	Don't
	Include any evaluation results Provide a separate executive summary that can stand alone Ensure complete synchronicity with your core content	Don't include or exclude different details for different members of the buying group. You'll cause offence. Include everything, but make sure that content specifics are clearly marked
Sales teams	Selling is a team sport; involve anyone and everyone in your company who can help Match your team with the buying team Make sales meeting or other schedules clear, and communicate them in good time to everyone involved	Don't abuse your colleagues' time Don't assume knowledge or experience; brief your team members properly on the role they are expected to play and with whom they are dealing
The presentation	Timing is critical. Make a careful judgment of when to go for the main performance Not everyone is a natural public speaker. Train yourself and your team members to be the best that they can be Set expectations upfront for timing, format, content, and follow-on Radiate empathy and understanding of the buyer's needs and challenges	Don't be rushed into it. Agree where you are in the sales process and present accordingly Don't assume that facilities that you don't own will be adequate. Find out ahead of time and have a back-up plan; then a back-up plan to that Don't avoid rehearsal; this is a performance Don't assume that you have met expectations. Ask, then make corrections fast if there needs to be some

The Takeaways and Lessons Learned From Chapter 5	Do	Don't
The tender or RFP	Get details early; help to shape the tender if you can Have patience with long timelines and slow decision making Understand the procurement procedure, but try not to be constrained by it	Don't be an also-ran; figure out your strategy to be the stand-out supplier Don't skimp on competitor analysis Don't try to cram all the detail into constrained formats. Use links to your online content

CHAPTER 6

Evaluation, Trial, and Closing

Overview

In the last chapter, we focused on making our pitch to the prospect and becoming a credible contender for the business. We have the knowledge of the market from Chapter 1; we have positioned and credibly branded ourselves in that market in Chapter 2. We've qualified our prospective customer in Chapter 3 and know with whom we are competing and have presented our credentials to them directly in Chapters 4 and 5. Now it's crunch time. In this chapter, our topic is the whole process of turning the prospect's awareness into a positive opinion, with sufficient confidence in you, your company, and your solution to give you the order. Why is this important? This is the stage at which many potential complex B2B sales are lost. Managing the customer's detailed assessment of what you are selling is an essential skill that will serve you well and lead to more closed deals. Every potential sale will differ at this stage; so an adaptable, personalized, and tightly managed process is needed. Professional and experienced managers of the sales process will comment on their relevant lessons learned in the field and we will draw some conclusions on the most effective approach.

Evaluation—Holding the Hand That Signs the Deal

Uncomplicated, large-scale B2B product sales are a rarity. The complex sale is more likely to be the one you encounter. Often, the buyer and his or her team will have an evaluation process in place or insist on a trial of your solution. Let's tackle evaluation first. Depending on the nature of the sale, the evaluation may well be in parallel to that of your main competition. How do you ensure that you come out the winner in what is essentially a remote and detailed competitive sales pitch? It takes *persuasion, monitoring, ease of use*, and *empathy*. Many technology companies, for example, have a specifically designed evaluation version of their product, together with a set of instructions as to how to use it. This is very useful, but still requires close control by the vendor. If appropriate and if you have the resources available, use this as an opportunity to introduce the customer to the high-quality team that they will work with when they choose you as the supplier. To provide an evaluation, the manager or team gives you the chance to initiate a relationship that will be long term if you get the deal. Make sure that the evaluation team is in no doubt that they are in a soft but vital selling role. Even if the buyer or project leader is keen to do this, it is likely that there will be resistance to the trial work from those users in the business who simply want to get on with their day jobs. Part of the technique in this, therefore, is to provide sufficient encouragement, guidance, and even manpower to make it as painless as possible, while selling the benefits of your solution throughout—persuasion, monitoring, ease of use.

In *Selling Is Hard; Buying Is Harder*, Garin Hess describes how his company, Consensus, developed auto-demo software that can enable the prospect to "see" the product and its capabilities without the expensive presence of a salesperson. This accelerated sales procedure helped to create a process buyers liked and helped them go through it at their own pace. Of course, this could be just as easily and cost-effectively applied at a much earlier point in the sales cycle, because of its low drain on sales resources and ease of use. The other major benefit he found was how quickly the automated demo was passed around the members of any buying group. This "buyer enablement" tool was developed to benefit both sides, but some control was lost in this way. It worked, but was not a solution for every sales situation.

At the evaluation stage, as we discussed, you will likely still be in a competitive situation. If the nature of your product is such that you can offer a prepackaged and remotely managed solution, then your competitor may well be doing the same. *You will need to know this.* Your competitive advantage will come from the ease by which the user can—on his or her own terms—compare the alternatives with the least disruption to the

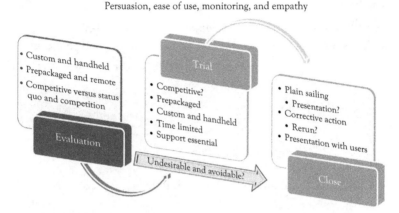

Persuasion, ease of use, monitoring, and empathy

- Custom and handheld
- Prepackaged and remote
- Competitive versus status quo and competition

Evaluation

Trial

- Competitive?
- Prepackaged
- Custom and handheld
- Time limited
- Support essential

Undesirable and avoidable?

- Plain sailing
- Presentation?
- Corrective action
- Rerun?
- Presentation with users

Close

Figure 6.1 The final steps to the close need careful management

day-to-day running of the business. It is worth the risk of insulting the user's readiness for this process by ensuring that they are, in fact, ready. If, for example, the process involves running an installed or cloud-based software solution (presuming that you are confident in the fundamentals of your product), the least that you should be offering is a properly resourced helpline. That should be online (e.g., chat-based) and on the telephone, with the capacity to support the expected number of interactions, whenever they may arise. Your higher aim is to provide help and reassurance both that the solution is the right one and that the company behind it really knows how to look after its customers. If it's a situation where your solution is a highly equipped office workspace, for example, your customer may send a team of their people to yours at the same time as they send others to that of your competitor. Ask for both teams to sample both offerings, to help eliminate bias. If your agricultural equipment is being used in evaluation alongside a competing set, then, as with the previous example, you can leave nothing to chance, in this case even the weather. Be prepared for all eventualities. Even with your remote option, putting some of your best people to handhold on site is a good move if you can justify it on the grounds of your own resources and the potential sale value, and persuade the user to allow it. If you can get this agreement at the last minute, you may well outfox the competitor.

Prior to the evaluation, as part of your sales process, you will have investigated and understood the precise nature of the evaluation. It is possible to be just a bit too keen and find yourself in overkill mode, when the process may well be a simple one. Gauge it right. As well as the detailed basis for the comparison of your solution with the existing system and the competing one, it will have been wise of you to establish what will happen afterwards.

You need to know:

- The duration
- The evaluation criteria
- The precise completion criteria and time
- The results
- When and how those results will be communicated both to you and to the competitor and within the customer's business

This is critical, because the user's personal response may well not be obvious from the formal evaluation. You need to know immediately any point of contention or competitive failing of your solution. That way, you may have the chance to put it right, explain the reason for it, run it again, or at least manage the wider communication about it before the deal is potentially lost. You are still selling at this stage, remember, and the intensity of the sales process that got you thus far must not be lost.

If you come out on top, don't miss the opportunity to shout about it. Arrange a presentation (see Chapter 5) for the buyer that fits with your proposal process, utilizing the user's own evaluation team to support your winning pitch with their positive experience during the evaluation. If you have come in not badly, but only second on the evaluation, still push for that presentation. Having seen the results, it is reasonable for you to request the chance to respond to the decision not to go with your solution. This will take some persuasive selling, but again, an agreement to be able to do this can be set up in the pre-evaluation stage, particularly if you have established the right kind of personal relationship with the buyer. Do not do this unless you have the full evaluation results, however, or you will not know exactly what you are fighting over. It could be that the point or points on which you have been marked down were simply misunderstandings over what you are offering and are easily rectified to your advantage. The deal is not lost until the ink is on the competitor's order form. This is where the confident salesperson does not take no for an answer and is not knocked back or out of the race because of this one setback. In any case, learn from the experience.

The Trial—The Judge Is on Your Side, But the Jury Is Still Out

When the evaluation decision has gone in your favor, the buyer may still insist that there is a trial or a trial period in using your product or solution to seal the deal. Let's look at how you can best manage this, so that you get the contract and the buyer gets the kudos.

First of all: push back. This will be a test of the relationship that you have formed, but the cost in time, money, and effort—for everyone—to run a full trial is considerable. If the buying decision has been made, the buyer should have the confidence simply to go ahead with the installation and implementation of your solution. From your standpoint, a trial of any kind is undesirable and probably avoidable.

Will the existing systems, products, or solutions be run in parallel? If that contract is signed and valid only with the proviso that the trial is successful, then are there specific, agreed criteria in place upon which to judge the success or otherwise of the trial? What would failure look like and what would be the result of that? These are the hard questions that need to be asked of your buyer in this situation.

But let's say that she insists and that you have to agree to a trial period. The race is well run, you are in the lead, the competitors are out of sight, and the last fence is in front of you. Let's make sure that you don't fall at this one. If you regularly face a trial situation with your product or solution, you will have it packaged and ready to go, like your evaluation one. If the sale that you have made is of your standard, unmodified software, service, vehicle, computer hardware, and so on, which you provide on a trial basis, then your task at this stage is easier. The keys to success are to ensure ease of use, monitoring, support, and control (see Figure 6.1). Be sure that both sides understand the timing involved, whether that is hours or months, and the precise nature of what is to happen—again, just as in the evaluation. Even though it is most likely that this is not a competitive situation any longer, your focus should be no less than it was in getting to this point. If the customer is provided with your product and then left to utilize it alone, that's fine, as long as you have a properly manned, fully available support system in place for them, as we discussed in relation to an evaluation. This time, though, with further implementation a near-certainty, you will be introducing to the user the individuals from your company with whom they will have an ongoing relationship. It's time to begin your transition from supplier to partner, which we discuss further in the next chapter. Don't make any of the classic mistakes:

- Don't provide any kind of reduced functionality product.
- Don't give access only to the hotline that normally supports experienced users.
- Don't lose focus and get involved with your next prospect to the degree that you are not in control or communication with this one.

Doing any of those things increases the possibility of something going wrong and bringing a halt to the proceedings. If the trial is all plain sailing, so that, at the end of the agreed trial period, you are convinced that the user is happy to sign off on it having been a success, then set up a meeting that will allow you to present the results to senior management—results that you will have monitored carefully and recorded, of course. Ideally, involve the internal individual or team that handled the trial in that meeting to do your final selling for you. Even consider using the users, if you judge that as appropriate. Anyone who is a cheerleader for you: get them involved! From here, your ongoing account contacts are going to change (see Chapter 8, Figure 8.1), so having a meeting to make the customer's users and management team feel good about their own buying team's decision is a very positive move.

But something may go wrong. The new office Wi-Fi in your facilities may not have functioned properly, the driver of the new truck may have found it difficult to maneuver, or the user interface on the software may have frozen when it was trying to pull data from the current system. Your close monitoring and control will likely have quickly corrected these problems, but that's not enough: you will need to put the user's mind at rest that this was a blip, not an ongoing issue. This is difficult to generalize across all of the possibilities, but whatever the case, make sure it is done, done fast and done well. Is there a need to redo the trial from the start? If so, don't argue or hesitate, just get it done. Don't let any degree of doubt creep into the user's mind about their decision to go with your solution. And still push for that posttrial presentation. Don't avoid the subject of the glitch that occurred: be honest about it and show how it was solved—fast, efficiently, and permanently. Show how good you are at support.

If the trial was a competitive one, then all of the above cautions are amplified. You will be doing the trial as a potential supplier, not a chosen one, so the whole tone of the exercise will be different. You will need to understand exactly what your competitor is doing and—as earlier in the sales process—do it better. Take all of the same precautions and make preparations as with the evaluation, described above. You will be one step back from the close, but still be in a good position to jump those last couple of fences in the race. So, let's now get that contract signed.

Closing Or Opening the New Relationship

For every salesperson, this is the most difficult skill to master and one of the points at which the biggest percentage of "leaks" occur from the effective sales process. I would generalize, at this point, in saying that B2B selling has moved on from the high-pressure, adversarial style of closing to a no less effective style that is more about *beginning* or *opening* a relationship between two individuals and their companies than it is about *closing* the sale and running off, respectively, to celebrate a win or experience buyer remorse. Studies by McKinsey and others have found that B2B companies have poorer customer buying experiences than B2C companies. The 2021 Gartner Digital Buying Survey showed a growing preference for a rep-free experience and complete end-to-end autonomy in their transactions, but the involvement of face to face sales interaction reduced the potential to make the wrong decision and to experience, later, that regret. Michael Wheeler, in *The Art of Negotiation: How to Improvise Agreement in a Chaotic World*, though he refers positively to the Roger Ury book *Getting to Yes*, and its focus on the "win–win" closing approach, emphasizes that this is not a simple process that will move smoothly along the rails laid down by any set of rules. His plea is the common sense one for salespeople to listen most intently to what the buyer is saying and to help that buyer come to a conclusion with which both of them can be satisfied. Time to blast another sales myth. We have all been told you never walk away from a customer. But you *can* walk away from a totally unsuitable prospect or a customer, and it can be the best thing you do.

Greg Adams in Conversation With Tom Cairns

Greg Adams currently serves as a partner/principal with a global professional services firm focused on marketing, sales, and service transformation programs for large cross-industry organizations. He previously spent over 25 years leading information technology sales teams, including time at both Salesforce and IBM. He has led teams in the United States, Europe (including four years based in London), and globally; he has led as many as 400 sellers and had revenue responsibility up to $700M. He holds a BA in marketing from Adrian College and an MBA from Eastern Michigan University. He and his family currently reside near Chicago, United States.

TC: Have you any comments or lessons learned about what links Marketing, Selling and Account Management to make them effective?

GA: *We call it marketing, sales and service in my world, and they really are highly related and highly dependent disciplines. In far too many organizations, sales and marketing rarely talk to each other. In highly effective organizations, they are tightly aligned with common metrics. I spend a lot of my time now talking to clients about how to use technology to align their front-office teams (meaning marketing, sales and service).*

I believe that most organizations will have a front-office and a back-office platform. The back-office platform is rigid by design, focused on consistency and tight controls. We tend to not want flexibility in the back office, instead focusing on adherence to well considered best practices. The front-office platform enables speed and agility, to allow for changes to how you market, sell and service clients/customers. Your front-office processes are a big part of an organization's competitive differentiation. How you compete today may change tomorrow, and the technology needs to enable this agility.

Marketers spend a lot of time and money creating interest in your solutions. Highly functioning marketing teams are able to track and measure the pipeline generated by their activities and follow that pipeline through the sales cycle to closed revenue. The more closely you can track pipe gen to closed revenue, the more marketers can ask for additional investment in marketing.

The evolution from new to established client/customer is similarly important. It's a bit of a cliché, but also true that it's easier and less expensive to sell to an existing client than a new client. This is where account management comes into play. Companies need to be deliberate about the levels of service they provide and have systems and processes that allow service levels to be tracked and maintained.

Many of the same focus areas previously discussed apply when you're talking about account management. The best sellers continue to refine their point of view of how their solution can continue to add value to their client. They bring new ideas and stay close to their client's evolving business. It's almost guaranteed that your competitors are targeting your existing business with the client. Complacency and a bad service experience are some of the biggest reasons I see customers switching vendors. It's also important for sales managers to challenge their territory mapping decisions and ensure that the right sellers are on the right accounts. A rep that is great at closing new accounts may not be great at growing them (hunter versus farmer). Longevity on an account has a ton of value, and we all can probably agree too many companies make changes too quickly. That said, matching sales skills to client needs is important.

Clients are also better-informed today about solutions out there than they were a generation ago. By the time they start an active RFI or RFP process, they've likely already done their homework and have an initial preference for vendors. There is a lot of independent third-party information out there that helps validate thinking around RFIs. The marketing team can play an important role in shaping how your company shows up before the sales team gets engaged.

Going back to the theme of platforms, I'm a big believer that there is value in establishing a long-term relationship with a small number of vendors. Customers should test market pricing and keep abreast of new *capabilities, but be careful about chasing what I call "shiny pennies." Especially in the tech industry, there are new players that will come along and disrupt, but I've seen a lot of clients struggle with integrating a lot of disconnected tech. They may have a bunch of "best of breed" solutions, but they don't work together and don't solve the problem. Great account management is how you maintain these relationships over many years.*

I was recently involved in an application selection process for a large client. The easy answer was to stick with their incumbent provider that had very deep relationships across the organization. The incumbent vendor's solution was viable, though not the best. Ultimately, the incumbent vendor lost this business because they had a "B" sales team that approached the sale with the assumption that there was no way they could lose. A new vendor had a great sales team, established relationships across the executive team, and was just easier to deal with. When the decision was made to switch vendors, the incumbent vendor's leadership finally reached out to ask why they had not received some notice that this was going bad for them, with the inference being that had they known they would have put a better team in place. This was a failure in account management, and an expensive one.

TC: What is it that is pivotal in added value? What do you mean by value? Is it in financial terms?

GA: *I started my career selling industrial products in Detroit into large manufacturing plants, mostly related to the auto industry. We had a branch manager that called on the same large auto plant for decades, and pretty much had 100 percent market share with this customer for the components he sold, and even had sign-off rights on new equipment coming into the plant to ensure replacement parts were available (from him). He was seen as part of their team, and as someone that helped them anticipate needs and problems. It was well known that they paid a premium, and they were happy to pay. It was the only parts relationship that never went out to bid, and they had a blanket open-ended contract. When this branch manager retired, the customer hosted his retirement party. I always think of this when I think about account management best practices and value. He added a ton of value to their organization, and that value earned him market share and a premium price.*

Value can be expressed in a lot of different ways. It's best when it's measurable and specific. When I did big deal reviews with my sales teams, I used to always ask for the business case for our solution. We're asking the client to pay "x" ... and they are getting "y" value. The more specific the better. If the teams can't answer this, and answer for how our value is differentiated from our competition, I know we're in trouble. If you're selling a commodity, you had better be adding value on the service you provide in support of the product. If there is no value-add around service, you're competing on price, and that is a tough way to make a living.

TC: Is there a different sales process when selling a higher priced or a lower priced solution? Or is it a similar selling process?

GA: *The basic process is the same, though the timeline can change with the size of investment required. In some ways I think it's easier to sell bigger deals, because the decision makers are involved sooner, and they tend to engage more strategically. I've never seen anyone lose a deal because they called too high. You just have to be prepared for those discussions and focus on value.*

TC: How important are sales managers and executive leaders with sales experience?

GA: *I used to work for a company whose founder used to say two things that have stuck with me. First, "nothing happens without a sale," and second, "in this company, there are those that sell and those that support those that sell." That second one may be a bit of an extreme, but the point is valid. Nothing happens unless a customer decides to buy your product or service.*

First-line sales managers have the toughest job in most companies and tend to be the first line of defense around many of the best practices we've discussed. Having sales managers that have successfully sold themselves is important, and having senior leaders that have spent their careers (and still spend their time) in front of clients is really important. From time to time, I see companies put people that have never sold into sales leadership roles, and I find it rarely works. Just like you'd never ask a seller to manage a group of software developers or auditors, the reverse should also be true.

While there are certainly examples of products that have sold themselves (IBM mainframe computers in the 1960s, or iPhones today), I go back to something I said earlier. A good solution with a great sales team will usually beat a great solution with a bad sales team!

TC: Do you have any final thoughts to share?

GA: *I go back to where we started: sales is both an art and a science.*

Running a large sales team is a tough job, and technology like CRM can be a huge enabler to drive growth and efficiency. Technology helps leaders have a much better understanding of what is happening across their organization and can do amazing things to help drive new ways of working across teams. For large organizations, technology is the best answer to enable speed in terms of identifying opportunities or risks, and in linking teams (marketing, sales and service). When done right, the ROI for these investments is significant.

The art of selling is also really important. Sellers that understand their client's buying process, the competitive landscape, and your value proposition, and who aren't afraid to ask for the order, are really important in many industries.

Investing in front-office capabilities and professional sellers that know how to leverage them will provide an outsized return on investment for most companies.

You might discover during the evaluation stage that what appeared to be a well-thoughtout and specific performance brief or set of requirements from the customer for the solution in question is nothing of the sort. Sales experience seems to dictate that the failure of the buyer adequately to define the problem is the biggest barrier to the seller's ability to help them to solve it. Let's imagine that your robot filling and packaging unit was designed for 1000 units an hour processing rate, and a basic maintenance pause of 30 minutes in every 24 hours of working. You have confidently put it forward for evaluation in the buyer's production facility because these performance specs exceed those that you have been asked to meet. Your installation team then discovers that 1000 units is only the average, and in fact, the peak processing requirement is 20 percent greater than this. Also, although you have been told that the production-line schedule is such that individual units are required to run daily for just three six-hour shifts—leaving plenty of time for your essential maintenance—you discover that overstretched maintenance crews only get to that part of the process every 48 hours. Your evaluation result is bound to be negative; you run the risk of an embarrassing system failure. You do have a unit that could withstand the extra burden, but it is considerably more expensive, moving you outside of the restricted budget that the buyer has declared. You are aware that the competing unit that is being evaluated against yours is a similar spec and usually considerably less reliable. It will not perform better in the unexpectedly more challenging trial run. You realize that, in this instance, the customer is not always right. This is now a test of your relationship with the buyer. Can you confidently return to him or her at this stage and confront them with the harsh reality? That is, their attempt to keep the acquisition cost within the budget will expose the production line to a high risk of failure. You will have to convince them to loosen the budget constraints to move up to the necessary level of equipment. Have you established yourself sufficiently as a trusted adviser in this situation to be heard on the issue? If the answer is no and your buyer is determined to put his own production line at risk for the sake of coming in under budget on this project, it is time to walk away. The inevitable failure of the installation of an inadequate solution will almost certainly be blamed on you and your company's equipment if you allow it to go ahead. Let the competition in, to suffer the failure. Walk away.

The B2B sales landscape has changed. As a marketing or sales professional, you are more likely than ever before to encounter procurement professionals, leading a team which is constantly feeding them information relevant to your negotiation (see Chapter 4, Figure 4.2). This will be from a myriad of sources that you cannot entirely monitor or control. It is also possible that you find yourself in front of a professional negotiator, who is trained to, and focused on, negotiating the best financial deal for his or her company. This might happen after you have got to a point in the sales process where you had felt you were merely a signature away from closing the deal, all selling, evaluating, and proposing having been done. The negotiator's focus will be on the negotiation itself, not the product or service you've successfully sold to the buying team. The net price to be paid assumes the primary importance in this situation. Usually, there will be more price pressure, because the negotiator will consider that he or she is there to get the lowest price on a commodity, not to evaluate the business benefits of your finely honed and positioned solution. Your value-based selling (VBS) approach (see Chapter 5) may not have permeated through to this final guardian of the company's purse strings; you have to be prepared with a clearly presented set of tools to swing the discussion back to value. Establish whether the negotiator has seen any of your prior work on this. The supportive evaluation results and the individuals—managers and users—who have accepted your VBS arguments now become your essential allies. Ensure that you have a way of getting their acceptance of and support for your value proposition in front of the negotiator, who will not want to be accused of ignoring their professional opinions. The negotiator will certainly not want to be seen as an unwanted barrier to what now should be a much-anticipated new solution for their company, or to force any more investigative, analytical, or evaluation work back to them.

Bearing this in mind, you can use it to your negotiating advantage. Prepare alternative solution options with differing prices. So, for example, option one may be the complete, value-rich solution. The second may be priced lower, but will exclude one aspect of support or maintenance. The third—at the lowest price—could be a stripped-back, product-oriented solution. But this is not a game or a scam: each of these must be viable alternatives that you would be happy to sell, not false or impractical sales ploys. Your job—supported by all the backup data and material that you have at your disposal—is to negotiate an acceptance of the best deal for you and your customer, while showing your flexibility on price in this viable way. In this way, although you may not interact with the negotiator again over this particular sale, you are helping to create a positive relationship on which to base future business with the user. You are not so much closing the deal as opening the relationship, a much better way of looking at it. Both parties should walk away feeling good about what has been agreed. For the follow-on business you hope to gain, the negotiator will know that you both can work together.

Do not kid yourself. You have had prospects—everyone has—who, even after contacting them what seems like a hundred times, would never buy from you. You may well find yourself in a situation at this stage, when you are apparently a real contender for the business, just being used as a counterweight for an argument in favor of a competitor whose success has already been decided upon. Or is someone internally trying to justify the status quo and the "do nothing" option? Constantly asking questions about the state of the sale and how you are being compared to the competition is essential. Despite what people will say about never giving up on a prospect regardless of who they are, you do need to be selective. It comes down to key things you need to evaluate:

- Size and critical, strategic importance of this deal to your company
- Probability of closing – including the strength of the competition
- Longer-term profit potential of this account
- Number of other potential prospects in your pipeline and the opportunity cost of pursuing this one

Do not under any circumstances make your decision an emotional one. This gets people into trouble and will have you either cutting off a great opportunity too soon or wasting valuable time. Keep your pipeline full, but make sure each opportunity has earned the right to—and has the qualification to—be there. Let's imagine that the sale you are in the process of making has very few complications. The buyer's internal business case is clear and your competition is pitching on a purely cost or cost–benefit basis. Whether this is a sale of high-value products, value-intensive services, or performance-based solutions, it will still be clearly be decided on a value basis. But VBS is an art in itself, and the ability to quantify and communicate value in B2B sales is more important than ever. We discussed VBS in detail in Chapter 5. At the evaluation stage, it's not only by the workings and effectiveness of your product or solution that you are being compared to your closest competitor. Your buyer will be looking out again into the world of information at his or her fingertips and be checking back, in the cyclical, iterative way we saw in Chapter 4 (and Figure 4.2), to the decisions and conclusions reached by the buying team up to that point. Things may change for you if the buyer finds something convincing that may alter his or her opinion. In its recent study of B2B buyer behavior, Gartner found that the level of "buyer regret" in high-value deals was lowered by a factor of three when that buyer considered that they had received high-quality information and sufficient of it to support and facilitate the buying decision. As a cautionary point, however, the words "overabundance" and "overwhelmed" were used, as buyers in that study sought to prioritize and "deconflict" all of the data, opinions, and perspectives with which they were presented. The conclusion is that the canny salesperson can act as a valuable human filter for all that the buyer and team are being bombarded with, from all sides. This cannot be achieved, though, without first having established a highly trusted relationship that might be tested like in the example above.

Joy Armstrong in Conversation With Michael Grant

Joy is an Executive Account Director within the life sciences industry. Her roles throughout her career have been to sell clinical trials, focused on pharmaceutical product development, around the world for U.S.-based companies. Joy was based in Australia for 10 years selling to APAC countries and now sells out of the United Kingdom to both Europe and APAC.

Joy is currently commuting to the United States and advising/training the sales team on successful international selling.

Joy, you achieved global sales sales success for your pharmaceutical companies, often by selling a 'trial concept' rather than a product. Can you highlight some of the different approaches to this that you have adopted in various parts of the world?

The US divisions find it very challenging selling into Australia, New Zealand and Asia as the sales process differs greatly between the US, Europe and APAC.

The US sales process is based on dinners and golf courses and is more orientated toward the social aspect. I tend to find that the fundamentals are not there and to some degree it seems "falser." European and APAC sales are a lot more formal and "work focused" and they start from the fundamentals up, just as in life you start at a lower stage to build a relationship.

In selling drug trials, you are focused on long term relationships. They are not transactional sales but partnering sales. You need to spend a lot of time face to face in the prospect's country.

On moving to Australia, I was not sure how the sales process was going to go. In theory the Australians are more "laid back" but it is also a very tight-knit community. Everyone knows everyone. It was easier for me as an English person than if I was an American because of the perceived bravado that goes around an American sale; that increases resistance in Australia.

Common sense tells us how to sell to Asians far better than a training course could do. Each culture has different things that they value. For the Koreans, Chinese and Taiwanese you build a relationship on trust and honesty in your business dealings, but it is ingrained in their respective cultures always to expect a discount.

In India clients give a lot of transparency to the process and who else they are working with, and they share competitive information and pricing with your competitors. This can be very uncomfortable for a salesperson! Conversely, in Korea and China if they know that you are working with a competitor down the road, they are likely to exclude you from further business. Secrecy and security are the local bywords, in my experience.

It's all about understanding the human element of a sale and the people you are talking to. I would emphasize some key sales tips that I have learned:

- *Always go slowly in the sales process and don't run headfirst in as you will miss important factors.*
- *You have two ears and only one mouth. Always listen more than you speak in the sales process.*
- *Don't tell the client what you can do until you have asked the questions and then tailor what you say.*
- *My first question to a client is in which country they want the pharmaceutical study to be run. I never push a US offering until I understand the clients" preferences for where in their world they would prefer, or eventually want to market their drug. If you get off on the wrong foot this early it can change the whole sales process.*
- *Never think that you know it all, as I might be the dumbest person in the room. But I always know where to get the best answers from.*
- *You must be able to cope with rejection and not take it personally. That's a harder thing than winning the sale.*

- *You must always have a genuine interest in the person you are selling to, rather than merely be servicing your own personal needs.*

Unlike most successful salespeople I am not mainly motivated by the money. Yes, I like money, but for me it's all about the fun of building the relationship and seeing something good come out of it for both my company and for the client at the end. If you add both value and knowledge to a client, they respect you more. Scientists often work alone in a laboratory in their own world, you can add great wider experience and knowledge, especially in helping them to get a product to market.

I am not convinced that you can teach someone to sell, but it must be in their blood or character to have a genuine interest in people. You can teach them the tools, but without innate compassion and empathy they will not succeed. You do need something "special" about everyone in your sales team.

Always have the courage to stand up to a client who is going down the wrong track. Salespeople are programed to think that the client is always right and that they know what they are talking about. This is often untrue and can lead to disaster. I once lost a big deal that later went seriously wrong for both the client and the winning competitor. In a way this was perhaps my biggest win, as the client came back to me, bigtime!

What I am most proud of in my sales career

Selling to a huge global pharmaceutical company with 30,000-plus employees can be formidable, and different from selling to a medium size biotech company with a few hundred. When asked to lead the sales into a mega global company I was both hesitant and uncomfortable. They eventually became my best and biggest client—and it was not just taking orders. It certainly taught me a lot and the need to be talking with more people in the process from different areas of the organization and at different levels. The sales process was the same, but the implementation was longer and more challenging.

I am most proud of where I have got to and now have the confidence to reach for even greater success and responsibility. I have no degree or any of the qualifications that I was told were needed to progress. I am dyslexic but have proved that you don't need to write superb reports to be a successful salesperson. I love helping others "up the ladder" in their careers through mentoring and training them.

On returning to Europe from Australia I was given the role of selling into Europe having been absent from this market for ten years. All went well and, the company—realizing the relevance of my APAC experience—gave me that additional territory and overall responsibility for both regions. I lived on an airplane but had the satisfaction of knowing that five salespeople covered North America, whilst I simply covered the "rest of the world!"

Reaching a Satisfactory Conclusion: The Mutually Acceptable Close

We are at the end of the new sales process. As Figure 4.1 describes, we have informed, influenced, motivated, and sold to our prospective buyer. We got our targeting right; we found our prospect with the need and the ability to buy. Our presence and our promotion were pitched at the right people, at the right time, and at the right intensity to inform and educate them but not to overwhelm them. The strength of our brand has made them feel comfortable that we will be a reliable supplier with whom they can be proud to do business and who will become a long-term partner for them. The product or solution that they have chosen has been thoroughly evaluated against its closest competitors, been seen to be superior, and has been personally and enthusiastically praised by respected members of the customer's own industrial community. They have been helped to see past the basic price of the deal to the value that it offers in bringing substantial business benefits in the future. Your company—be it the original manufacturer or developer or a trusted third-party organization—is precisely the source with which they are most comfortable. The company is buying the solution that best meets its perceived and actual needs.

But you don't yet have the signature on that contract. You've had to go to the sales review meeting and say that you still haven't closed it. Why is that? The same reasons recur often:

1. Your ultimate buyer—the signatory—has left the position or the company. Their replacement has ordered a review of all new procurements.
2. A desperate competitor has offered their solution at half the price or free for a year.
3. The buyer has received some bad news about your company that rocks his or her faith in you as a supplier.
4. The company is in financial trouble: their latest set of results has put their shareholders in a spin and their share price has crashed. All spending is frozen.
5. The company is the subject of an aggressive takeover bid by a rival, possibly prompted by the reason above. No new contractual commitments are allowed.
6. The political or economic situation in the market or the country has drastically changed overnight.
7. The evaluation or trial went badly.

What do you do to still reap the rewards for months of marketing and sales effort?

- Find out the truth of the situation, first hand.
- Communication is everything. In situation 1, get in front of a new buyer as soon as possible, offering more help than pressure to buy. Make them see a way to be an instant hero by going ahead with the deal.
- For 2, get back on your value hobby-horse, steer away from the cost arguments, and reiterate the reasons that the decision had been made to choose your company as the supplier.
- For situation 3, be honest about that bad news. Whatever it is, get the company response across clearly. Depending on the nature and severity of it, involve your most senior management to restore confidence.

- If the situation is at a macro level, as with points 4–6, beyond what you can directly influence, speak to the highest level of contact that you have in the business and make it clear that you are keen to go through with the deal, will help in any way that you can, and are willing to engage with new management at any time. Find out who that is and make sure that they receive your message.
- Depending on the nature of the holdup, evaluate your position calmly. There would be no point, for example, in forcing through a contract to supply what you have proposed, to a company that cannot pay for it.

Summary

Any marathon runner will tell you that the middle of the race is the most complex and that the last mile is the hardest to complete. Many races are lost at the last gasp—so it is with sales cycles, that's why this stage is no less important than the earlier ones. Your good work in all of the earlier, complex stages of the sales process leads you to this point, where attention to detail, persistence, and a real understanding of the customer's buying process are critical. The key word in the evaluation stage is *control*. Many a supposedly certain deal has been lost when a slipshod evaluation process has been allowed to happen. An evaluation is still most likely to be a competitive situation, so you need a competitively oriented approach, with parameters for success that you have agreed with the customer. When the evaluation is done successfully, shout about it! Make sure the whole buying team knows that they are now expected to sign the order; ask for it. If your solution has not met expectations, don't delay: be clear about why that is and put it right, if you can.

A trial situation is different, though the essential principles of parameter-setting and control remain the same. Do your very best to sell past the necessity for a trial. If the buyer is not convinced that your solution is going to do what you have promised, then something is missing from your sales approach. If there is a trial, be clear about what is expected, for how long, and what success or failure means for the progress of the order. Is it signed but subject to withholding of payment until after the success of a trial? Is it signed and paid for but revokable if the trial is unsuccessful? Is it unsigned until the trial is successful? There has to be mutual agreement that the terms are reasonable, before the trial begins.

Buying teams, CTOs, CFOs, and professional negotiators are all out to get the best deal for their company. It is not uncommon for evaluations and trials to be followed by an attempt to beat you down on price. Use the successful results of those processes and your best VBS techniques to push back and close the deal. Like you, your prospect wants to get through the sales process, satisfactorily, and get on with the job.

It can sometimes be surprisingly difficult for the salesperson to set up the closing meeting and ask decisively for the order. Set up that meeting in the prospect's mind from a very early stage—get the right person or people in the room and don't spring any surprises or have them sprung on you! Make paperwork clear and concise and ensure that it has been read and understood in advance by anyone who has authority for or veto over signing it.

The Takeaways and Lessons Learned From Chapter 6	Do	Don't
Evaluation	Work with the customer to set the parameters Maintain control as best you can Provide easy access to hand-holding and support, on-site if possible	Don't use a reduced-function or feature-cut version of your product or solution. You are likely still to be in a competitive situation Don't forget that you are still selling Don't assume that your customer is good at this. Make it easy for them
Trial	Avoid this altogether if you can Set stringent guidelines and establish a clear picture of what success looks like and when it should be achieved	Don't assume smooth running: monitor, check, and control at every stage Don't brush off problems; fix them immediately

The Takeaways and Lessons Learned From Chapter 6	Do	Don't
	Set a date for a results round-up presentation to confirm what has been achieved	Don't be too eager to provide more than has been agreed, if the customer's requirements estimation proves to have been inadequate. Renegotiate the deal
Closing	Aim for a mutually acceptable conclusion to the sales process, to avoid buyer remorse, later If there is last-minute hesitation, be persistent in seeking the real reason for it Establish early in the process all necessary preconditions for getting that signature	Don't be pressured into last-minute price discounting Don't lose your faith in your value proposition Don't be afraid to walk away if there is an insurmountable obstacle. There's always the next deal

CHAPTER 7

Installation and Support

Overview

In the previous chapter, we used our detailed and closely integrated marketing and sales process to close the sale and secure the order, creating our new customer relationship. But we're not finished. We'll now examine the art of helping your new customer to hit the road running. Why is this important? Because it's all too easy to close the sale and lose attention on having the customer realize all of the business benefits that you sold to them. Whatever your product or service offering, a smooth transition into the customer's existing systems by properly managing the installation process is essential to avoid buyer remorse, customer support problems, and any early damage to a new relationship for which you have long-term ambitions. We'll also examine the importance of successful implementation by the user.

We also discussed in Chapter 6 the importance of "the customer's detailed assessment," critically involving the technical team. With sales, marketing, and the technical team working together, we'll now examine the art of achieving consistently successful post-sales relationships. Experienced practitioners will discuss relevant lessons learned in the field and we will draw some conclusions about how best to work with your user on the implementation of your products or solutions into their business.

Installation—Becoming Part of the Solution

In the afterglow of a successful major sale and account acquisition, it is easy to underestimate the attention that needs to be paid to integrating a new system (or service, or solution of any sort) into your customer's business. The user will certainly have been planning and constantly reviewing what he or she will need to do to interface your solution into their existing systems, from the very beginning of their requisition process. No doubt, as we discussed in Chapter 6, this was a major topic during the trial or evaluation phase, but it will have been in the user's mind earlier and all along. This is where—with diligent work—you head off any chance of buyer remorse. That is the feeling, after the contract is signed, that they have committed themselves to something that might not be all that they had hoped for. The most frequent cause of unhappiness is the failure to meet expectations. It's your job—together with your team—to make the integration of old and new (or the replacement of old with new) as smooth and painless as possible for both sides. Your aim must be to create good feelings of accomplishment and kudos for a job done well, among both the user team and your own. Those expectations will, of course, be the ones that you set during the early part of the sales process, so bear that in mind when you are describing the business benefits and value proposition on which you closed the deal.

The customer's board members will be looking at the realization of business benefits as their priority, throughout the project. It will probably be necessary for your team to be reminded that the user's senior management will focus their attention on measuring the business improvements. They will know that measuring them makes them happen. That means your own team will need to be properly briefed on these expectations and to be seen as part of the team making those measurements and achieving those benefits. Benefits come from exploitation by the system users. Smart management will know that installing the new solution or technology achieves nothing on its own—they will not expect the supplier of the technology to deliver the business benefits. It should be your aim to be seen as *part of their* team that will produce the expected results. Skeptics and others in the user base will be saying "show me"; it will be up to you to have planned in advance how to do that. Take this as a positive statement of need, rather than a negative challenge. Include in your implementation plan specific points at which you can show the benefits of the new solution over the old.

Interview With Kenton Turner by Tom Cairns

Kenton is currently Chief Technology Officer of BPD Zenith Global Group, with responsibility for Europe, North America, and Asia Pacific. His company remit is to deliver IoT- and AI-based asset management solutions across all business and industry sectors. His technical and commercial knowledge of infrastructure, middleware, and applications, gained over 25 years in the IT industry, provides the real-world experience required to know how solutions are created and delivered effectively.

TC: Based on your extensive in-depth experience, what do you feel is the key factor in delivering to the customer his desired solution and business outcome?

KT: *The thing I would like to get across as you see changes in modern day business and sales is the importance of pre-sales and post-sales technical personnel being engaged as part of the sales team in the early stage of the sales cycle and process. Having a technical person understanding the customer requirements along with the salesperson working as a team is critical. Once the commercial aspects are complete and the deal is done, the successful handover to the delivery teams and the post-sales teams are the critical success factors. If that is done well and you get consistency throughout the sale and delivery cycles, then you end up with a happy customer.*

TC: What are the pivotal moments, the critical bits?

KT: *It's getting in and engaging early. In my experience the salesperson should work with the pre-sales technical architect. A relationship develops. The technical pre-salesperson gets to know the seller. You become a double act. This means that, when you leave the potential customer, you don't leave unanswered questions. The salesperson will understand the commercial and business issues. The pre-sale techie is listening for the little "gotchas," the little things that are going to make a real difference. The techie will understand his own portfolio and how it maps to the customer's business demands. When you return to the client you can talk to them in their language. You don't talk about your product features; you talk about how it applies to their business. That is the strength of a good sales and pre-sales combination.*

We are starting to see more technically orientated salespeople doing the pre-sales job. The salespeople are now doing more technical demonstrations to show how the product works. The more complex the product, the more senior the client you are engaging, then the subject matter expert needs to come in. Working as a team, the sales, pre-sales and delivery team who are mapping into the support side will provide complete consistency all the way through. This teamwork is how you get a good customer.

TC: In today's business world, how is this all pulled together effectively?

KT: *It's just having the capacity across the team. You either have subject matter experts or not. It depends on your product portfolio. If you are a single product vendor, your salespeople should be able to answer all the technical questions, deal with the commercial issues and demonstrate the product. If you are selling complex or multiple solutions to the customer, then I think you need more skill sets. This is the person who generates the sale, understands the commercial relationship, understands the customers business, gets under the skin of all that, and looks at it as a workable solution.*

An important fact today is that, nine times out of ten, there is no single vendor of the required solution. There are multiple technologies coming together, in which case you need that architect type approach that is going to help you understand that. The successful projects that I have worked on as a technical person in the field as a pre-sales architect is when I have then formed a relationship with the other two or three vendors and presented a single front to the client.

The complexity of the solutions required today with, for example, software as a service delivery, cloud delivery, mobile technology, etc. drives the customers today to ask for an integrated solution to their business problems. The opportunity today is for those sales organizations that can integrate multiple vendor technology to meet the customer's needs.

TC: Given that complexity, how do sales organizations deal with the increasingly virtual selling and business world? What is the real challenge now?

KT: *Well, the technology has helped. For example, the virtual technology we have today allows us to have multiple stakeholders and multiple* *vendors on at the same time with break out functions. Though the same principles of providing the solution via the team still apply.*

TC: At what stage do you need to go from multiple virtual meetings to face to face?

KT: *There is an example I had recently. A UK client. A broad business problem requiring a broad solution with multiple stakeholders. A large opportunity with the full tender process. Multiple bidders and proposals. Huge amount of documentation and lots of sessions. We would get point by point calls on Zoom to answer a question with a specific response. Often, we would go through a demo virtually. When we moved to the last two or three potential suppliers, the customer wanted face to face meetings. In the room we had the customer with three decision makers, three department heads and various stakeholders. We had our sales account team, technical team, implementation, delivery and support team in the room. We all got round the table. That meeting was when you started to see people sparking off one another with innovative ideas and solutions. You don't get that in virtual environments. There is something about face to face interaction in a room. For example, one of the stakeholders jumps up and, off script on the whiteboard, starts to describe where he thinks they want to go and what he wants us to do. We all chipped in and suggested ideas. The result was we significantly increased the size of the opportunity and the scope of what we could achieve for the client in that meeting. A signed contract quickly followed.*

I believe that would not have happened virtually. We needed all the different stakeholders physically in that room together face to face at that stage in the sale.

TC: What would you say you have learned about managing the customer relationship before and after the sale that are the critical and pivotal parts?

KT: *The biggest single thing, and it may seem basic, is effective communication. It's about talking to people and making sure you get a regular contact point and having something valuable to discuss. Whether that is via a virtual medium or face to face depends on what you want or need to achieve. Regular communication after the sale is critical. Too many people will deliver the sale, have implementation people do their bit, then* *everyone moves on to the next project, leaving the customer behind, still dealing with his problems. Consistency of continued client contact going forward is critical. That is a key account management skill.*

If you have lots of small accounts, then organizations tend to sell and move on. There is no ongoing account management. If you are in the business of providing integrated enterprise solutions, then the salesperson must maintain the relationship with those client accounts. There will be ongoing business. It's a balance.

TC: What is the most important part of the account management relationship?

KT: *Trust. For example, if your solution or service does not fit the client's needs, then you need to advise them of that and be open with them. You might lose the sale today, but you will gain a customer for the future.*

TC: Have you any final thoughts?

KT: *You need to have that trusted consistent contact point throughout the sales cycle. The sales cycle does not end when you get a contract. The end of the contract is in fact the beginning of phase two of the same sales cycle. What we are seeing more and more today is industry-based solutions selling that requires industry-based knowledge. There are a set of common factors in each industry, and the better the seller can articulate that and show deep knowledge and understand how business needs interact with everything else then that can differentiate you as a business.*

Deeply experienced subject matter experts combined with sellers (or alternatively more technically competent sellers) is the best model. Senior decision makers who are technical want to talk to equally knowledgeable people. That level of pre-sales skill tends to get missed and can be very costly to the sales organization. Don't underestimate the ability of the technical community and its value to the potential customer. Get the technical team into the sale as early as possible. It's not just selling which matters, it's about selling the right product for the right purpose with the right technology.

If users feel wary and nervous about using what is new to them, you should intensify your preparation and training schedule, together with the user management team. If there is some resistance to the changes that you will be bringing about, you will need to address this and remove it as best you can, as early as you can, otherwise they will not exploit the system effectively or achieve the planned business benefits. In an extreme situation, you may even experience a degree of virtual sabotage from those in the company who never wanted to change from the status quo. You never want to hear someone say "I told you this wouldn't work"! Recognize that, in addition to the expected benefits, there may be other positives that will emerge as the capability of the new system becomes better understood. In Chapter 8, we look at how you can go still further on this path by jointly enhancing the new system to achieve unexpected additional benefits.

Whatever your product or solution, it is likely that the implementation and use of it will involve changes in the user's company or their way of working. Your implementation team's understanding of what that means for each particular user should be sufficiently deep for you to feel confident that your solution is not only being used correctly but also enabling your user to apply best practice in that specific industry. They will also be working with a new supplier—you—who has sold them on the business benefits that working with you will bring (as discussed in Chapter 4). It is generally accepted that an astonishing 70 percent or more of all major change initiatives fail to deliver on time, on budget, to the specification that was planned and anticipated. Your objective is to be the supplier and strategic partner that ensures you and your customer are part of the successful 30 percent.

Experience and research have shown that B2B vendors show a reasonable level of competence in getting their new product, solution, or system installed. As we have discussed previously, the plans for a smooth installation—including ironing out or eliminating incompatibilities and ensuring that any lack of new skills is solved—are part of the best sales plans, early on. But your new customer organization is likely to be experiencing challenging changes in every aspect of their business. To remain efficient, to be competitive, to gain market share, and ultimately to satisfy their shareholders, they have to make your solution work alongside many others, so they are under pressure, no matter what their area of business. Your earlier segmentation work (see Chapter 1) will have helped you to learn, to understand, and to empathize with the unique challenges faced by a player in that particular industry. That almost certainly helped you to get the deal and will now help you to empathize with your new users.

But it is the user, not you, who will have to ensure that any installation drives the planned business changes that justified the investment.

Your route to developing a long-term, mutually profitable relationship relies on your being able to help that to happen. It may seem a stretch too far to take on the responsibility—even if only in part—to initiate real business change in your customer's organization, because the most often cited reason is the failure in *behavior* change.

> *Your most unhappy customers are your greatest source of learning.*
> Bill Gates, Co-Founder, Microsoft Corporation, Founder,
> The Gates Foundation

Implementation Management Associates (IMA) listed what their research and experience had found to be the main reasons that *installation* did not lead to successful *implementation*, including:

- Projects are poorly defined and metrics for success are not commonly understood.
- Users don't adopt new processes or accept new tools and methods, so operational efficiencies aren't realized.
- Resistance generated from the degree of work disruption is covert, unmanaged, and slows down change.
- Leaders at all levels don't take an active role in change implementation or accept accountability for implementation success.
- Use of multiple approaches for enterprise-wide change reinforces "silo" mentality.
- Organizations are seduced by the frenetic activity of project teams—unfocused "busy work" masks a lack of progress.
- Organizations confuse *installation* with *implementation* and therefore declare success too early.

We are assuming, for the sake of this section, that the major sale your company made puts you in a position to be a business-critical partner to the user organization. In this case, it is not sufficient for you—representing a vendor that has committed major resources to securing a deal and has put your reputation on the line—to designate these failings as "their problem." The difference between a business that gains and maintains long-term and mutually beneficial relationships with the world's leading companies and one that does not is that they do *not* walk away from giving follow-up work as much attention as the sales and marketing that got the deal in the first place. Simply getting your product or solution into the building is not enough.

Mark Robinson, one of our expert interviewees, recommends the appointment of a "Client Adoption Officer" whose role from a very early stage is to focus on how the client will use the product/service to deliver value/benefit and change. This individual can lead that team and be the key liaison between them and the user base (see Figure 8.1 in the next chapter).

The best companies recognize their obligation—their duty of care, if you will—to their customers to achieve a successful implementation, even when the mechanics of doing so go far beyond the product or solution that they have sold. What often happens is that the vendor project team go their separate ways on the "go-live" date, no matter what the actual state of play, and the customer is left to fend for itself.

What does success look like? Some elements are obvious: the project needs to be on time, under or on budget, with all technical and business objectives met. The IMA would add that "all human objectives" also need to have been met. Your customers will be more demanding than ever, as their own customers become more demanding of them. Enthusiasm is infectious, but sometimes you will encounter some degree of failure at this stage, so knowing how to keep things positive while correcting a problem is yet another essential sales support skill. Some have been heard to say that customer service is the new sales—an exaggeration, but the point is well taken (Figure 7.1).

Figure 7.1 Secure the deal but cement the relationship

What If There's a Problem?

> *It takes months to find a customer, seconds to lose one.*
> Vince Lombardi, American football player, coach, and executive

You have been tested in every way, possibly through rigorous competitive evaluation and a trial period (see Chapter 6), so you expect a smooth post-sales experience. But with highly stressed, fast-moving businesses, things can go wrong. What potential stumbling blocks are there and how can you tackle them?

Let's look at some examples:

What can go wrong	How you can fix it
A radically new user management team arrives. The people you had the relationship with are gone	Treat this as an opportunity to be regarded as part of their induction team. Get your introductions early to make sure that you and your firm are seen as part of the future, not of the past
Poor financial performance forces your user to curtail the planned installation or cut back on your services	Be part of the solution. Quickly understand the extent of the problem and do whatever you can to help your customer to meet reduced budgetary levels. Devise a new payment plan or extend credit terms, for example
A hitherto unforeseen technical problem emerges with your product	Ensure that you investigate and define the problem early. Assuming it's fixable, give your customer a definite but realistic plan and timetable to put things right
There is a clash of personalities between your installation and support team and the customer's people	Investigate thoroughly and impartially to understand what has happened, as far as you can. Don't assign blame, just mediate, report to user management candidly and honestly, reassign your people if necessary, and move on as quickly as possible
The performance review is not positive	Act quickly. Get the full details and get in front of the customer management team to understand where the problems lie. Produce an action plan that is agreed from top to bottom and communicate, communicate, communicate

The customer made an investment based on what they believed the ROI would be, as you enthusiastically told them. Proving it, even after the contract has been filed away, remains an essential part of the sales job.

Implementation: The Key to ROI

We discussed in Chapter 4 the extent that you may well have gone to in promising or guaranteeing that, together, you and the customer will help the company to realize the business benefits and the ROI of which your solution is capable. This ROI comes only with full use of your solution by the users. The best project managers will have already planned how to use your solution to achieve the optimum payback, operationally as well as financially. Perhaps, Mark Robinson's suggestion of a "Client Adoption Officer," would be better titled "Customer Success Manager"! This is the person, as the title would clearly suggest, who will work with the internal project manager to ensure that the promised business benefits are realized through efficient use of your new solution.

This is when you will need the attention to detail and relationship management skills that make the difference between this being the start of a beautiful friendship or the beginning of a customer support and relationship nightmare. In this model, regular communication, between your project manager and his or her opposite number in the customer business, assumes very high importance. Both of these individuals will probably need to be particularly careful that promised resources remain in place as the installation of your solution moves to full implementation within the business. Make no mistake, this is, once again, a key element of the complete sales process. Success here is the difference between a one-off sale and a long-term, profitable relationship.

What now constitutes success will be different from the installation phase. The users of your product solution will now become the focus of your attention, not those with a budget to buy it. This phase is more of a challenge, because it's even harder for the vendor to control than the pre-sale and installation ones. Your installation manager and the team now need to be skilled in becoming accepted as part of the customer's own team, understanding and being focused on the least disruptive way to integrate what you have sold into the customer's new way of working.

Of course, the vendor cannot be too intrusive; this would not be welcome. The internal implementation manager is in charge. His or her team is going to be asked by the users why changes are happening and what is now expected of them. Your team is there to provide the answers and the support for the customer's team, to be formal and informal reinforcements for successful implementation. It is essential that all parties maintain enthusiasm to move to what everyone must be convinced is an improved solution. Your team is still selling! It is likely that the customer team will have been given a clear message about the necessity to succeed and the dim view that would be taken if that success—and the promised payback—is not achieved. The vendor team needs to be clear about that also. The IMA (*ibid*) uses the term "blended plan" to describe how the human and technical sides of the implementation should run together, to ensure minimum disruption to the business and the highest chance of success.

At some stage, there will be a formal review of the extent to which your solution has helped the company to achieve its intended business benefits and the value that you promised. You will probably not be able to control this, but you must be a part of it. To sit passively awaiting the results is not an option. Ideally, earlier on in the sales process you will have suggested a review format as part of your value proposition (see Chapter 4). The best of these has a rolling review approach, so that any problems that occur are found and dealt with early on, rather than festering until they emerge as critical at a quarterly or six-monthly assessment. Your objective—you are still selling—at such a review is to use it as a platform to expand the implementation. Customer Division A—where the implementation has been judged a success—becomes a reference site, in effect, to help sell the solution to Customer Division B. Every corporation is different, but it could be that, in your customer's firm, departments, divisions, or countries have a high degree of autonomy over their investment in your kind of solution. If this is the case, Division A's happy users become your most effective salespeople. If senior management people have seen positive results, they will support you, so form a sales team and plan with them on how to extend the benefits that they have seen. Make them heroes in the wider business: innovators, pioneers, progressives, however they wish to be perceived. If possible, use their own scheduled internal meetings to make your pitch. Leverage your trusted insider position to the hilt.

Most big corporations have subsidiary and associate businesses with whom they have a particularly close relationship. Get your marketing team to investigate how far that applies to this customer and whether your solution is relevant to them. You have great industry credentials behind you now and an undeniable authenticity as a trusted partner to the corporation. Marketing can target the associated businesses and begin contact and information flow to get your content in front of their buyers. It's time to exploit this customer success story.

Exploitation

Is this too harsh a description of wanting to drive hard for more business from an existing customer? I don't believe that it is. You have worked hard to get this far and now, with your customer's help, you can exploit your success—and their realization of the benefits that you have provided—to secure more business. The most obvious instrument is that of the *reference site*. In the earlier part of the marketing and sales process, as described in our earlier chapters, backing up your claims to being able to provide a workable and highly beneficial solution to your customer was an essential element of your success. No one wants to be a guinea pig, unless you are pitching a new technology that early adopters are eager to be the first to use, as Geoffrey Moore's "Crossing the Chasm (*ibid*)" explains. A buyer wants to get some assurance that "people who are like me" have proven the benefits that you claim. The reference account is at the core of this. Your PR effort will undoubtedly have broadcast your win of this visibly important marquee account (see Chapter 1) and included the user story in your content (see Chapter 4), but you can go further.

It's back to the old principle of "show and tell." Nothing can be more reassuring for a cautious potential buyer than to talk with an industry equivalent who is facing the same challenges as him or her every day. If they can show the benefits that they have achieved with your product or solution, then all the better. This has to be handled sensitively, but you will almost certainly find that your user advocates will be eager to show how they have benefited their business by dealing with you. Agree a mutually acceptable schedule or number of appointments and the preferred method of hosting your prospects. Be sensitive to the use of your own users' time. Some recommend always being present when the user and prospect meet; others the opposite. You have to decide for yourself what is appropriate. Can you reward your user for his or her help? Again, a sensitive topic. Personal reward will normally be taboo because of company policy, but perhaps you can offer additional or discounted product or service, providing more benefit for the business and by which the user advocate can justify their time to their management. Many vendors find that the creation of a user group—made up of members of the customer management and user teams of your products or services—is a very good additional way to keep in touch with them and to encourage the shared positive experience of dealing with you.

Perhaps we can move the enthusiastic user from a position of reference to *advocacy*: from passive to active support of your sales and marketing. As before, company guidelines and policies will dictate how far you can go with this, but you may be surprised what you can get. If pitched correctly, the effort of your user in advocating your solution can be used *by them* to promote their own forward-looking attitudes. They will be pleased to show themselves as innovators to their own shareholders, industry colleagues, and potential employees. Make it easy for them to do it: provide templates for press releases, case studies, and presentations for their use. Make them feel good about being your business partner and glad to be showing what they have achieved with your help. As ever, be sensitive to their internal politics, making sure that you do not upset their own marketing department.

With the most willing reference customer, you can go still further. As your user does their own sales and marketing to acquire new accounts and to increase their sale, it may be the case that your solution has become part of their USP. If, for example, your scheduling and loading services were the deciding factor in the deal, providing the real value behind your truck sales, then surely the efficiency of their own services is a key selling point for your freight services customer. Gain some extra visibility and credentials by proposing joint marketing activity. Together, you can create even more compelling industry-specific content and give even more impressive presentations. It's also another brick in the defensive wall you are building to protect this valuable account from your competition.

That high-visibility partnership is difficult to unwind and is another competitive advantage.

Can you go further still? It is not unusual for users of specialized software solutions, once they are comfortable with the initial implementation, to want to improve upon them. Even the most expert systems integrator (SI) will admit that, sometimes, the user will be better qualified to specify how the solution can be improved. They may well, not, however, be better qualified to do the necessary software surgery. The result is that codevelopment often takes place. The benefit to your company is getting even further embedded with an enthusiastic user of your product who, as a result of the enhancements, will implement the solution on a much broader basis in the company. Further, perhaps to subsidiaries, or to associate companies and more. It is important to formalize developments like this, so that the expectations and commitments on both sides match up as well as they did on the initial agreement. It is very easy to get sucked into an "improvement" cycle that can spiral out of control and suck in an unintended level of resources. Make sure that the benefits are mutual. This level of cooperation is yet another competitive strategy and yet another source of brilliant content. Be sure that you get proper permissions from your user to release to the public any details of what is happening—you may be helping them to build a piece of their own competitive strategy that they want to keep to themselves.

Still further? Sticking with our software solution example, there have been many examples of firms who never saw themselves as solution providers, packaging and taking to market what was previously their internal system. With reference to the comment above, as long as this is not a part of their advantage over their own competitors, why not—as the SI with the experience to do so—help them to do that? Your combined expertise could well be a winner in the marketplace in which you both operate.

An example: one of the world's biggest global energy companies had a substantial in-house systems group. One of its many contributions to the giant group was the development of Kalido, a 3D database application that helped to manage the overwhelming amount of complex research data that they stored and used. Clarity International, a management consultancy working on team building and business process management, saw an opportunity. Specializing in the development and execution of plans for software and systems marketing, Clarity shared the enthusiasm of the energy giant's management team for the advanced Kalido app. They sold the idea to them that, since it was an enormously useful internal tool—but did not play a significantly strategic role—its commercial potential could be exploited. Clarity's expertise in taking new companies and their products into new markets was applied to packaging, positioning, and marketing the database for commercial use. A joint program of recruitment of expert SIs and value-added resellers (VARs) across Europe was the basis of a successful year-long project that saw significant sales and the later spin-off of Kalido as a separate software development company. The customer moved from buyer to partner, with much mutual benefit gained.

As mentioned earlier, this kind of proactive cooperation can sometimes lead to merger or acquisition, as in the case of IBM and PwC.

Summary

We've learned here that the signing of the order, the contract, or the granting of the tender is the beginning of a customer relationship, not an end to it. Like the last disappointing chapter of what was a good book, or the unsatisfactory ending to a film that you have spent two hours watching, poor post-sales installation and support can easily become a bad ending to your sales success. The art of helping your customer to hit the road running can be a difficult one to master, but is worthwhile for any vendor. Watching your product shipping into the customer's premises or seeing your solution being installed is gratifying, but does not signify the end of the sales and account management process. Achieving consistently successful post-sales relationships (see the next chapter) begins with excellence in implementation, securing the relationship in depth throughout the buyer's business. This is a great example of your becoming a marketing and sales business, not just a team. As we have discussed, success at this stage is often driven by every function in your company focusing on the customer's success, playing out those core brand values that got you started.

The Takeaways and Lessons Learned From Chapter 7	Do	Don't
Installation	Be the holder of the expectations for your solution Maintain the intensity of your contact with the user. You are still selling Act fast to solve any problems.	Don't assume that the job is done when your product or solution crosses the buyer's threshold Don't allow "drifting" from the agreed timetable. Everyone needs to see the business benefits as promised, when promised
Implementation	Balance your role as part of the team, both yours and the customer's Appoint a Customer Success Manager if you have the resource to do so. If not, develop a customer success plan that can be managed jointly by others	Don't underestimate the changes that might occur to the individual working lives of those to whom you have sold Don't lose control of the benefits analysis
Exploitation	Actively move the user from passive reference site, through advocacy to partnership	Don't overdo it. The user's prime concern will remain the management and growth of his own business

CHAPTER 8

Post-Sale Strategic Account Management

Overview

By following the interactive and integrated sales and marketing process of the previous seven chapters we have achieved the status of trusted business partner. All that hard work that we went through in the last chapter and those before it, to sell our product or solution, was worth it. It is welcomed and working as intended in the customer's business. Let's now reap the rewards of additional business from our installed base for the long term, by getting right all of the elements described here. This chapter is about managing your very best salespeople—that is, your happy customers.

In this final chapter, we introduce the vital roles of the SAM—strategic account manager or KAM—key account manager, who will produce highly profitable repeat sales. We'll look at becoming embedded as a strategic partner, assessing and realizing future sales opportunities, gaining enthusiastic endorsements and referrals, and fending off the competition by providing a great customer experience (CE). And the benefits here are applicable to organizations large and small. A major practitioner will discuss how they have had success in this area, and we will draw conclusions on how best to make it work.

Customer Account Management— Becoming a Welcome Insider

There are many different facets of the sales function. New business prospecting is hard and many salespeople dislike doing it, no matter how fundamental to the selling job it is. It's regarded as "the sharp end," so managing the targeted sales process and closing the deal tends to get the hero status. But productive large account management (LAM) requires a different set of skills. Such accounts are sometimes called key accounts, and therefore have a key account manager (KAM), and most often as strategic accounts, which require strategic account manager (SAM)— different acronyms: same job, no matter whether that is a global corporation or a much smaller business that is still a "large account" to you!

If you want to meet your most ambitious revenue and profitability targets from your best and biggest customers, then you must focus your limited resources on where they can produce the best returns. A surprising number of companies have policies based on maximizing profit from every customer, even though some of them should be lightly managed for top-line product sales revenue, some for broader solution and services value, and others should be heavily invested in, to build future competitive advantage. One of the quickest ways to go bankrupt is to overservice and "delight" *all* of your customers!

There will be recurring opportunities for repeat sales in any size of customer, of course, but the smart management of your biggest revenue providers can transform your company's fortunes by providing a regular stream of income from a known and friendly source. And don't forget those competitors! They will not have given up on their own attempts to get business from that precious account of yours. Your SAM plan has to be both proactive and protective. It's a well-accepted statistic (originally researched by Miller and Heiman within their large account management process, LAMP) that five percent of your customers bring in 50 percent of your revenue; 20 percent of them will be the overall source of 80 percent of your revenue. I haven't seen the comparative *expense* statistic in formal terms, but my own experience suggests that 25 percent of your customers will take up 75 percent of your support resources, paid for or otherwise. We'll discuss that later in this chapter.

Your SAM task is to make the difficult assessment as to which of those customers will bring further rewards and which are—and will continue to be—a drain on your profitability for little or no reward. But don't think exclusively of the size of those accounts or specific revenues earned from them. There is also the understandable element of your not wanting to lose them because of their strategic importance. It could be that a high level of service cost for a particular account is worthwhile because they are, effectively, helping you to improve your product or service. It could be that they are such a bellwether company, highly visible in your chosen target industry or segment, that having them as an account is highly promotable. Or they may have become a useful strategic partner, as described in Chapter 7. Losing them would be damaging to your reputation, so you don't want that to happen.

In Chapter 1, we looked at how to find, decide upon, and carve out your target niche. In Chapter 3, we put our efforts into making sure that we discovered and understood the hierarchy, the bureaucracy, and the buying process of each of our prospects, to win their business—a business that we understood because of our attention to detail in working through our market segmentation. Now that they are our customers, rather than forego that work, we need to intensify it. The lead major account manager needs to understand those accounts at least as well as those who work there, if not better. Malcolm McDonald, Emeritus Professor at the Cranfield School of Management in the United Kingdom, says in his "On Account Management" that "It's important to understand your Key Accounts better and in more depth than you understand your own organization." His KAM evaluation format is a useful tool. His categorizations derived from that analysis go from "manage for sustained earnings," through "invest in improving your competitive position (possibly at the expense of maximizing profits from them)," to "manage for cash and minimize costs."

> *I find that managing the customer relationship, post-sale, is a valuable skill that many newer businesses lack, even though their customer base can be by far their best source of creating higher customer value by "expanding the pond they fish in."*
>
> Chris Raman, serial venturepreneur, Founder,
> Ventures4growth, Belgium

Critical Changing Relationships

What about the people involved? Now that you are an insider, your regular interactions with your typical major account should be quite different—and driven by different members of your team.

I would categorize your ongoing relationships to be with three distinct groups of people:

- The customer project team—the user's people who were and continue to be responsible for bedding in your solution. They comprise the installers and the implementers—see Chapter 7 for a discussion on the differences. They are going to be the most familiar with your product and be the ones to whom you must ensure that your customer service people provide the very best support. This team may well be disbanded as optimum implementation is achieved. Your customer support manager (CSM) should be in charge.
- The customer user base—the company employees with whom you will probably not have had a relationship previously, but who are likely the most affected by the implementation of your solution. At the departmental management level, they

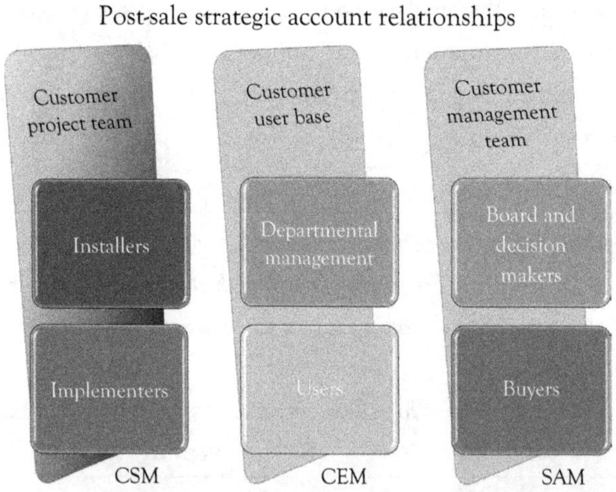

Post-sale strategic account relationships

Figure 8.1 Customer and seller relationships change during the process. The customer support manager (CSM), customer experience manager (CEM), and strategic account manager (SAM), each plays a role

will have been responsible for maintaining the efficiency of their department while managing the changeover to your solution at the hands of their team members. Those users' jobs will have been affected to some extent, perhaps to a very large extent, by what you have sold to the company. A highly skilled customer experience manager (CEM) should be your key point of contact, here.

• The customer management team—you took the customer's money on the premise that you could help them to realize specific business benefits (see Chapter 5) for their firm. The board and other senior decision makers have a personal vested interest in ensuring that those business benefits are realized. Your continuous task—best handled by the original strategic account manager (SAM) who made the sale—is to keep them comfortable with the decision they made and to maintain the positive relationship between your businesses. They and the buyers, who will potentially be a very disparate group, possibly including a specialist negotiator (see Chapter 6), remain very important to you. Your competitors will be targeting them continuously.

Though the managers will likely be the same, the buyers of your solution—or at least some of the buying group or committee that you had to sell to—will probably no longer be those with whom your time is best spent. The users of your solution described above, at any level, can now be cultivated to be your allies and champions.

Long term relationships with public sector accounts can be very lucrative, but it takes expert and diligent strategic account management skills to preserve those relationships. In government sectors like defence, redeployments of senior personnel can be frequent, so account managers must stay in regular touch with procurement teams. Those redeployments can also be positive for the account manager, as those with whom empathy has been established can make effective internal recommendations for new business opportunities in their new location.

Nichola Thurston-Smith, former Head of Public Sector
Strategic Accounts, Microsoft

It should be emphasized at this point that the thinking here can be applied to any size of vendor or customer and their respective teams. The long-term gains in prestige and lower-cost incremental sales can—relative to the size of the business—be greater for an SME than for a larger firm!

Judi Edwards in Conversation With Kimball Bailey

Judi Edwards has spent many years both buying and selling complex services and solutions. She has been a serial director of information technology (Global CIO for Burberry, CIO Europe for Levi Strauss, and IT director for jewelry chain Signet), becoming a "poacher turned gamekeeper" after her 11 years at IBM, which in turn she joined after nine years of management in the retail sector. Additionally, she spent a further eight years at Gartner as VP in the Executive Partner program, advising and coaching CIOs and IT leaders—a role where she was able to help clients with advice on strategic procurement and benefit realization and where her own strong relationships often led to the reintroduction of the Gartner sales team.

So, having worked on both sides, does she observe similarities between the behavior of a successful seller and a successful buyer?

Absolutely, says Judi. *A buyer has got to have absolute clarity of the outcome he or she expects from the service or solution provided, and a successful seller has got to share that clarity of vision—and deliver results that are fully aligned with it.*

It should go without saying that the seller must be able to deliver those results—and it's not worth pushing a solution that you know isn't going to work. It just wastes any relationship that has been developed. If you sell something to a client who is unhappy with the outcome or who doesn't realize the benefit that he or she was expecting from the investment, you will be bad-mouthed in the industry—which can be an awfully small world. You certainly won't get a second chance, and remedial costs are likely to be penal. And of course, a sales process that encourages bad sales behavior— even as an unintended consequence—is flawed.

Judi talks about the industry being a "small world."

Very much so, she says. *I don't necessarily expect a salesperson to be an expert in my industry, but I do expect some basic knowledge and interest. That is all part of building a relationship between buyer and seller, a relationship that can and should be invested in and which makes the whole process personal.*

Any idiot can follow a process, she laughs—and she knows; she has been on enough sales courses and delivered them herself. *A basic training scheme will tell you how to fill out a template, but it won't teach you how people work, or what hacks them off. What is difficult to teach or to acquire is the "soft stuff." So, while IBM's sales school was pretty proscriptive in terms of process, the success of attendees was measured on soft skills; they were differentiated on their adaptability and their ability to build a relationship. These soft skills usually equate to what was the most value to me as a buyer, and the hardest to articulate when it comes to defining a successful seller. But once I have a relationship with someone, a relationship that will cross over multiple organizations (both mine and that of the seller), and once they have built a track record and I can trust them, that is 90 percent of the job done—for both parties.*

Judi says that the soft skills are hard to define and articulate. Can she have a go?

I've mentioned a degree of industry knowledge. Do some research, enough at least to be able to appreciate the context and competitive environment of business change, and to demonstrate an understanding of the reason for the desired outcomes. It's a balance: some knowledge will help you to open up the conversation. If you are an expert, don't patronize; if you aren't, don't continually state the obvious or try to teach granny to suck eggs.

Then a really good salesperson will work in partnership with the buyer at a very early stage, looking at—and quantifying—the benefits that the buyer is looking for and making the solution part of the internal business case for change. So, help your sponsor—the buyer with whom you have a relationship—to sell your solution on to the CEO or CFO. I'm not talking about a free consultancy project to do all of this, but enough to make us feel that we are on the same side. That way, it becomes much more about influencing than just about selling.

And simply keeping in touch, including—or even "especially"—when clients change company. This gives us an extensive lifecycle of relationship. I used the same small team of advisory consultants to help me quantify, independently, what I had in place when I became CIO of a new company. This wasn't a service I was looking for more than once with each company I was with! But they had demonstrated competence and had kept in touch well and sensitively, including when they had also moved organizations. I have worked with large consultancies whose golf budget was bigger than the entire turnover of this smaller firm—but the smaller firm got the business.

So how do you manage the relationship throughout the "life cycle"?

Well, largely it is about consistency. I would usually want a long-term relationship with the supplier, so it's not just about selling, but implementation and proper follow-through. I get cross when the internal procedures of the seller company get in the way of that relationship. Too many firms have an "account management" process that actually reduces the quality of the relationship with individuals. I don't expect to see the sales director if the sales director adds no value, but it is worse seeing him or her only once when brought in supposedly to add "gravitas" to close a deal, and then never again.

The relationship is about trust and effective dialogue.

And while it is true that people do prefer to buy from people they get on with, and that chemistry is indeed important, that doesn't transcend the quality of the results.

As a buyer, does Judi have any pet hates?

It is so easy to pick out (and reject) a "cookie cutter" response, where a previous bid has been cut and pasted—sometimes without even changing the name of the company the bid was originally developed for. For the buyer, it is hugely irritating when the work you have done to develop an "agenda" for a supplier presentation is not followed; for the seller, it is lazy, disrespectful and a waste of time. It is far better not to bid than to do a bad bid. And seeing people do that is a pet hate as a sales manager too—it just negates the trust that may have been built up before that point. So, if the seller has produced a request for proposal, agenda or other tender document in a specific order, please follow it. It sounds simple, it sounds obvious—so why don't bidders do it?

Don't pad out a bid unnecessarily. Sorry, this may sound a bit "101" but we all learned about features, advantages and benefits very early in basic training. So why don't sellers focus on the real "a-ha!" content of the bid—the benefits?

And a pet hate as a seller is when the buyer doesn't make it clear what the priorities are and hence what the selection criteria are. Again, if you know you can't win it, why waste everyone's time? It's about having an effective focus—as buyer and as seller—on achieving the desired outcomes. And explaining why a seller has decided to "no bid" can only serve to increase levels of trust for the next time.

So, Judi strongly believes that successful selling—and often successful buying—comes from developing and maintaining a good relationship. Does she have a few key things that are relevant to remember whether you are a "beginner" on the sales cycle or an experienced seller?

The basics are important and remain so—just because the principles are "101" doesn't make them any the less valid. Trust—both ways, as buyer and seller. Don't make assumptions—again, as buyer or seller. Ask good questions but, more importantly, listen to the answers. Make sure that both parties benefit from any meeting in some way. Focus on what you can win—don't fritter away a relationship on something you can't. Basic courtesy—timekeeping is one thing to think about, but also do your research. More than once I have been the only woman in the room and the salesperson has therefore assumed that I was not the senior buyer present. You have to laugh.

And is there one thing above everything else?

Just one thing? Well, as a seller, link your solution firmly to the benefits that the buyer is looking for. As a buyer, articulate those benefits and make it easy for all parties to get to the right solution.

And this is all about good practice—in many ways it doesn't matter whether you are selling or buying at a strategic level or a commodity level. In all cases, you can still differentiate through benefit, especially if you find out what is most important to the buyer. Even when one might think that price is the key driver—and when it may be—there is almost always something that can make your solution stand out from the crowd.

In *Bag the Elephant*, Steve Kaplan talks about "recruiting great champions," describing what makes one of those as someone:

- Motivated by what's best for the business: makes decisions based on what's good for their employer, not on politics. Respected by superiors: management looks to them for solid business recommendations.
- Socially networked: people like a champion, so their endorsement carries extra weight and cachet.
- Able to navigate the company to get things done: they know how to sell ideas internally.
- Cut from the same cloth as you: you have chemistry because you share the same business philosophy, work ethic, or background. (See Kimball Bailey's quote in Chapter 3.)
- Willing to give credit rather than protect turf: they must feel that your success and the success of the deal reflect well upon him or her.

These apply at the initial sales stage, but are even more relevant for you once you are the incumbent supplier. It is likely that your champion was a member of that internal team that evaluated your offering positively in the first place (see Chapter 6), so the ongoing success of the project is in their interest. Dependent upon their sphere of influence in the company, it is worth involving your champion in the early stages of any follow-on business proposal that you may be planning to make. His or her understanding of the internal company procedures, timetables, hierarchy, and language will be a great help to you in persuading your customer to allocate more of their budget to your products or services.

> *The rapid and continued adoption of ABM programs will require significant investment in technology, media, data and employees.*
>
> Gartner

It's therefore no surprise to learn that account-based marketing (ABM) has been the fastest-growing go-to-market topic among Gartner

Technology Solution Provider (TSP) clients in the past year. The technology has improved and expanded. The new functionality (through both acquisition and development among developers and suppliers) has improved ROI and increased buy-in from marketing, account executives, and others. As a result, in their Magic Quadrant study on the area, Gartner estimates that the market grew at 29 percent during 2020 and more than 35 percent in 2021.

I would expect other industry sectors to reflect this. ABM offers a structured methodology for finding, engaging, and selling to multiple individuals in key accounts. As programs mature, coordination between sales and marketing is likely to increase, while tools for account selection, planning, engagement, and reporting will improve further. Existing major customers become a marketing segment in microcosm, wherein your targeting can be even more precise and be backed up by insider knowledge that you didn't previously possess.

> *Account based marketing is simply that instead of fishing with nets, we're fishing with spears. And for bigger fish.*
>
> Matt Heinz, President, Heinz Marketing

But man cannot live on the best 20-pounders alone. Five-pound fish can grow into 20-pounders. As the LAMP (*ibid*) process points out, your next 25 percent of revenue is likely to come from the next 20 percent of customers and the following group will contain the potential to grow to become part of the 20 percent or even the "core" five percent. As Henry Ford (a reasonably successful businessman) famously said: "It's OK to have all your eggs in one basket as long as you really do watch that basket!" The caution here is to allocate resources appropriately, while not ignoring potential where it may lie outside of your customer base. A large portion of the resources we're talking about are the skilled people from your company. The SAM function is not necessarily best handled by even the best frontline sales management team or individual. What was a prospecting, hunting, sales-closing exercise has now become a project management one. As a strategic supplier to your customer, your solution will now be the subject—at least in part—of board-level discussions. It may be that a senior manager or director with the relevant expertise from your company is now the better person to be involved at this top level. He or she should strive to be at those board meetings. To be accepted as a truly strategic partner, rather than a supplier, is a worthy KPI of your success in managing the account. I have seen this achieved to the point where someone in this position is made part of the evaluation team for new supplier bids, actually assessing the worth of a potential competitor's offering. Get to that point and then you really know you've become an insider!

A Profitable Relationship— The Continuous Business Cycle

Selling is hard, but so is buying, and both are continuous. We discussed the reasons companies buy in Chapter 3 and how to get your solution installed and running at its best in Chapter 7. Your buyers will have breathed a sigh of relief when their decision to go with you and your product or service is vindicated by its company wide adoption and successful use. Now your account plan looks different. It has new goals, concerning customer support, strategic advice, and more. These will not necessarily be numerical and certainly will be longer term than before. You're probably no longer under pressure from a short-term sales target deadline: you're planning with your customer on how to develop both your business and theirs over the next few years. So, your plan is to reposition yourself in your large account from a supplier to a partner. The core of this is to set goals that both you and the customer understand and agree to. This will need to be on an account-by-account basis, as personalization is the route to success. This is not to say that your company should be making commitments to be what it is not, but rather to be coordinated in supporting and developing your solution together with the user. Having left behind the tensions associated with making the sale, you will find that your relationship can be more open and candid. As mentioned above, it might be between different individuals, but you will be able to tune accordingly both your mutually agreed goals and the strategies you develop to achieve them. Remember, you're an insider now and should strive to be treated as such.

It's worth constantly reminding yourself that your customer doesn't want to be "managed," no matter how many times or ways we use that word. As some of our interviewees say in this book, what they want to be is successful and anyone who can help them to be so will get their attention. Let's be blunt: while you're useful, you're useful; when you're not, you're not. Empathy in business is not like personal friendship, although sometimes that will be the result of a long-standing business relationship. Trust is very important: it is not unlikely that your key contact will at some point be under pressure to defend their relationship with you as a supplier and will need your help to maintain your preferred status with his or her firm. Any absence of trust in you, personally, or in the authenticity of your company, its solutions, and ongoing support will see that trust dissipate very quickly. The same applies between any sizes of business and in any industry. Our senior practitioners have all encountered bumps in the road and have had to work hard to smooth the way, as you will have seen by their comments in the interviews. You have to stay useful and be part of the success of the individuals and their company for the long term. Professor Andrew Sturdy discusses this in his extract, next.

Supplier and Buyer Relationships

Contribution by Professor Andrew Sturdy

Professor Sturdy is currently the Research Director at the School of Management at the University of Bristol. His distinguished academic career also includes spells at Warwick and Imperial College Business Schools and the University of Melbourne. His first degree and PhD were at Manchester University; since then, he has published widely on management, and in particular consultancy, where his work is highly cited; he is a critical friend of the industry.

His research has engaged with different aspects of the relationship between suppliers and buyers of consultancy, and this academic rigor supports some of the views expressed elsewhere in this book. For example, Professor Sturdy stresses that effective selling and buying are—as part of timeless tradition—known to be a long game, with specific "rites" and "rituals" associated with both parties. The frequent difficulty of specifying precisely the nature of the service means that people often buy from those with whom they feel affinity, perhaps through education, class, or background, even if this can also bring a risk of being too close or familiar.

Some of Professor Sturdy's conclusions from his paper "Guess Who's Coming to Dinner" focus on how sellers seek to gain increasing levels of information about a buyer and how this shapes the relationship. This is not abuse or bribery, of course, but what used to be considered normal behavior—and still is, in many contexts. The rites of communication and entertainment associated with both the sale and service delivery, and the ongoing relationship that he identifies, are also picked up by Yvette Taminiau in various papers such as "It Looks Like Friendship, But It's Not." These address informal client relationships within "Big 4" accounting and consulting firms and show how informality in business relations continue to create long-term, trust-based relationships, even as professional procurement practices shape the sector.

However damaged in recent years by the interference of a client's compliance department, a relationship between prospective seller and prospective buyer should, indeed must, transcend time periods, and there are specific "rites" that can make that happen. Mike Ames, in an earlier chapter, supports this when he says that a relationship should be nurtured even when the prospective client is not in the "buying zone."

Professor Sturdy shows how successful relationships continue between individuals (or between firms and an individual) even when those individuals change jobs. There is also research on the subject of "networked reputation" or "word of mouth" (Glückler and Armbrüster), whereby this behavior leads to the development of a network. So, for example, a consultant may leave McKinsey to become CEO of a client company, but still remain in the "tribe." This becomes a self-fulfilling closed shop, much more structured than those informal relationships discussed by Mike Ames and Judi Edwards elsewhere in this book.

Professor Sturdy also talks extensively about "knowledge asymmetry" (Lonsdale, Hoque, Kirkpatrick and Sanderson), whereby, for example, in any transaction, the buyer and seller have unequal information. In other words, the seller of an item of goods may know more about the item's true worth than the consumer. Potentially, in this case, a commercially naive consumer might pay more to an opportunistic vendor than the item's actual worth, had they known the full information. At the same time, in professional services such as consulting, client knowledge of the local context can often be crucial to effective service delivery.

As was mentioned earlier, ABM systems are available to help you manage the process, but although the detail is important, you need to keep your eyes on the prize of achieving complete symbiosis with your customer. Your ultimate aim as a true business partner might be to have an improved solution for this industry segment that you and your customer effectively co-market to businesses like theirs: a joint venture. Not every user will want to do this, but some may surprise you with their enthusiasm to do so. A significant number of large companies have developed in-house systems for which they have realized the market potential and, so, become resellers of those systems to companies like themselves. At a lesser but still important level for your company, your user may want to enhance their own reputation as a thought leader and advocate of the solution that you have jointly developed or enhanced. It is a huge competitive advantage for you to be able to articulate your credentials and your own expertise and experience as a supplier of such a solution, with the full and highly visible backing of an industry leader in the segment within which you are selling. This is likely to involve considerable application of resources, so you will need to ensure as far as possible that the payback will achieve the goal that you have set and be worth that investment. Treat the goal, the strategy to achieve it, and your detailed tactical plan of activities as you would any other major business project. This is not a "soft" or nonspecific objective you are setting: it must form part of your expense and revenue forecast, like any other sales or marketing initiative. Establishing this will help to galvanize the appropriate parts of your company behind the account management plan. You will be likely to involve technical support, R&D, finance and other colleagues to make it work, so there must be an understanding that a project like this for a single existing account is worthwhile for the business as a whole. A key "appointment" in your strategic account management team is the project manager, so get that one right! You will need an experienced practitioner for this, someone who can plan, allocate, and manage resources both from your own company and from the user, to achieve the goals that you have set.

The health of any customer relationship is hard to quantify: while many companies rely solely on common metrics, such as sales and profit, to gauge performance, those metrics can mislead. Business relationships, like personal ones, evolve continuously. Your company must not only assess a relationship's current state but also anticipate potential ups and downs. And, most important but least understood, not all CRM efforts work equally well in all stages of a relationship, but many do. Making a big investment in a customer-specific product line, as Corning did with Apple, might help realize the full potential of a promising partnership. Corning makes Gorilla Glass, which is in the screen of every iPhone, and the two companies have been together since the iPhone's introduction in 2007. Each has made extensive commitments to the other, after Steve Jobs agreed to buy from Corning if they used a new, expensive, and largely unproven technique to strengthen the glass for iPhone screens. Corning's CEO, Wendell Weeks, initially hesitated but took the risk—taking six months to achieve the required standard—to get the massive deal with Apple. Apple responded in kind by making a $200M research and development investment in Corning and its plant in Harrodsburg, Kentucky, that specializes in making cutting-edge glass.

Zhang, Watson and Palmatier found that customer relationships can evolve through four states, which they defined as *transactional, transitional, communal, or damaged.* In each of these states, through which customers can move in either direction, your sales and marketing efforts have to be tailored appropriately.

The *transactional* state is where most relationships begin and where most remain. Transactional relationships are the most common, and many relationships never mature beyond this stage. Some customers simply prefer conducting business at arm's length and do not want, or have a policy of not having, deeper entanglement. This is particularly the case with the public sector, where formalized procurement is prevalent. These accounts can be regarded as needing less ongoing CRM resource. It's an undeveloped relationship with low to medium levels of trust, commitment, dependence, and (from the vendor's point of view) sales. That dictates a watching sales brief, using regular communication and the use of your constantly updated and relevant content (see Chapter 4), designed to maintain a high brand awareness and spark interest in further sales, especially of your newly introduced products and services.

The research findings in this case showed that 60 percent of transactional relationships do deepen, entering the *transitional* state. The understanding by both seller and customer of how to best communicate and cooperate grows; they learn to trust each other and to make greater commitments. They become familiar with each other's corporate cultures and idiosyncrasies, resulting in sales growth for the vendor and the identification of even greater potential. This does, however, take work and careful attention. As the study showed, 40 percent went nowhere further. The most effective way to secure this level of interaction and the possibility of moving to the *communal* state is to appoint a dedicated sales manager (or team) who becomes the conduit for all communication and interaction with the account, taking a proactive approach to seeking further business. This is at the core of the role of the CEM.

Communal relationships produce the highest sales as well as consistent sales growth. These are the kind of accounts that we discussed earlier, comprising a minority of the customer base but a majority of the sales. Communal relationships were found to be the most stable (61 percent remain year to year), but the closeness and mutual reliance meant that transgressions, such as inadvertent neglect of customers or betrayals of trust, are all the more harmful. Again, you can see the similarity to personal relationships. The study found that it is more likely to become *damaged* (21 percent) than merely to slip back to, say, transactional status. Communal customers are typically highly profitable, so managers will want to avoid neglecting them and to give them their full attention. As the study says, the *damaged* state was seen to be marked by customer dependence, but by low levels of trust, commitment, and relational norms. Essentially, you and your customer stop talking to each other. The customer may want to leave, but can't: there's some short-term reliance on a critical part, support, or input. This dependence, though awkward for the customer, represents the potential for saving these relationships. Exiting the damaged state is difficult; 56 percent of the relationships in the study remained stuck here, with low sales growth and poor relations. Previously justifiable support costs may start to look out of proportion to the revenue being generated by the seller, but making the effort to reconcile differences will almost certainly pay off. Putting numbers on this, on average, it costs five times more to acquire a new customer than to keep a current one, and a 5 percent reduction in churn can increase profits by 25 percent or more.

That world of pervasive information that you harnessed and utilized to inform, influence, motivate, and sell to your customer in the first place is still important. Refer back to Chapter 4, Figure 4.2. Your competition will still be wanting to break in, and your customer remains open to influence by all of the available information about your company, your solution, the marketplace that they are in, and what their own competitors are doing. Sorry, but there's no let-up in the necessity to be the funnel and filter to them, so use this to your advantage! Having regular account reviews is a given in SAM. These are to ensure that you have your finger on the pulse of the customer, but also—and it's easy to forget this—to evaluate constantly each customer's net value to your own business. We have just examined a view of the states that a major account may be in, but whatever the stage or state of that relationship, your own profitability must remain paramount. Is the shape of the deal that gained the account with your customer still the one that is appropriate? Of course, you cannot renege on contractual commitments, but it's worth reviewing everything from product and solution pricing to the services that you are providing. As discussed previously, it is all too easy for an account to move from being your largest and most profitable to your most burdensome.

Are you giving away services, for example, in a way and to an extent that, although it initially made sense, has now grown out of proportion? In their examination of this conundrum, Ulaga and Michel ask the question for each service that you provide to your customer at no charge: "Should you bill it, kill it, or keep it free?" One of the easiest ways to increase revenue and increase profitability from an existing account is to make the "free-to-fee" (F2F) transition. This is not an easy conversation to have with your salespeople, distributors, partners, or major accounts, but it is an essential one. Value-based selling (VBS) may have got you the deal in the first place, but did that value you committed to provide involve what has become an overly generous provision of free services? As ever, my advice here is to find out—proactively—what the current situation is. You will need to know if the customer values each of those free services. What may have looked to them as your providing good value for money in the first instance may have become a "freebie" that they take for granted and that is not valued as highly as it once was. It may have reached the point in some cases that you still are incurring the cost for something that is now neither highly valued nor effective, for you or the customer. It can also be the case that your own deliverers of that service have let the standards slip, because the perception has evolved that it's free and therefore worth nothing. This is not a route to maintaining your reputation for excellence in an important account.

In the report mentioned earlier, the authors designate four categories for free services:

1. *Profit drains*, which don't create value for customers and should be abandoned
2. *Distributor delights*, which customers do value but which third parties would do a better job of delivering
3. *Competitive weapons*, which need to be offered for free as strategic differentiators
4. *Gold nuggets*, which can be delivered in-house and for which customers are willing to pay

You cannot categorize your own free services in this or any other way without input from that vital, regular customer survey. Of course, subtlety is the watchword when asking the customer about these things, as you won't want to send the wrong message and initiate resistance. And there will be resistance, on multiple fronts: from the customers, but also from your own salespeople and potentially from partners. Work through your options, what you would like to do, and what the effects would be of "billing it, killing it, or keeping it free." Get your sales, marketing, CSM, CEM, and finance people involved from the beginning of the discussion. If there is to be a change that benefits the business, it must be clearly articulated to all parties involved in making it a success. Once a decision is made, communication needs to be clear, concise, and unambiguous, again, to all parties.

Changing Phases

As time goes on, your strategic account's business and your own company will change. The confidence that you have built up will evaporate quickly if your people, products, pricing, or positioning undergo any substantial change that the customer then hears about from elsewhere. That applies equally to good and to bad news! Similarly, if your customer account undergoes radical change—say, a merger or an acquisition—and you as a supposedly strategic partner hear it on the news, rather than from the CEO, your confidence in your position will—rightly—be considerably undermined. Two-way communication is key. Institute a regular program of information exchange between your company and the account. Don't hold meetings for their own sake—this becomes a burden for the customer—but use the platform of a new product announcement, a change in senior personnel, a major industry or technology advancement, or even a new and relevant research report as a reason to get together. Enhance that reputation that you have built as the go-to guys for filtering the world of information that you all exist in. Add value continually. As we've discussed before, that is a valuable function.

In Chapter 1 and throughout this book, we have recognized the vital ingredient that is your market, industry, and customer knowledge. The broader this is, the more it can form a major advantage for you and your business. Coming into contact with many and varied buyers as you do means that your view of the industry's competitive landscape—the environment in which your customer does business—is likely to be better than that of the customers themselves. As Dawar and Vandenbosch described in their *MIT Sloan Management Review* article "The Seller's Hidden Advantage," sellers know things about their customers' businesses that the customers don't know and can't find out on their own, yet value immensely.

> *This isn't a matter of divulging confidential aspects of clients' businesses to their competitors. The challenge is to translate an industrywide perspective into knowledge that customers can use. Companies that can do this successfully reduce their customers' costs or operating risks and are rewarded in turn with customer loyalty, pricing flexibility or both.*
>
> Dawar and Vandenbosch

Your customers are embroiled in running their businesses in demanding circumstances. They rarely have the time or expertise to measure how they compare to competitors or peers. In effect, they have a restricted view, but you have a broad one that can bring them immense benefits in cost reductions and time saving. This often-overlooked advantage is one that you can utilize all the way from your branding and positioning, through your core content development, to your proposals and invitations-to-tender responses, to your post-sale strategic account management. This is not to underestimate or undervalue your customer's expertise—they do, after all, run a successful business in that sector—but your breadth of experience across the industry is likely to exceed their own simply because it is your business to act more broadly across the industry and to learn from every interaction. Dawar and Vandenbosch have a good example to illustrate these points: Hilti. Hilti Corp. is a Liechtenstein-based maker of high-end power tools and fastening systems. Their customers are professional builders, contractors, and construction companies. The construction industry remains constrained by national boundaries owing to national building codes and local needs. Hilti's customers generally, therefore, lack the geographic span continually to monitor building and maintenance practices elsewhere. Hilti can help its customers fill their experience gaps through its presence in more than 120 countries. Logging more than 100,000 customer contacts each day, many of Hilti's 11,000 customer-facing employees refer to the company as an information network that just happens to sell tools and building systems. Few of their competitors can match this kind of information integration and the resultant ability to recommend proven solutions based on customer experiences. Hilti and its customers consider Hilti's customer orientation, application know-how, and advisory skills to be strengths that justify its premium prices: the ultimate goal of successful brand positioning. They are viewed as true industry experts, who are listened to when they communicate in any way about the market.

Your industry knowledge can give you the ability to benchmark company and solution performance in a way that a single business can find very hard to do. *BusinessWeek*—the top-selling business periodical—has long been a source of credible business information. In its regular ranking of business schools, however, it has gone beyond being merely a useful source of information. Many prospective students and recruiters now use the metrics that the magazine has established for its ranking study to evaluate schools. They have used their broad scope and resultant expertise to become the owners of the industry benchmark. Hilti and *BusinessWeek* are great examples of the creation of customer value through industry knowledge and the resulting strong competitive positioning.

In "Clients for Life," Seth and Sobel cite the quality of *empathy*—commonly defined as the ability to perceive other people's emotions and thoughts—as the key to personal effectiveness in client relationships. These were some of the supportive comments to that point made by their corporate contacts in relation to their external suppliers and advisers:

- "The really empathetic professionals listen to what I mean, not what I say."
- "A session with a good adviser is a discussion, not a lecture."
- "The professionals I deal with must be genuinely interested in my issues and problems."
- "The adviser must know how to contextualize recommendations, making them both relevant to my company's unique problems and understandable to my executives and me."
- "The truly great advisers gain a deep understanding of my industry, of my organization, and, most important, of me as an executive and as a person—that's when a long-term relationship develops."

Achieving this level of symbiotic relationship takes time, patience, and skill. But it's worth it. As you and your strategic account get to know one another better, that means the individuals on both sides become more familiar with each other's companies. It is not unusual for employees to consider switching sides: moving between companies. This can be a positive development, but if there is active silent recruitment encouraged by either side—in other words, plain old poaching—that can lead to trouble. As ever, open and honest communication between all concerned is the best approach.

You may well be using a third party on this account. As your partner—the SI, the VAR, the consultancy—deepens their relationship, it is important that you as the vendor maintain your account contacts. You're not trying to undermine your partner—make that plain by good communication with them about what you are doing—but you do need to ensure that your strategic plan for the account is being followed and supported. Your third party is an independent business, and they may well see their own interests in the account differently to yours. It is even possible that another of their suppliers—one of your competitors—could use them to infiltrate your customer. If, during one of your regular account reviews, you discover that your partner is going off the rails in any way, tackle this quickly to ensure that you maintain your hold. In the worst of circumstances, you may find that something has gone so wrong that you want to swap out that partner for another, or that the customer insists on this. That's a challenge, but one that you must take on and be seen to be doing what is best for the customer, his or her experience with your solution, and the long-term relationship that you want to nurture. Sustain a partnership with the partner if you can—making enemies is never a good result.

Understand Your Customer's Experience

Your CSO, CEM, and SAM (see Figure 8.1) need constantly not only to do their jobs well but to communicate with one another. In an SME, these roles may be wrapped up in the job of one person, but the principles of recognizing the changing relationship landscape are sound and still apply. As with the sales process, this is easy to theoretically oversimplify as a linear one, when in reality, each part can be happening simultaneously. As the CSO manages the installation and implementation of your solution, guiding the new users to use and maximize the benefit of your product, the CEM will already be working with the customer's departmental managers and the users themselves to ensure that they are benefitting positively from the innovations that you have brought to their business. It could be the case that the CSO is managing and supporting a process that extends over a long period, so delaying the CEM's involvement would be unwise. If your solution has been installed and is in daily use in the customer's firm, any issues that need to be elevated above the support function for resolution need addressing quickly and efficiently. The challenge is to cost-effectively respond to the customer's current needs. And current needs are constantly changing, possibly driven by the implementation of your new solution. Customers don't want to waste their time. CCMC's two wonderfully titled *National Customer Rage* studies in 2015 and 2017 showed that severe problems are more associated with wasted time (a median in their studies of five hours) than out-of-pocket financial loss. Customers value their time more than their money. *Proper handling of complaints retains customers.* In almost all business sectors, a customer who complains and is satisfied by the complaint's resolution is 30 percent more loyal than a noncomplainer, and 50 percent more loyal than a complainer who remains dissatisfied. The customer service function, as well as addressing complaints and providing support to the new users, should be executing and absorbing the input from your customer surveys—now often called the voice of customer (VOC) input—to improve that service. If you do have a customer experience (CE) function, then that constantly updated and analyzed feedback should be fed into it. If that dedicated function (CE) does not exist, then it is the CSO's job to act as a consultant on customer attitudes, experience, and satisfaction to the rest of the company, driving through whatever changes are necessary to improve the CE to the best of your ability. This is where a culture of continuous improvement can be created for your business. Unfortunately, many companies gather a mass of relevant data but lack the expertise or will to analyze it properly, so it becomes a wasted effort, without payback for the business.

Summary

Strategic account management is the vital skill that can keep your company on its planned growth trajectory. As we have cautioned earlier, managing your best and largest accounts well does not take away the necessity for the continued active prospecting, marketing, and selling that has got you to this point. You do not want overreliance on a handful of them. But astute management of this vital part of your customer base will contribute heavily to your profitability, brand image, and longevity. Do it badly, and all of those benefits are reversed.

Strategic accounts tend to be big, dynamic, demanding, and challenging. Yet still, it is the individual relationships that you form and nurture within them that will guarantee your success. Constant analysis of the balance between the cost of servicing them properly and the business that they generate is essential. If you use channel partners to service them, ensure that the three-way relationship is trusting and tight, to everyone's benefit.

The sign of achievement in strategic account management is that outside onlookers at both your company and your customers constantly see your two logos supporting each other in every communication, with both businesses proud of the relationship and its longevity.

The Takeaways and Lessons Learned From Chapter 8	Do	Don't
The welcome insider	Maintain as much regular contact as you did when you were making the sale, providing that you have judged there to be sufficient potential to justify it	Don't assume that your competitors have given up on the account Don't be complacent, or get taken for granted
Relationships	Recognize that, as the incumbent supplier, you will have different relationships with different sets of people Empathy is a vital character trait for your SAM. It's highly valued by your customers If channel partners are involved, another level of strategic management and communication is essential to avoid conflict	Don't think that every new face in the company will immediately know all about you and your firm and be comfortable to be your user Don't let new users miss your communications. Have your marketing function ensure that relevant new contacts immediately receive links to your content Don't ignore problems: tackle them fast
Additional business	There is no substitute for continual listening to your customer Maintaining regular personal contact is vital New business opportunities may come from unexpected quarters of the company	Don't overservice your account in relation to the profits they produce for you Don't assume that the board and decision makers will automatically turn to you for the next order

The Outro

Our seamless process delivered the results!

We signed the profitable deal and established a long-term customer relationship that will serve us well for a long time, whether we work in a large or small enterprise.

How did we manage this?

- We defined and found our market.
    - We used formal market research techniques and the science of market segmentation to discover to whom we should be selling and what they want from us. We checked that there was a strategic fit with our business and the revenue and profits potential in our chosen market segment to achieve our business plan.
    - We worked on our core values and used them to establish our brand and the identity we want to communicate. By closely studying our competition and their activities, we fine-tuned our proposition and the messages we want to communicate, establishing a unique positioning for ourselves.
    - We analyzed our target customers in detail and compiled our target list.
- We established a sound and error-free marketing and sales process, tuned to the buying behavior of our customers.
    - Choosing between all of the many options, we selected our primary promotional and social media channels. We insisted on obsessive attention to coordinated branding in all of those activities. Our sales team was trained in virtual and face to face selling techniques. Using our core content in many different ways, we perfected our approach to proposals, tenders, and RFPs. We trained all of our customer-facing personnel in presentation skills and prepared flexible materials for them.

- ○ We decided that having a network of third-party partners was the preferred GTM (go-to-market) strategy and our customers' preferred WTB (where-to-buy) option.
- ○ From throughout the company, we assembled a team that could rival any of our competitors when called upon to face an evaluation of our solution. Despite being skilled in avoiding one, when it was necessary for a trial of our solution to take place, we knew how to manage it to a successful conclusion.
- We managed the customer relationship for our mutual benefit.
  - ○ Our installation team became experts at working with our customer to install and then to implement our solution across the business, with minimum disruption and maximum benefit. Our focus on the customer experience and uncompromising excellence in support quickly secured our long-term relationships and kept out the competition.
  - ○ Using those excellent relationships, our customer base soon became our most lucrative and profitable source of new business, both from those customers and from those to whom they helped us to sell.

Along the way through the book, we heard and learned from the experience of others who had operated in the same world, before us. They shared their wisdom, their tips for success, and their experience of overcoming barriers and difficulties.

We also referred to the enormous body of written work that provides theory, practical advice, and research data to inform and support our marketing and sales efforts.

With all of this, how could we possibly fail?

Of course, failure is still a possibility. Strategies don't come together; marketing efforts do fail to achieve their objectives; sales funnels fail to deliver well-qualified prospects; and deals fall through at the last moment. In *Seamless*, the authors have tried to bring together guidance on all of the ingredients for a successful mix of skills and resources applied to actions, avoiding the failures and ensuring that your sales process produces the results you aimed for. Our experience and the experience of the contributors to this book tells us that this is not easy. In order not to complicate matters, we have talked throughout as if there is one deal on the go—as if the process applies to one proposition to one potential customer. That's necessary in order to make the book readable, but we know that, in practice, any marketing and sales team or small business owner is constantly juggling a myriad of prospects and ongoing potential business. That's the job, after all!

Seamless is designed to help and guide you, no matter what the size of your firm or your team. Take your current primary marketing, selling, or account management challenge and look back at the summary of the *Seamless* chapter that best addresses it. Look at the "Dos and Don'ts" block for that chapter and tick off how they apply to your particular problem or situation. If there is something in there that helps you, investigate that chapter again, for the detail. For the view from the sharp end, read the interviews with our senior practitioners—their successes will inspire you; their guidance will help you to replicate those successes for yourself and to avoid the pitfalls.

Then step back and do the thing that this book is focused on: look at the whole process you are going through. Figure 4.1 and Figure 4.2 will help you to do that. Be honest with yourself. Do you know how far you have progressed with this deal? Have you skipped or missed anything? If so, repeat the earlier instruction: look at the summary and the dos and don'ts. We are confident that this will help guide you to greater success.

Good luck and remember to have fun along the way!

Peter D. Bayley
With Kimball Bailey, Tom Cairns, and Michael S. K. Grant

Bibliography

"Brand Values." October 12, 2021. Statista Research Department.

Aaker, J.L. 1997. "Dimensions of Brand Personality." *Journal of Marketing Research* 34, no. 3, pp. 347–356.

Alsher, P. August 2015. "How Do You Define Project Success? A Guide to Installation vs. Implementation." Thursday, August 27, 2015 and "Why Do Change Projects Fail? How Can You Prevent Your Project from Becoming a Statistic?" Friday, August 14, 2015. *Implementation Management Association (IMA) Blog.*

Ansoff, H. October 1957. "Strategies for Diversification." *Harvard Business Review* 35, no. 5.

Bacon, T.R. 2005. *Powerful Proposals: How to Give Your Business the Winning Edge.* AMACOM.

Barber, N., L. Ivy-Rosser, A. Lozada, and M. Bakalar. February 16, 2022. "The Forrester Wave™: Digital Asset Management For Customer Experience, Q1 2022." *The 14 Providers That Matter Most and How They Stack Up.*

Blount, J. 2020. *Virtual Selling. A Quick-Start Guide to Leveraging Video Based Technology to Engage Remote Buyers and Close Deals Fast.* US: Wiley.

Broetzmann, S.M., M. Grainer, and J.A. Goodman. 2017. *2017 National Customer Rage Study.* Alexandria, VA: Customer Care Measurement & Consulting.

Chaffey, D. 2019. *Digital Marketing.* Pearson.

Challenge, Inc. n.d. "More-B2B-Decision-Makers-Want-In." www.challengerinc.com/blog/more-b2b-decision-makers-want-in/.

Champy, J. 2008. *Outsmart: How to Do What Your Competitors Can't.* UK: Financial Times Series.

Dawar, N. and M. Vandenbosch. January 15, 2004. "The Seller's Hidden Advantage." *MIT Sloan Management Review.*

De Meyer, A., C.H. Loch, and M.T. Pich. January 15, 2002. "Managing Project Uncertainty: From Variation to Chaos." *MIT Sloan Review.*

Dietmeyer, B. 2011. *B2B Street Fighting.* Think! Inc.

Eder, S. July 11, 2022. "Seven Tips for B2B Voice of the Customer Research." Quirk's Media. New York, NY: NewtonX.

Fisher, R. and W. Ury. 2016. *Getting to Yes: Negotiating an Agreement Without Giving In.* Cornerstone Digital.

Forsey, C. November 12, 2020. "18 Core Company Values That Will Shape Your Culture & Inspire Your Employees." and "Company Core Values Glossary." Originally published November 12, 2020 10:19:00 AM, updated September 03, 2021. @cforsey1/Hubspot. www.hubspot.com.

Frambo, M.B., H. Kok, and B. Fon. March 2022. "What Do Consumers Know About Corporate Responsible Management? A Case Study of Eight World-Leading Brands and Their Branding Strategy." *Journal of Human Resource and Sustainability Studies* 10, no. 1. The Hague, The Netherlands: International Business School.

Gärtner, S. and S. Schurz. n.d. "Statista Marketing Compass Report 2022." *Statista Design/Contentmarketing.com/Media Research* 42.

Gartner. 2020. "2020 Marketing Data and Analytics Survey."

Gartner. 2021. "Digital Buying Survey, 2021."

Glückler, J. and T. Armbrüster. 2003. "Bridging Uncertainty in Management Consulting: The Mechanisms of Trust and Networked Reputation." *Organization Studies* 24, no. 2, pp. 269–297.

Godin, S. February 5, 2007. *Permission Marketing: Turning Strangers Into Friends and Friends Into Customers*. UK: Simon and Schuster.

Goodman, J.A. and S.M. Broetzmann. 2019. *Strategic Customer Service*. HarperCollins Leadership, an imprint of HarperCollins.

Hedley, M. n.d. "China Market Entry Strategy: A Guide To Entering Chinese Business-to-Business Markets." B2B International. www.b2binternational.com/publications/china-market-entry/

Hess, G. 2020. *Selling Is Hard, But Buying Is Harder—How Buyer Enablement Drives Digital Sales and Shortens the Sales Cycle*. River Grove Books.

Hoffeld, D. 2016. *The Science of Selling: Proven Strategies to Make Your Pitch, Influence Decisions, and Close the Deal*. Tarcher Perigee.

Implementation Management Associates. n.d. "The Mini-Guide to Implementation vs Installation." www. imaworldwide.com (accessed 2022).

Kaplan, S. March 2008. *Bag the Elephant!*, Reprint ed. Workman Publishing Company.

Keegan, B.J., D. Dennehy, and P. Naudé. 2022. "Implementing Artificial Intelligence in Traditional B2B Marketing Practices: An Activity Theory Perspective." *Inf Syst Front.* https://doi.org/10.1007/s10796-022-10294-1.

Keränen, J., H. Terho, and A. Saurama. September 1, 2021. "Three Ways to Sell Value in B2B Markets." *MIT Sloan Management Review.*

Kim, W.C. and R. Mauborgne. 2005. *Blue Ocean Strategy: How to Create Uncontested Market Space and make the Competition Irrelevant*. Boston: Harvard Business Press.

Kotler, P. 2001. *Kotler On Marketing*. UK: Simon and Schuster.

Larry Steven Londre. n.d. *The Nine P's/9P's of Marketing ©2007*. Londre Marketing Consultants, LLC.

Livestorm. 2022. "Marketing Manager Mindset Report." https://livestorm.co/.

Lonsdale, C., K. Hoque, I. Kirkpatrick, and J. Sanderson. August 2017. "Knowing the Price of Everything? Exploring the Impact of Increased Procurement Professional Involvement on Management Consultancy Purchasing." *Industrial Marketing Management* 65, pp. 157–167.

Mark Hunter, C.S.P. 2021. *A Mind for Sales: Daily Habits and Practical Strategies for Sales Success*. HarperCollins Leadership, a division of HarperCollins Focus, LLC.

McCarthy, E.J. 1978. *Basic Marketing. A Managerial Approach*, 6th Revised ed. US: Irwin (Richard D.) Inc.

McDonald, M. and B. Rogers. 2017. *Malcolm McDonald on Key Account Management*. Kogan Page.

Miller, R.B. and S.E. Heiman. 2005. *The New Successful Large Account Management: Maintaining and Growing Your Most Important Assets—Your Customers*. Grand Central Publishing.

Moore, G.A. January 2014. *Crossing the Chasm, 3rd Edition: Marketing and Selling Disruptive Products to Mainstream Customers*. US: Collins Business Essentials.

Porter, M.E. 1980. *Competitive Strategy: Techniques for Analysing Industries and Competitors*. New York, NY: Free Press.

Porter, M.E. n.d. *Competitive Advantage: Creating and Sustaining Superior Performance*.

Prahalad, C.K. and G. Hamel. May–June 1990. "The Core Competence of the Corporation." *Harvard Business Review*.

Pugh, D.G. March 16, 2021. *Profitwell—The Pricing Strategy Guide*. www .profitwell.com.

Pun, R. and C. Ferguson. January 4, 2022. *Gartner Magic Quadrant for Account-Based Marketing Platforms*. Sheth, J. and A. Sobel. 2000. *Clients for Life—How Great Professionals Develop Breakthrough Relationships*. Simon and Schuster.

Shore, J. 2020. *Follow Up and Close the Sale*. McGraw-Hill Education.

Sinek, S., D. Mead, and P. Docker. 2011. *Start With Why. How Great Leaders Inspire Everyone to Take Action*. UK: Penguin.

Slywotzky, A., R. Wise, and K. Weber. 2003. *How to Grow When Markets Don't*. New York, NY: Warner Business Books.

Smith, W.R. 1956. "Product Differentiation and Market Segmentation as Alternative Marketing Strategies." *Journal of Marketing* 21, no. 1, pp. 3–8.

Sturdy, A., K. Handley, T. Clark, and R. Fincham. 2009. "Management Consultancy: Boundaries and Knowledge in Action." Oxford University Press.

Sturdy, A.J., M. Schwarz, and A. Spicer. 2006. "'Guess Who's Coming to Dinner? Structures and Uses of Liminality in Strategic Management Consultancy." *Human Relations* 59, no. 7, pp. 929–960.

Taminiau, Y. and A. Wiersma. 2016. 'The Process of Trust Creation Between Business Partners at the Golf Course: A Long-Term Process." *International Journal of Strategic Business Alliances* 5, no. 3/4, p. 245.

Taminiau, Y. January 2013. "'It Looks Like Friendship But It's Not', the Institutional Embeddedness of Informal Client Relationships of Big 4 Accountants and Consultants Compared." *International Journal of Management Concepts and Philosophy*.

Textor, C. April 20, 2022. "IMF World Economic Outlook Database April 2022."

Trout, J. and S. Rivkin. 2000. *Differentiate or Die—Survival in Our Era of Killer Competition*. McGraw-Hill Companies, Inc.

Trout, J. and S. Rivkin. 2010. *Repositioning: Marketing in an Era of Competition, Change, and Crisis*. McGraw-Hill Companies, Inc.

Tussell report, 2021. "Local Government Procurement with Tech SMEs—Trends and Opportunities."

UK Government. September 8, 2020. "How to Bid for UK Government Contracts as an SME Effectively." www.gov.uk/.

Ulaga, W. and S. Michel. October 30, 2018. "Bill It, Kill It or Keep It Free?" *MIT Sloan Management Review*.

Vladimirovich, M.K. 2020. "Future Marketing in the B2B Segment: Integrating AI into Sales Management." *International Journal of Innovative Technologies in Economy*.

Weinberg, M. *2012 UK New Sales. Simplified: The Essential Handbook for Prospecting and New Business Development*. Amacom.

Wheeler, M. 2013. *The Art of Negotiation*. Simon and Schuster.

Wunker, S. 2011. *Capturing New Markets: How Smart Companies Create Opportunities Others Don't*. McGraw-Hill.

Zhang, J.Z., G.F. Watson, IV, and R.W. Palmatier. May 1, 2018. "Customer Relationships Evolve—So Must Your CRM Strategy."

About the Authors

Peter D. Bayley, Author and Business Writer, WriteAllAlong

 **Peter Bayley**'s career includes unique, long-term achievements in brand-building and marketing for global IT businesses, including Compaq, Commodore, Lotus, 3-Com, and Wall Data. A highly successful high-tech sales management career preceded his years in marketing. As an experienced public speaker, he has presented business strategy, products, technology concepts, and business training courses to a wide variety of audiences. He has extensive entrepreneurial and broad consulting experience for both small and large companies, based in the United Kingdom, Europe, and the United States. He is a published author and business commentator.

Peter studied graduate and postgraduate business studies and marketing at the University of West London, Southend Business School and Anglian Regional Management Centre. He is a freeman of the City of London, through the Information Technologists' livery company, and was previously a member or Fellow of The Prince's Trust Technology Leadership Group, the Institute of Directors, the Institute of Sales and Marketing, and the British Institute of Management. He was an international board member of the Seattle Software Association.

Kimball Bailey, Consulting Director, Alastor Consulting

Kimball is an experienced strategic advisory consultant and consultancy director who specializes in helping clients—from the largest corporates to small technology companies and charities—to ensure their benefits from investment in business change achieve planned outcomes.

His 35 years of consulting experience includes strategic development, business transformation, and procurement work across a range of sectors in the United Kingdom, Europe, the United States, and the Middle East. After several years in the financial services industry, he worked in senior consulting roles at Ernst & Young, Gartner, Pagoda, and Compass. He founded the independent management consultancy Alastor, which advises on the improvement of business performance, the realization of business benefit from change, and the effective management of IT.

He is a liveryman at the Worshipful Company of Information Technologists and a freeman of the City of London. He is a published author and holds an MA in law from Cambridge University (Magdalene College).

Tom Cairns, Founder, SalesTechnique Ltd.

Tom is an experienced senior business executive, entrepreneur, and management educator with over 40 years of consistent achievement with multiple global companies including Apple, Lotus Software, and IBM. Focused on leading sales organizations and their business partners to success across international territories, he consistently produced high-performing teams and increased revenue and profit.

He later moved from executive corporate management to become one of IBM's elite global sales performance coaches to help create leading-edge sales execution programs for the sales force and channel.

As founder and managing director of SalesTechnique, Tom continues to follow his passion to research and deliver practical proven methodologies, tools, and techniques that deliver high-performance sales execution and successful key account management skills.

Tom graduated in pure science from Glasgow University, is a Fellow of the Higher Education Academy and Advance HE, and is a fully qualified lecturer in Learning, Teaching and Management Education.

Michael S. K. Grant, Past President BCS: The Chartered Institute for IT

As president of the BCS, **Michael** chaired the board of trustees and, as immediate past president, chaired the BCS Nominations and Remuneration Committees. He represented the IT profession in the United Kingdom, leading the 64,000 members globally. Today, he sits on the strategic marketing team for "ifip," the global IT organization of professional institutes. A past clerk and master of the IT Livery Company, and a member of Chichester University Multi Academy Trust, he also founded an ICT specialist recruitment company for senior executives in marketing and sales across Europe and, more recently, spent five years as an associate director of Harvey Nash plc.

Prior to this, he worked for over 30 years in senior international marketing and communication roles in Gateway, Lotus, Commodore, ICL, and Prime Computer and in the FMCG industry with HJ Heinz. He has lived and worked in the United States, Australia, and the Republic of Ireland.

Index